THE SHAPE OF
BATTLE

THE SHAPE OF
BATTLE

THE ART OF WAR:
From the Battle of Hastings to
D-Day and Beyond

ALLAN MALLINSON

PEGASUS BOOKS
NEW YORK LONDON

THE SHAPE OF BATTLE

Pegasus Books, Ltd.
148 West 37th Street, 13th Floor
New York, NY 10018

ISBN: 978-1-63936-193-9

10 9 8 7 6 5 4 3 2 1

Printed in the United States of America
Distributed by Simon & Schuster
www.pegasusbooks.com

The events of all wars are obscure.
History is only roughly right at best.

John Masefield, *Gallipoli*

The history of a battle is not unlike the history of a ball. Some individuals may recollect all the little events of which the great result is the battle won or lost, but no individual can recollect the order in which, or the exact moment at which, they occurred, which makes all the difference as to their value or importance.

The Duke of Wellington

Battles are won primarily in the hearts of men.

Montgomery of Alamein

CONTENTS

Part Four

SWORD BEACH

The Battle for the Bridgehead

6 June 1944

169

Part Five

IMJIN RIVER

The Battle for Honor

22–25 April 1951

261

Part Six

HELMAND

Operation Panther's Claw:
The Battle for the Population

19 June–27 July 2009

311

LIST OF MAPS

PREFACE

The Shape of Battle isn't meant to be a coda to Clausewitz (*On War*) or a companion to Keegan (*The Face of Battle*), but is rather a study of why some battles were fought as they were, and as battles to one degree or another will always be fought.

No one battle is quite like any other in its shape and course. Each takes place in a different context – the war, the campaign, the weapons, the people. Nevertheless, battles across the centuries, and the continents, have much in common, whether fought with sticks and stones or advanced technology. War is, after all, an intensely human activity; human nature doesn't change, and men are no more intelligent now than their predecessors of a thousand years ago.

Trying to seek the present, or the future, in the past is perilous, not least in using examples from history to confirm one's own preconceptions and prejudices. The past has first to be engaged with on its own terms. Yet if battles didn't have anything in common, why would professional soldiers study them? What other than diversion would they find useful in old battlefields? That most assiduous student of the soldier's art, Field Marshal Bernard Law Montgomery, 1st Viscount Montgomery of Alamein, 'wanted to study the great captains of the past to learn how they thought and acted, and how they used the military means at their disposal'.* He was, he said, less interested in the detailed dispositions than in understanding 'the essential problem which confronted the general at a certain moment in the battle, what were the factors which influenced his decision, what was his decision – and why'. In short, he 'wanted to discover what was in the great man's mind when he made a major decision. This, surely, was the way to study generalship.'

This isn't a manual, though. I don't labour the similarities between the six examples. I don't 'compare and contrast'. I don't try to draw over-arching conclusions that are in any way prescriptive. Military *savants* have been doing that for centuries, and yet in any battle one side always loses – there really is no such thing as a drawn battle in the perfect sense – so the formula for victory, unlike that for defeat, clearly isn't definitive. (How could it be, given the dialectic and dynamism of war?) The narratives speak for themselves. As Thucydides, the greatest of the ancient Greek historians, wrote: 'If he who desires to have before his eyes a true picture of the events which have happened, and of the like events which may be expected to happen hereafter in the order of human things, shall pronounce what I have written to be useful, then I shall be satisfied.'†

As I shall, indeed, if what I've written simply serves to show what an enigmatic business is war – the most complex human interaction ever known.

---

* Montgomery of Alamein, *A Concise History of Warfare* (London, 1972).

† Thucydides, *History of the Peloponnesian War*, ed. and trans. Benjamin Jowett (Oxford, 1881).

INTRODUCTION

'Movement of Bodies'

Those of you that have got through the rest, I am going to rapidly
Devote a little time to showing you, those that can master it,
A few ideas about tactics, which must not be confused
With what we call strategy. Tactics is merely
The mechanical movement of bodies, and that is what we mean by it.
Or perhaps I should say: by them.

Strategy, to be quite frank, you will have no hand in.
It is done by those up above, and it merely refers to,
The larger movements over which we have no control . . .

Henry Reed, *Lessons of the War* (1942)

Modern military theory divides the practice of war – 'warfare' – into
three levels: strategic, operational and tactical. This division has its
roots in the Napoleonic Wars, especially the works of two generals
in opposing armies: the Prussian Carl von Clausewitz, and the
Swiss Antoine-Henri Jomini, who served in the French.* These ideas

---

* *The Shape of Battle* is not about war as a phenomenon, but about its practice. Although
there are several, sometimes competing, commentaries on the nature of war – war as

developed further with the American Civil War, and were then codified by the German general staff after the Franco-Prussian War. They reached their practical maturity with the Soviets in the 1930s following the experience of the First World War and Russian Civil War. In Britain, meanwhile, the levels were perhaps more instinctively understood than articulated. It was only really towards the end of the Cold War that anything was promulgated with authority – in the 1989 document *Design for Military Operations: The British Military Doctrine* published by the (Army) General Staff – although, as usual with British doctrine publications, it prompted more debate than it resolved.

Field Marshal Montgomery put it this way:

Grand Strategy is the co-ordination and direction of all the resources of a nation, or group of nations, towards the attainment of the political object of the war – the goal defined by the fundamental policy. The true objective of grand strategy must be a secure and lasting peace. Strategy is the art of distributing and applying military means, such as Armed Forces and supplies, to fulfil the ends of policy . . . Tactics means the dispositions for, and control of, military forces and techniques in actual fighting.

Montgomery implies that the 'operational level' is the less well-defined zone of overlapping strategy and tactics – the level of command where strategy is 'geared' into tactics (and sometimes, indeed, vice versa); the level at which a *campaign* is devised and executed. 'In a campaign,' he wrote, 'the commander should think two battles ahead – the one he is planning to fight and the next one. He can then use success in the first as a springboard for the second.'

---

catharsis, war as a cataclysm etc. – I take as a simple definition Clausewitz's 'War is . . . an act of force to compel our enemy to do our will.'

That said, argument is endless as to whether the level at which a campaign is designed, and that at which the design is put into execution, are or should be the same. In essence, the operational level is concerned with employing military forces in a theatre of war – or, especially in a conflict short of war, a 'theatre of operations' – to gain advantage over the enemy in order to achieve the strategic goals. Indeed, the operational level might be better called the 'theatre of war level', or 'theatre of operations level', or perhaps simply 'campaign level'. Gaining advantage over the enemy at this level is achieved through the design, organization and conduct of campaigns and major operations. A campaign is in essence a series of related military operations in a given time and space – almost certainly involving *battle*.

Montgomery didn't underestimate the problems of this, not least because of the continual intrusion of the 'political' – the policy – into the military, and vice versa: 'The strategical background to a campaign or battle is of great significance [to me]. What was the aim? What was the commander trying to achieve? An object may be very desirable strategically; but that which is strategically desirable must be tactically possible with the forces and means available.'

Put crudely, strategy is about picking the right battles to win the war, while tactics is about using the means at one's disposal to win the battle. Strategy is about balancing overall objectives (or 'ends') with the ways and means of achieving them. But it's very much a business of give and take. The leaders of the state set the policy, but military officers must apprise policy-makers of the extent to which those objectives are achievable with the ways and means available. If the necessary ways and means can't be found, the objectives must be modified. This is a dynamic process – not least once the campaign begins – needing continual dialogue to make sure that ends, ways and means remain in balance. 'Politics' can't be excluded from tactics, or vice versa. But without strategy, tactics fumble blindly, bloodily and with no assurance of success.

In pre-modern times, of course – the times of Hastings and Towton – the leaders of the state were also the leaders of the military. This made for an interesting short-circuiting of the dynamic process. Similarly, at Waterloo the Duke of Wellington was simultaneously both the operational-level and the tactical commander; indeed, he was also, in some respects, key at the strategic level. Across the valley, his adversary, Napoleon, combined all three levels in a single saddle (and failed conclusively in all of them).

But let us at least be clear about what is a battle, the subject of this book. The *Shorter Oxford Dictionary*, the British defence establishment's lexical authority, defines 'battle' in its medieval sense as 'a fight between (esp. large organized) opposing forces'; to which the *Concise Oxford* adds 'a fight between armies, ships or planes, especially during a war; a violent fight between groups of people'. In other words, a battle is a period of intense, continuous or near-continuous fighting over a relatively short period in a distinct geographical area, ending usually, but not always, in a clear result – victory or defeat.

Nothing too precise, then; nothing certain. Indeed, Montgomery, who'd seen his fair share of battles, in defeat and victory, put it bluntly: 'Only one thing is certain in battle, and that is that everything will be uncertain.'

PART ONE

HASTINGS

The Battle for England

14 OCTOBER 1066

Then King William came from Normandy into Pevensey . . .

The Anglo-Saxon Chronicle

The battle of Hastings was just about as unique as a battle can be. It was completely and utterly decisive (although not immediately recognized as such by either side); it changed the course of history in a single day (and with no preliminary manoeuvring to speak of); and it was the last time that a British army fought as a single arm – entirely as infantry. Yet remarkably little is known about the battle for certain, only the place and the date; of its shape and course we have only an outline. The result was not a foregone conclusion by any means. Indeed, the odds were in King Harold's favour. Something, however, made the last Anglo-Saxon monarch play his hand uncharacteristically poorly. Something shaped the battle to the advantage of his opponent, Duke William of Normandy. If, as Montgomery said, 'battles are won primarily in the hearts of men', was Hastings primarily a failure of heart?

1

JUS AD BELLUM*

All battles are won before they are fought.

Sun Tzu

By rights, a seasoned campaigner like Harold Godwineson shouldn't have lost the battle of Hastings. What was it that led him to fight when and as he did that day on the ridge north of the town? Was it a sort of mental exhaustion; or sudden alarm, perhaps; hubris, even? Or was it something more existential, compelling him to submit to, in effect, a personal trial by combat with William, Duke of Normandy? In 54 BC, Caesar had by his own account crossed the Channel with 800 ships; in 1066, according to the twelfth-century English-born Norman chronicler Orderic Vitalis, Duke William sailed with 900 (though his contemporary, the Norman historian 'Maistre' Robert

---

* The right to go to war – the concept, set out by St Augustine of Hippo in the fifth century AD and developed later by figures such as Thomas Aquinas, determining whether resort to war was morally and lawfully justified, and known generally as 'just war theory'.

7

Wace, says 700). Caesar made some gains and local allies, yet every Roman soldier was back in Gaul the following year. In 1066, however, as the German poet Heinrich Heine wrote eight centuries later,

> Fate willed the Duke of Normandy
> The fatal day should gain,
> And on the field at Hastings lies
> King Harold 'mongst the slain.

Fate – the elaboration of events predetermined by a supernatural power: divine providence . . .

Within the span of a single month, the Anglo-Saxons – the Old English – would fight three major battles, two of them epic and decisive. Harald Hardrada, King of Norway, the most seasoned military leader in Europe, invaded northern England with a huge force of Danes and Norwegians, and after first defeating an English army outside York, was in turn utterly defeated – and killed – at Stamford Bridge east of the city. Indeed, if Hastings hadn't occurred, that battle would have been celebrated as *the* historic, decisive English victory. In the event, Harold's defeat at Hastings made Stamford Bridge an historical – strategic – irrelevance; yet in campaign terms, Stamford Bridge is central to what happened at Hastings. Indeed, the events of 1066, the year of the two invasions, are an object lesson in the complete art of war – strategy, campaigning and battle. Hastings and the two battles that preceded it show not just the hazard of combat, but just how much battle is shaped by strategy and the campaign undertaken to implement that strategy – as well as, of course, by the enemy.

Yet strategy – *grand* strategy, the coordination and direction of all the resources of a nation – is itself shaped by the nature of the nation (and vice versa). The late Professor Sir Michael Howard, a man who'd seen war at close quarters and then spent the rest of his life thinking about it, suggests that this seemingly self-evident fact hasn't always been appreciated: 'The history of war, I came to realise, was more than the operational history of armed forces. It was the study of entire societies,' he wrote. 'Only by studying their cultures could one come to understand what it was that they fought about and why they fought in the way they did.'*

The two armies that fought at Hastings were radically different in both these respects – what they fought about and how – because their cultures were radically different. That indeed is the starting point to understanding why, at the end of what may have been the longest battle fought to that date – a full eight hours, and perhaps more – King Harold lay 'mongst the slain.

But painting a faithful picture of England in 1066, especially its military organization, isn't easy. The sources are scant compared with those of the years after the Conquest. It's only relatively recently that the term 'Dark Ages' fell out of favour, not least because of the implied value judgement on the period as one of intellectual darkness and barbarity. Another aspect of the 'darkness', however, was the dearth of information about the period, including its military organization. Indeed, the eminent Victorian historian Frederic Maitland wrote that 'no matter with which we have to deal is darker than the constitution of the English army on the eve of its defeat'.† Yet it's clear, not least from the great audit carried out fifteen years later, the Domesday Book, whose data were collected in about seven months, that on the eve of that defeat England was one of the richest kingdoms in Europe, its wealth based on farming and trade, and that it was very highly organized.

---

* *Captain Professor: A Life in War and Peace* (London, 2006). Howard, formerly Chichele Professor of the History of War, and Regius Professor of Modern History, at Oxford, and Professor of Military and Naval History at Yale, had won the Military Cross in 1943 serving with the Coldstream Guards in Italy.

† *Domesday Book and Beyond* (Cambridge, 1897).

It was also comparatively peaceful, although there were fault-lines. King Alfred had in large part checked the Viking raids in the late ninth century, and his grandson Athelstan (King of Anglo-Saxon Mercia and Wessex, 924-7, and of the English, 927-39) had driven out the most warlike of them from the 'Danelaw', consolidating his rule over the whole of what is now England – indeed, in effect creating 'England' – although the more assimilated were allowed to stay on their farms and in places such as York where their trades were valued (the 'settled Danes'). The weak rule of Aethelred the Unready (978-1016) encouraged the Danes to return, however, and Cnut (or 'Canute') and his sons ruled England from 1016 to 1042. The throne then reverted to the House of Wessex, to Edward (the 'Confessor'), the son of Aethelred, and of Emma of Normandy who on Aethelred's death had married Cnut and borne his heir Harthacnut. From the accession of Cnut to Edward's death in 1066, England faced no great – certainly no overwhelming – challenges. The northern earls had always remained more than a little uncertain in their allegiance to the Wessex crown of England, however.* On the eve of the Conquest, Athelstan's creation still remained something of a work in progress.

England in Edward's reign was therefore a place of *byrig* (the Anglo-Saxon plural of *burh* or *burg*), the fortified settlements that Alfred had established as a defensive network. Yet the country was essentially a rural one. The towns that had grown around the *byrig* were small, with most people depending on the land for survival. This in turn

---

* Earls ranked directly below the king and were his right-hand men in the shires, each of the greater earls being the prefect of one of the major divisions of England, usually a former kingdom (such as Mercia). The position was not hereditary, though by the tenth century it was customary to choose earls from a small number of great families. Indeed, the crown itself was not absolutely hereditary, each monarch being approved by the Witan – council – which included the earls.

shaped military strategy, which was based not on any large standing force but on the mobilizable potential of the population as a whole. Although there were occasional forays to chastise the Scots and Welsh, the object of strategy was essentially defensive and therefore, as long as there was good intelligence and coastal vigilance, the king had no need of a large standing army. There was from time to time something approximating to a standing navy – foreign ships hired for 'the duration' of perceived danger – but ultimately naval defence too relied on commercial vessels and their crews.

There were, however, permanent professionals bearing arms. These were the housecarls (Norse *húskarl*, literally 'house man').* They were the household troops and executives, the king's bodyguards; perhaps some 2,000 tough and practised fighting men, with high morale and a strong *esprit de corps*. Probably a good many had Danish blood. In addition, each earl had his own housecarls. Indeed, some historians judge that pre-Conquest England had the finest infantry in Europe; 'Fortunately', from Duke William's point of view, as the French Marshal Bugeaud would observe of the Duke of Wellington's infantry in Spain several hundred years later, 'it is not numerous.'

The housecarls, then, fought on foot, their preferred weapon the two-handed broad-axe (adapted from the Danish axe, some 1.3 metres long, the height of an average man at the shoulder at that time). However, for even closer combat some carried a sword and buckler (small round shield), or the kite-shaped long shield for protection against heavier weapons and arrows. This is not to say they had no horses, however. Besides the practical need for speed on occasion, the status of the king or earl meant that he travelled mounted, and his household troops had to keep up. They had their armour and

---

* The *Anglo-Saxon Chronicle* uses *hiredmenn* as a term for all paid warriors, whether housecarls or butsecarls and lithsmen (the latter two also having some competence as sailors).

camp kit to carry, too. But all the evidence is that the housecarls almost invariably fought dismounted. The Vikings were the threat, and the shield wall was the best defence against even a *berserker* charge.* The Vikings themselves, when unable to attack, didn't as a rule like to stand their ground. They were, after all, essentially raiders.† Besides, cavalry – men who fought *on* horseback, i.e. from the saddle – were both expensive and difficult to train. Only the regulars, the housecarls, would have been likely to achieve any proficiency. Even the Romans hadn't used their mounted arm for fighting, much, but rather for scouting. No doubt the Anglo-Saxons did their scouting on horseback, too, but there's no real evidence of a separate mounted arm, certainly not at the time of the Conquest. If, occasionally, a housecarl used the saddle to gain advantage – to throw a spear, say, or to run down a fleeing enemy – that wouldn't merit description as a cavalry action. It would have been more like the work of the dragoons (mounted infantry) of the Commonwealth period and later, who had responsibility for scouting, than that of the 'horse', the real cavalry.‡ The problem with dismounting to fight, however, is that someone must hold the horses. As it would have been a waste of a fighting man to have a housecarl do this (one

---

* From Old Norse *berserkr* (bearskin); these were members of warrior gangs, noted for their particular bloodlust, who attached themselves to noble households as bodyguards and shock troops.

† John Peddie, *Alfred the Good Soldier: His Life and Campaigns* (Bath, 1989). There were always exceptions, of course, perhaps most notably at Brunanburh (937); but as no one can agree even where the Battle of Brunanburh took place, accounts of a Danish shield wall are speculative.

‡ Nor was recent experience of trying to fight mounted likely to commend the practice. The *Anglo-Saxon Chronicle* records how in 1055 King Edward's (Norman) nephew, Earl Ralph, was routed by the Welsh near Hereford: 'Before a spear was thrown the English fled, because they had been made to fight on horseback.' Whether they had been made to do so by Earl Ralph or by ambush is unclear. They appear to have been worsted by archers.

horse-holder for three horses was the rule of the British cavalry in the early twentieth century), we can assume that there were a good many 'grooms' accompanying them and the *thegns*, the second order of nobility.

Although there is some (thin) documentary evidence, as well as that of the Bayeux Tapestry, that the Anglo-Saxon army had archers, there's nothing to say who exactly they were and how many. There are claims that the 'mystique' of archery was one carefully guarded by the aristocracy, being a part of their sport – hunting – and that bows in the hands of *ceorls* (free peasants) were discouraged, even prohibited. It seems unlikely that the archers were housecarls, however, whose forte was the melee. But were archers important anyway in Anglo-Saxon tactics? To be able to stand off in a fight and inflict damage on an adversary was an obvious advantage, but only so far. Battle was decided in close combat by the opposing hosts. There was every incentive for one side or the other, or both, to come to grips as quickly as possible. Besides, a moving target, even a large one, wasn't easy to aim at. Almost certainly there were no crossbowmen in the English army of 1066. They'd have been useful at Hastings, for although slow to load, these weapons could have inflicted real damage on the Norman cavalry at upwards of 100 yards, while the 'selfbow', smaller than the later longbow of Agincourt fame, though faster to use, wasn't nearly as lethal. But as the shield wall appears to have had little difficulty in standing against Duke William's horse, the absence of English archers at Hastings can't be counted as significant.

The housecarls were, then, the professional core of the king's military force. The remainder were levies, usually referred to as the *fyrd*. The word *fyrd* isn't quite as precise as is sometimes suggested. In several sources the Old English *here** (army) is used interchangeably

---

* Cf. the modern German *Heer*, the land force element of the Bundeswehr.

with *fyrd*, though some authorities have it that *here* is an offensive – raiding – army and *fyrd* a defensive force. They also suggest a connection therefore between *here* and the verb *hergian*, 'to act like a raiding army', usually translated today as 'to harry'. It seems that in referring to those in the shires liable to *fyrd* (i.e. army) duty, the word has come to mean the levies themselves. A semantic point, perhaps; in any event, when the king, or an earl, took to the field with an army, whether *fyrd* or *here*, the force would invariably consist of both regulars and militia.*

The *fyrd*, as the militia, comprised two echelons, which historians have come to call the 'great *fyrd*' and the 'select *fyrd*'. The great *fyrd* was in effect the nation in arms, albeit in practice almost always in localized form.[†] Every freeman was obliged to serve in the event of an emergency – primarily invasion. As it was a defensive duty, and a largely territorial one (most probably confined to the boundaries of an earldom – such as East Anglia – or perhaps even a shire), it was unlikely to have been much resented. How effective it was, this army of men who'd rarely if ever borne arms, is open to question, but in battles at this time numbers usually carried the day. The function of the great *fyrd* was to be a large and reasonably quickly assembled force to counter sudden attacks from the sea. Mass made up for arms. Three hardy freemen with clubs and scythes might well overpower an exhausted raider. Some, too, would have been useful bowmen, adept at taking – perhaps poaching – deer. But the real value of the great *fyrd* was in reinforcing, or multiplying the effect of,

---

* Militia: a force raised from the civilian population to supplement a regular force in an emergency.

† 'Only in the darkest days of the Danish attacks in the reigns of Aethelred [978–1013 and 1016] and Edmund Ironside [1016] is there an indication that this general obligation was enforced on anything like a national scale': Charles Warren Hollister, *Anglo-Saxon Military Institutions on the Eve of the Norman Conquest* (Oxford, 1962).

the select *fyrd*. This was a more active, and almost certainly nominated, militia, roughly equivalent to modern reservists. As far as the evidence goes, in most parts of England – certainly those outside the old Danelaw – the select *fyrd* was recruited on the basis of one man from every five 'hides'. The hide was a variable unit of land based originally on the acreage sufficient to support a household.* It could be as small as 40 acres (16 hectares) in counties such as Berkshire and Wiltshire, or elsewhere as large as 120 acres.† It was simply a measure of value as a basis for taxation and civic obligations (such as maintenance and repair of bridges and fortifications), and manpower for the select *fyrd*. Towns were also assessed in hides (in the Domesday Book, Tewkesbury for example was assessed as ninety-five hides, Northampton as twenty-five).

Hides were grouped into hundreds, the standard subdivision of a shire for administrative and legal purposes. The origin of the term 'hundred' is again uncertain, although initially at least it suggested an area of a hundred hides. These groupings – hides and hundreds – were an obvious basis for mustering and organizing not only the great *fyrd*, but also the select *fyrd*, and especially for determining the latter's financial support. Each five-hide unit and its equivalent in the old Danelaw had to provide the pay and subsistence of its fyrdsman when summoned for duty, and probably his equipment – helmet, spear, and axe or sword as a minimum. So who exactly was the select fyrdsman?

---

* From the Anglo-Saxon *hid* (or its synonym *hiwisc*), believed to derive from *hiwan*, 'family'.

† Here again there is dispute as to the measure of an acre, as it was originally associated with the amount of land that a team of eight oxen could plough in a single day. Regional variations were considerable, according to Bede, and in some places it would have been as little as half the area of the modern acre, which was set by an ordinance of *c.*1300 as measuring one furlong by one-tenth of a furlong – 4,840 square yards.

There's no consensus on this question either. The obvious answer would be the best warrior in the five hides. He might be a *ceorl*, a free peasant who either owned land or worked it, or he might be a *thegn*, a member of what would later be called the gentry or minor nobility. A *thegn* derived his status almost exclusively from the ownership of land – a minimum of five hides – which in the first instance would have been acquired by gift of the king, an earl or perhaps a senior churchman, but which might then have passed to him by inheritance. Or indeed by purchase, for there was social mobility within the system.* By 1066, such had been the increase in the number of *thegns* that there were three observable classes within the order. First were the king's *thegns*, closely associated with the royal court as either gentlemen-at-arms or administrators. The second class were the middle or median *thegns*, who probably held their land through a superior lord. Third were the ordinary *thegns*, who'd bought, been gifted or inherited the minimum amount from a higher *thegn* or churchman. Clearly, some of each class might have been found in the select *fyrd*. How many or in what proportion to the *ceorls* is impossible to say. Historians are divided on whether a *thegn* had a personal or a territorial obligation to the king – whether the obligation attached to his rank or to his holding of five hides (though, of course, most seem agreed that his rank rested on his holding of land in the first place). The important point is that the fyrdsmen of the select *fyrd* would have been men of either substance or military competence, and probably of both. It seems unlikely that when the select *fyrd* was called out, a process of selection would begin; there wouldn't be time. The owner of the five hides (which might have been but a

---

* 'And if a *ceorl* prospered, that he possessed fully five hides of land of his own, a bell and a castle-gate, a seat and special office in the king's hall, then was he henceforth entitled to the rights of a *thegn*': Commentary of Archbishop Wulfstan of York, taken to be the law of Aethelred and Cnut, referred to as the 'promotion laws'.

part of a king's or median *thegn*'s extensive holdings) was ultimately responsible for making sure an acceptable man reported to the constable of the hundred. Continuity was therefore best. In the case of a five-hide *thegn*, it was probably he himself who fulfilled the liability. At this time, all but the greatest *thegns* – those close to the status of earl – would have been used to physical work on their estates. As a result, it's safe to conclude that in the main the select *fyrd* comprised tough, intelligent men with some experience of military service over several years. Some may even have seen action against raiding parties. Their liability was limited to two months *in expeditionis necessitatem* (on necessary campaign), though in a continuing emergency this could be repeated. For example, in 1016, the year of disputed succession on the death of Aethelred, Edmund Ironside summoned the *fyrd* five separate times. Alfred had divided the Wessex *fyrd* into two in order to maintain an army in the field indefinitely. But there's no evidence that the select *fyrd* could be summoned merely for training. Indeed, the records stress *in expeditionis necessitatem.**

This, then, was King Harold's army – the society from which it was drawn, its organization, its weapons and terms of service. How did it compare with that of Duke William?

Leaving aside the question of numbers for the moment, the signal difference between the two was that William's army had cavalry – or rather, mounted knights – and a body of archers. Further, it had perhaps a fundamentally different attitude to war. Normandy was a small country compared with England, not as big even as Wessex. Its population at the time of the Conquest was probably around 700,000, while that of England was some 3 million.

---

* To be precise, the obligation was threefold, and known as the *trimoda necessitas* (obligation in three forms); but whether it was the obligation of the select or the great *fyrd* is uncertain, if of little importance ultimately. The *trimoda* were military service, repair of bridges and maintenance of fortresses.

The dukedom of Normandy had been founded at about the same time that Athelstan unified England (937). In the ninth century the Vikings had established a colony along the River Seine, which in a treaty of 911 was recognized by the Frankish king (who subsequently ceded further territory in the west) in return for their leader, Rollo, agreeing to accept Christianity and preventing other Vikings from entering the Seine. Normandy was bordered by polities of various sizes and degrees of allegiance to the king of France (or 'of the Franks'), whose alliances and enmities were in constant flux. While in the eleventh century, as a generalization, England was coming to enjoy peace, the Normans were much more warlike. This was something of an inevitability in a country with a long land border and restless neighbours, but it had come to be more than that. In its system of proto-chivalry – that is, medieval chivalry without, yet, its ideals of virtue and godliness – it was little more than a cult of horsemanship and war. And that cult had plenty of members, for an aristocratic youth had little choice but the church or apprenticeship as a *chevalier*. From an early age these would-be knights were trained to ride and fight together in groups known as *conrois* – to begin with, five to ten; then up to fifty. They wore shirts of chain mail – hauberks – much the same as the Saxon housecarls, but split front and back to allow them to sit astride, and likewise, helmets with noseguards. Each was armed with a sword and a lance, the latter as much a totem as a weapon, and perhaps better described as a javelin or spear, for few *chevaliers* seem to have fought with the lance couched – that is, under-arm to drive home the point using the momentum of the charging horse, with the rider secure in the stirrups.*

---

* This is an unresolved subject. The few illustrations – not least the Bayeux Tapestry – suggest that the lance was a jabbing, thrusting – both over- and under-arm – even a throwing weapon, shorter and lighter than the later one beloved of jousts. (Roman cavalry hadn't used stirrups, so using the couched lance with any force risked

'Chivalry in later ages may have had its merits,' writes one historian, 'but in the eleventh century it was a social disaster. It produced a superfluity of conceited illiterate young men who had no ideals except to ride and hunt and fight, whose only interest in life was violence and the glory they saw in it.'* There was evidently, then, a ready supply of eager men who disdained fighting on foot, even if occasionally they were forced to do so. And evidently too a ready supply of horses bred for the purpose that could bear the weight of a mailed *chevalier.*

Little is known about William's archers, except that at Hastings there were perhaps some 800 of them, including many Bretons. The Vikings had always used the bow as well as the blade, and the Normans were of course Vikings at one remove. William's archers were evidently highly trained in volley firing at a range of about 100 yards, which was short by later standards but well out of range of anything that could be hurled by Harold's army.† They didn't as a rule wear armour, though some did wear leather and helmets, and carried a knife or short sword for personal protection.

William and his allied princes had their equivalent of the housecarls, the *familia regis* (king's military household). They were fewer, almost certainly, than Harold's and his earls', and by all accounts not quite in the same league, perhaps because of the pre-eminence of the

---

unseating.) The couched lance was at its most effective when there was a line of them, otherwise the bold individual lancer could be hacked down from the flanks by the foot soldiers into whose ranks he'd driven. How far the *conrois* trained to charge in line isn't known. They were probably too much the individualists to perfect the knee-to-knee charge of, say, Napoleon's Polish lancers.

* David Howarth, *1066: The Year of Conquest* (London, 1977).

† The selfbow, which appears to be what the Normans used, had much less draw weight – and therefore range – than the longbow, which the Normans would meet to their cost in Wales the following century, and which defined the battles of the Hundred Years' War.

chevaliers (or *milites*, as some chroniclers have it). On campaign William appears to have used both Norman levies and mercenaries from adjoining states: well-armed and protected heavy infantry, known as *pedites*.

Clearly, then, although Harold would have a qualitative and perhaps quantitative advantage in infantry, William would have the advantage in being able to maintain the pressure in battle, and thereby the initiative, by attacking in turn with his three separate arms, though much would of course depend on the ground. Taking on a Saxon shield wall was not an attractive proposition.

But why was Harold's shield wall being put to the test in the first place? Why the battle? Why the invasion?

King Edward, 'the Confessor', so called for his piety, had died on 5 January 1066. He was the eldest son of King Aethelred ('the Unready') from his second marriage, to Emma, sister of Duke Richard of Normandy. But Aethelred had sons from his first marriage, and when he died in 1016, the eldest surviving, Edmund 'Ironside', was challenged by Cnut, son of Sweyn of Denmark. Edmund died later that year, leaving Cnut to take the throne. Twenty years later, on Cnut's death, there was another succession dispute, for he too had been twice married. Edward succeeded to the throne only after seven years of battling. Alfred the Great's line was now restored to the English throne, but only by the support of the powerful Earl Godwine of Wessex. To make sure of that support, Edward promptly married Godwine's daughter, Edith. Alas, the marriage was without issue.

Godwine himself died in 1053. Harold, as his eldest surviving son, succeeded to the earldom, while the other sons in turn became provincial lords of much of England. With such Godwineson power in the land, Edward prudently maintained good relations with the Norman court, now ruled by Duke William. Indeed, at some stage, it seems, he gave William to understand that he was to succeed him. On Edward's death in January 1066, therefore, there were three – perhaps four – candidates for the throne. Harold was the brother-in-law and friend of the late king, and, of course, brother of the widowed queen. Though he'd no royal blood he'd been at the heart of English government (in late years the *subregulus*, 'under-king') and had a formidable military reputation, gained principally in Wales. But to complicate matters he'd also burnished that reputation in Normandy, which he visited in 1064. Why he made that visit, no one can be certain. The pro-Norman sources claim that Edward, who was then sixty-one and increasingly sickly, sent him to confirm the offer of the crown to William. Some English sources suggest that he was going to France for an unspecified purpose and was blown off course – or even shipwrecked on his way – and ended up in Normandy. Some historians have suggested it was to negotiate the freeing of his brother Wulfnoth, who was a hostage in William's court. Another writer, with a distinguished naval background, and also a knowledge of small boats and Channel currents, suggests that France was never his destination, that he had simply embarked at his estate in present-day Chichester harbour for a sporting expedition – fishing off the Isle of Wight or hunting in the forests to the west (the Bayeux Tapestry shows him embarking with hawks and hounds) – and was caught in a northerly or westerly gale.* The *Anglo-Saxon Chronicle* is silent on the matter.

What is certain is that Harold landed in the Norman vassal province of Ponthieu, where he was promptly arrested. When William heard of it, he sent messengers ordering the Count of Ponthieu to hand over his prisoner, which he duly did. William then took Harold with him on campaign against the new Duke of Brittany, with the probable, if not obvious, intention of impressing his likely rival to the English throne. The plan evidently failed. The Bayeux Tapestry, a work of propaganda after all, portrays the campaign as a triumph.

---

* Howarth, *1066*.

However, other sources paint a different picture, in which William exhausted himself and his supplies in a futile chase around Brittany and was finally forced to withdraw. The only person to come out well in all accounts was Harold, who personally rescued some of William's men from the quicksands at Mont St Michel. If the latter accounts rather than Bayeux are to be believed, Harold might reasonably have concluded that the Norman war machine did not live up to its advance billing.

The succession was not, in any case, entirely a matter of birth or nomination. Ultimately it rested with the Witan, the ancient council of the Anglo-Saxon kings in and of England, consisting of the most powerful secular and spiritual lords. At Edward's death, Harold Godwineson was about forty-five, 'very tall and handsome, remarkable for his physical strength, his courage and eloquence, his ready jests and acts of valour', wrote the chronicler Orderic Vitalis. Harold claimed that on his deathbed Edward had named him his successor. In the Bayeux Tapestry, the king is indeed shown reaching out and touching Harold, who is kneeling beside him, but the text above doesn't explain the meaning of the gesture. The claim was enough for the Witan, however, which looked not merely at the blood relation but at the claimant's ability to defend the kingdom. The Confessor died at Westminster on 5 January. Harold was crowned king in the abbey the following day – the day of the old king's funeral. The haste looks unseemly, now; it probably did then, too. But in Anglo-Saxon England, it was election by the Witan that made a man king, the coronation being the ceremonial celebration. Continental doctrine, however, held otherwise; God, not an assembly of men, through the coronation made a king. And if the coronation was thought unseemly, then it would probably have nagged away quietly at those involved – not least Harold. For the Pope could declare it null and void.

Yet if Harold had a claim and the succession principles were not clear-cut, then what of his brother Tostig? A decade earlier, Edward had made Tostig Earl of Northumbria, but in October 1065 the Northumbrian lords had risen in violent rebellion against him, and Edward had sent Harold to put them down. Unusually, Harold had failed in this and Edward had had to acquiesce in the rebels' demands, exiling Tostig and giving the earldom to Morcar, younger brother of Earl Edwine of Mercia. (By the time Harold had reached Northampton, where Edwine's forces and the rebels had combined, it was probably clear that opposing them was futile, and that all he could do was negotiate a deal to save his brother's skin rather than his earldom.) Tostig believed, possibly correctly, that Harold had conspired at his exile to strengthen his own position. The marriage shortly afterwards of Harold and Edwine's sister could hardly have looked apolitical.

The claimant with the strongest blood title was Edgar 'Aetheling' ('royal prince'), grandson of Edmund Ironside, and thus in the direct English royal line. But he was only fourteen (perhaps younger), with no significant backing and so no immediate prospect of being able to rule independently. This all added to Duke William's belief in his own cause. After all, the late king's mother, Emma of Normandy, was the sister of William's grandfather, making William and Edward first cousins once removed.

The first challenge to Harold came from Tostig. With the help of his brother-in-law Count Baldwin of Flanders, he assembled a fleet and in April began raiding the south coast. When Harold moved against him, Tostig sailed north to the Lincolnshire coast. Here he was met by the forces of Edwine and Morcar and severely beaten, fleeing to Scotland with just twelve ships. Tostig was by no means finished, however. If he doubted he could seize the throne, there was at least his earldom to recover.

Harold, meanwhile, was preparing for the expected challenge from Normandy. (How much direct intelligence he was receiving from Normandy is unknown.) According to the *Anglo-Saxon Chronicle*, by early summer he'd 'gathered such a great naval force, and a land force also, as no other king in the land had gathered before'. It almost certainly included a substantial number of housecarls and the select *fyrd* of Wessex (which included Sussex and Cornwall) and Kent. Given that there was as yet no actual invasion, it seems unlikely that any part of the great *fyrd* was mobilized. There must have been some sort of constant watch all along the Channel coast; but, rather than dispose his forces in 'penny packets', it seems that Harold assembled the army on the Isle of Wight, whence he could use the prevailing southwesterlies to descend on the Normans wherever they landed. However, with no appearance of William or reappearance of Tostig, in early September – on the feast of the Nativity of the Blessed Virgin Mary, a date that would have been prominent in the mind of every *thegn* and *ceorl* – he stood down the *fyrd*. Their two months' liege service, which had probably been extended by a few weeks in any case, was coming to an end, as was their food supply, and they were needed on their farms to gather in the last of the harvest and begin the autumn tillage. Besides, the winds were unfavourable for invasion, and soon it would be the season of storms in the Channel, the *Sueth-Sae* (South Sea) as Harold's men knew it.

Duke William, however, wasn't constrained by either terms of service or the weather forecast. As soon as his spies told him that Harold had stood down the *fyrd* he made ready to strike, transferring his army to the mouth of the Somme for the shorter crossing. For surely the ill wind couldn't remain against him for ever?

2

THE NORTH WIND DOTH BLOW

Unfurl the sails, and let God steer us where He will.

The Venerable Bede

It was an ill wind for William, but not so ill as to bring him no good. At least it had helped his spies get back across the Channel, and in turn frustrated Harold's.* But when Harold turned away from the watch on the *Sueth-Sae*, he was confident the wind was in his favour; and, indeed, William was becoming anxious. Yet the same prevailing northerlies that kept William in Normandy were Viking weather, and with them now came Tostig again – and with him the most feared Viking warrior of the age, Cnut's grandson Harald Sigurdsson, king of Norway – Harald 'Hardrada' (Hard Ruler). Tostig had been licking his wounds and gathering a new army in Scotland, and

---

* It seems that the messenger pigeon was unknown to the English, although the Greeks had used them to proclaim the winner of the Olympics, and a century after Hastings there was a regular service between Aleppo and Cairo.

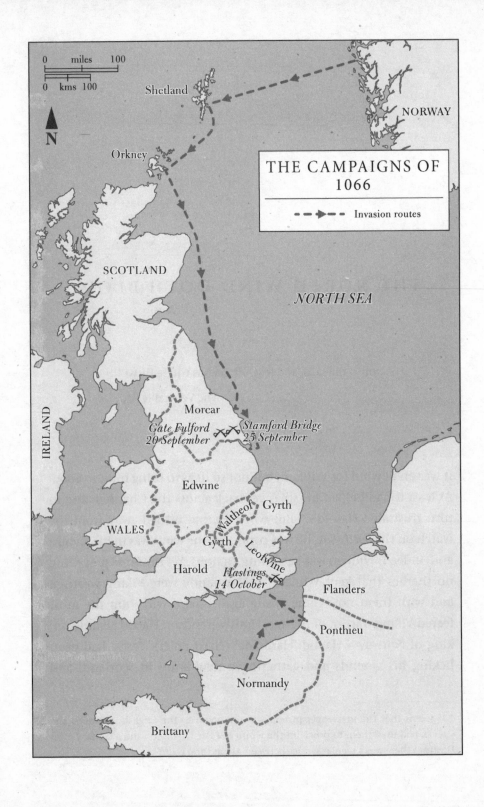

THE CAMPAIGNS OF
1066

- - -▶- - - Invasion routes

NORWAY

Shetland

Orkney

SCOTLAND

NORTH SEA

IRELAND

Morcar

Gate Fulford
20 September

Stamford Bridge
25 September

Edwine

Gyrth

Waltheof

WALES

Gyrth

Leofwine

Harold

Hastings
14 October

Flanders

Ponthieu

Normandy

Brittany

0   miles   100

0   kms   100

N

evidently had decided to back Hardrada's claim to the throne in the hope of recovering his earldom. Indeed, by some accounts he went in person to Norway to persuade Harald that conquest would be easy.

Their combined numbers were probably 10,000 at least (Hardrada is said to have had 300 ships, and some modern historians reckon he could have brought between 12,000 and 18,000 men from Norway), and in true Viking fashion they began raiding the north-east coast, burning Scarborough. This was a mistake. It alerted Morcar, who called out the Northumbrian *fyrd* and sent word to his brother Edwine for help – as well as to Harold. On about 16 September (by some reckonings, perhaps even a week earlier), having entered the Humber and sailed up the Ouse as far as Riccall, 9 miles from York, Hardrada and Tostig disembarked to march on the capital of the earldom of Northumbria. The Viking fleet could certainly have taken to oars on entering the Humber, but it would have been hard pulling the 40 miles to the confluence with the Ouse, and then another 30 to Riccall. That it didn't suggests that the wind was already veering south and east.

What happened then, precisely, isn't known, although it seems that Hardrada made no immediate assault on York. Instead his men were probably foraging, and forcibly. However, by the third week of September Morcar and Edwine had gathered an army strong enough to take the offensive – either that, or they fought a 'meeting engagement' (one in which both sides run into each other while on the move) with the invaders. Whichever it was, on 20 September, just outside the old Roman city walls at Fulford (sometimes 'Gate Fulford'), 7 miles north of Riccall, Morcar and Edwine were decisively beaten. Some sources have it that they were only just able to escape. Sir Frank Stenton, author of *Anglo-Saxon England*, the third volume of the *Oxford History of England* (first published in 1943), says that Fulford was 'a murderous and protracted struggle' which destroyed the English army of the north, so that Edwine and Morcar 'were unable to take any effective part in the campaign of Hastings'.* There are few details of the battle, however, and even fewer reliable ones. The Irish monk Marianus Scotus – Marian the Scot ('Scot' at that time still including the Irish) – a contemporary chronicler, though a distant one, being then at the abbey in Mainz, says that more than a thousand were killed in the battle, as well as a hundred priests. The priests were unlikely to have been Hardrada's, for there's still dispute whether he was a Christian or a pagan. (If the former, he certainly wore his Christianity lightly.) How exactly the thousand non-clerical deaths are apportioned, Marianus doesn't say, but as the burghers of York at once sued for peace and opened the gates to Hardrada, it was plainly an emphatic victory.

To what extent the city was pillaged is also unclear. The 'C' version of the *Anglo-Saxon Chronicle* says that Harald and Tostig 'went into York with as large a force as suited them, and they were given hostages from the city as well as provisions'. With its significant population of settled Danes it certainly appears to have been spared the worst, but a Viking army after a bloody victory couldn't have been entirely peaceable on entry. Be that as it may, having come to terms with the city, at some stage Harald moved out with his force some 10 miles east-north-east to a crossing of the River Derwent known today as Stamford Bridge to await the usual hostages (and probably more tribute).

With him went Tostig. This is puzzling, for if Tostig had reclaimed his earldom, why then didn't he remain in his capital? Its walls could have seen off any counter-attack by Morcar. According to the *Chronicle*, the terms agreed to by the inhabitants of York included the provision of men to join Hardrada in his march south. These would in effect be Tostig's *fyrd*. Why did he not remain to oversee their

---

* 'English Families and the Norman Conquest', in *Transactions of the Royal Historical Society* (London, 1944).

assembly? Perhaps the battle of Gate Fulford had inflicted more damage on the combined army – Tostig's men and the Norwegians – than is usually supposed?

Another puzzle is why Morcar and his brother rushed to battle in the first place rather than waiting for Harold and his army. Certainly, the sack of York, had it come to that, would have been a serious humiliation, and no one could criticize an earl for opposing a Viking army. But might there have been another consideration? Although Harold Godwineson had married their sister, the two earls may have feared that the king would trade Northumbria for his own purposes, as indeed some sources suggest he tried to, offering Tostig his earldom back if he changed sides. Mistrust of allies, especially mutual mistrust, is lethally corrosive.

Like so much else, when exactly Harold learned of the invasion, or what he made of it at first, is uncertain. There's no evidence that he'd expected a challenge from Hardrada; if he had, then the northern *fyrds* would surely have been on watch like those in the south. He appears to have been in London when the news reached him, which was fortunate, and at once sent out summonses for the *fyrd* to assemble – the select *fyrd* at least, probably chiefly that of East Anglia, his brother Gyrth's earldom, and perhaps even for some of his brother Leofwine's (of the home counties) to *re*assemble. He wasted no time waiting for them, however, setting off at once with his housecarls up the old Roman road, a road with which he was certainly familiar, having gone twice to York in the previous twelve months (the second time not long after his coronation, perhaps to make sure of the northern earls' loyalty).

It's sometimes said that he covered the 200 miles to York in four days, but although Harold was noted for swiftness, this would have been next to impossible on foot, and highly improbable on horseback without relays, which wouldn't have been available in any number for the housecarls. Six or seven days is more realistic, but even so, the fyrdsmen who made it to Yorkshire from the Wessex and East Anglian shires, joining en route, would have been hard pressed. It seems certain, in any event, that Harold reached Tadcaster, 10 miles south-west of York, on 24 September. By all accounts, Morcar and Edwine were nowhere to be found. What is clear is that at Tadcaster he learned that Hardrada was at Stamford Bridge, 20 miles to the north-east, and that there were no enemy in York to threaten his flank and rear if he marched to engage him. Centuries later the Duke of Marlborough would write that 'no war can be made without good and timely intelligence'; and this for Harold was indeed war-winning intelligence. What is not known is whether he was also made aware that the Norwegian fleet was at Riccall, which was just half the distance east-south-east, for it would perhaps have been tempting first to burn Hardrada's boats. That said, he would still have had to defeat Hardrada's army, and with a force perhaps weakened by battle at Riccall. Besides, how might the defeated invaders be expelled without their longboats? Were they all to be put to the sword? Whatever the intention, if Harold did know of the whereabouts of the fleet, he took the bolder course in going straight for Stamford Bridge – and he took it quickly.

Whether he also knew that Hardrada was still unaware of his march north, let alone his proximity, again we don't know; nor why Hardrada had chosen to camp by the Derwent instead of at Riccall. It seems that after York's submission he and his army had returned to the boats to divest themselves of their chain mail – or had had it taken there – and went confidently to the rendezvous at the crossing of the Derwent with just helmets, swords and shields (some accounts say without even shields).

Why? Two accounts say it was because the weather was warm and sunny.* Perhaps, but Gate Fulford must indeed have been a crushing

---

* The Icelandic chronicler Snorri Sturluson, writing 150 years later, and also Marianus Scotus.

victory for the great warrior to expose his army thus; and clearly he could have known nothing of Harold's approach. Rarely can surprise have been so great, therefore – *surprise*, the commander's greatest tactical asset – than when late the following morning, 25 September, having marched at dawn from Tadcaster, Harold appeared on the road from York. Or rather, a cloud of dust appeared, which Hardrada seems at first to have thought was raised by the approaching hostages. The alarm when he realized his mistake, and the frantic rush to get word to Riccall for his coats of mail and reinforcements, can only be imagined.

Again there's little reliable detail of the battle among the obviously fanciful stories. It was quite evidently a vast, unsophisticated brawl, a business of battle-axes and swords, although some accounts say the English had archers. Or at least a few bowmen. But they weren't firing distant volleys, as they would at Agincourt three and a half centuries later; they were firing 'direct', that is, at low angle and closer range, aiming at individuals or groups. If there was indeed a bridge at the crossing site, as its modern name suggests, the fighting would have centred on it, the river acting as a shield for Hardrada, who must have been hoping to gain time for help to come from Riccall. The *Anglo-Saxon Chronicle* ('D' version) says it was 'a very stubborn battle', while the 'C' version says it was 'fierce' and continued until late in the day. With dusk at about 6.30 p.m., and battle joined at, say, eleven o'clock, this would indeed have been a long battle by medieval standards, though the culminating point probably came well before last light. For we know that at some stage both Hardrada and Tostig were killed in the fighting, Hardrada reputedly by an arrow in his neck. Once the Norwegians had lost their king, it would have been *sauve qui peut* – a flight to the boats at Riccall. Some accounts have them chased by Harold's mounted housecarls all the way, which wouldn't have been practicable after dark. The author of *Vita Ædwardi Regis* ('Life of King Edward'), written the following year, says the

'Ouse with corpses choked', and that the Humber 'dyed the ocean waves for miles around with Viking gore'. It appears that only those who made it back to the boats were eventually given quarter, including Hardrada's son Olaf. From Stamford Bridge to the Ouse at Riccall is 11 miles as the crow flies, and at some point the Derwent had to be crossed. The fugitives could hardly have reached the boats in daylight, and so it seems likely that it wasn't until morning that Harold closed with them and offered terms – on sworn promise never to return. Even so, there were few left to swear an oath. By all accounts they'd come with three hundred ships; but they left with just twenty-four.

Harold now marched to York, probably on the 26th or 27th. Not only would he have wanted to recuperate – there would have been many a wound among his housecarls and fyrdsmen to be dressed – but he had also to deal with the matter of the city's hasty capitulation to Hardrada. Who knows whether he attended his brother Tostig's funeral? The body, according to William of Malmesbury's *De Gestis Regum Anglorum* ('On the Deeds of the Kings of the English', c.1125), was brought to York for honourable burial. It seems unlikely that Harold himself, though, would have honoured a rebel, even if he'd wanted to exalt his own royal house. If, however, he did stand by the grave as his brother's body was lowered, perhaps he felt the wind change, for on the 27th it was no longer blowing south. Not, at least, in the Channel.

Having learned that Harold had stood down his army earlier in the month, and having been just about to make the same decision, it appears that William now took a gamble. The wind was blowing a little more westerly, and so he embarked his army at Dives on about 12 or 13 September. But at first he could make no headway – suffering several wrecks, indeed – and so instead clawed his way along the coast to the harbour at St Valery. On the 27th, however, the wind freshened and at last backed to the north just enough. He set sail for the English coast after dark so as not to risk running into Harold's fleet – which in fact had been laid up for the winter – and also to make landfall with plenty of daylight ahead.

Next morning at about nine o'clock the greatest invasion fleet to cross the Channel until 1944 beached at Pevensey, 8 miles west of Hastings.*

At this point William's plan of campaign was probably not yet settled. It was enough to get the army ashore unopposed. It's sometimes said that when William sailed he didn't know which Harold he'd be facing. This is true inasmuch as it could either have been Harold Godwineson or Harald Hardrada, but it's highly unlikely that William himself could have known of the Norwegian invasion, or even Hardrada's intention to claim the throne. And suggestions they acted in collusion make no sense. It's safe to assume, though, that soon after landing he learned of Hardrada's arrival, and of Harold's march north; and that is the point at which he wouldn't have known which Harold – if either of them – would next be marching south.

Whoever his opponent turned out to be, though, William had to establish himself firmly in what was enemy territory. This meant marching east and fortifying an encampment, an Iron Age hill fort on the cliffs of the Hastings peninsula, and throwing up a 'motte and bailey'.† Then he had to feed the army. Being William, he set about this not as a transactional business, rather one of taking – and taking

---

* 'Then King William came from Normandy into Pevensey, on the eve of the Feast of St Michael' (Michaelmas – 29 September). The *Anglo-Saxon Chronicle* (Worcester MS) for the year 1066 is the only contemporary English account of the battle of Hastings.

† The motte (Old French *mote* – mound) was surrounded by a ditch (which in Late Middle English became 'moat') and surmounted by a stockade and primitive keep. The bailey (Old French *baile* – enclosure) was a forecourt surrounded by another ditch and stockade to protect the horses and other domestic animals, entered by way of a drawbridge.

with considerable violence, according to the Bayeux Tapestry and other sources. But then what? If whichever Harold had decided to stay fast in London, William's only option would have been to march on the capital, either directly through the heavily wooded Weald, or indirectly via Dover and Canterbury, or perhaps Chichester and the valley of the Test towards the Thames. Marching through the Weald would have risked going the way of Varus in the Teutoburgerwald, whose three legions were annihilated in ambushes by the German tribes in AD 9. Going by Canterbury would have exposed his flank to the Saxon navy and risked a fight trying to cross the Medway or the Darent, while the westerly route via Chichester would have risked marching straight into the Wessex *fyrd*. In each case the Normans would have had to live off the land, which would have slowed their progress and exposed them to attack as they spread out to forage. It's not difficult to conclude, therefore, that early on William saw his best course as staying put and drawing Harold on to him for a decisive battle, or at least one in which the English army was repulsed, allowing him then to advance with more assurance.

News of the Norman landing would have travelled fast to London, a distance of 60–70 miles – in a single day, possibly, two days at most; by the evening of the 29th, therefore. It would then have speeded north by relays along 'Ermine Street', what remained of the old Roman road via Lincoln to York. A reasonable estimate is that it reached Harold late on 1 October – a Sunday in the old Julian calendar – or on the next day. Henry, Archdeacon of Huntingdon, born twenty years later, to the Archdeacon of Lincoln – and perhaps therefore more than usually reliable – states that while Harold 'was at dinner, a messenger arrived with the news that William, duke of Normandy, had landed on the south coast, and had built a fort at Hastings'.*

---

* *Historia Anglorum* ('History of the English People'), *c*.1154.

Others have it as a feast, making comparison with the Duke of Wellington at the Duchess of Richmond's ball before Waterloo irresistible. No matter: whatever the interrupted meal, the shock can only be imagined.

'The king,' adds Henry of Huntingdon, 'hastened southwards to oppose him.'

3

THE KING HASTENS SOUTHWARDS

No one is so brave that he is not disturbed by something unexpected.

Julius Caesar

The march back down the Great North Road can hardly have been much faster than the march up it, and quite probably was rather slower, given the rigours Harold and his army had just been through. Some sources have it that he rested a while 20 miles north of London at Waltham Abbey, which he'd founded six years before. He'd certainly have had plenty of time en route to make an appreciation of the situation, and possibly more detailed intelligence of William's strength and movements would have reached him. We can assume that his intention was straightforward: to defeat Duke William by destroying his force or compelling him to flee, as he had Hardrada. We can also assume, because of how events turned out, that he concluded that he should give battle as soon as possible.

Why would he conclude this? Perhaps because his success against Hardrada had been a triumph of celerity, regaining the initiative by striking unexpectedly quickly. Although he couldn't expect to achieve the same complete surprise against William, confronting the invader at speed might at least unnerve him (or even, as one chronicler, William of Poitiers, suggests, gain tactical surprise in a night attack).* Harold may also have been anxious that reinforcements might soon arrive from Normandy. At any rate, he couldn't have feared for the loyalty of the Wessex gentry, as he had with the Northumbrian. This was not just part of his kingdom; it was his own earldom.

Therein also lay a limitation, however. He might take the plundering of Sussex as a personal affront, and thus make his moves precipitately. Indeed, it seems that William understood this perfectly, perhaps having judged his opponent's temperament two years before in Normandy, and therefore turned his foraging into despoliation to draw him to Hastings. The Bayeux Tapestry shows his men burning a house, a woman and child fleeing.

Either during the march south or in London, and quite possibly both, Harold's brother Gyrth urged that he adopt a fabian strategy: allow him, Gyrth, to take what troops were immediately available to Hastings to harry the invaders, while Harold himself gathered a much larger army – the great *fyrds* of Wessex and East Anglia, along with Morcar's and Edwine's troops (what was left of them) – to be ready for William when he began his advance inland. With the autumn storms approaching, William could expect few reinforcements from France, or supplies. Duke William had his back to the sea, where Harold's ships, called out of their winter moorage, would soon be able to intercept his lines of communication and block any retreat, or even to strike while they were still at anchor. Time was not on William's side, and Harold must have been able to see this.

He rejected the advice, however. Perhaps he believed he could deal

---

* *Gesta Guillelmi II ducis Normannorum, c.*1070s.

with the Normans as he had with the Norwegians. Harold had seen William on campaign and may have thought there was nothing excessively to fear from him as a battlefield commander. Besides, just how reliable were Morcar and Edwine? Perhaps he also believed it the duty of the king to be in the forefront of the action. And in any case, recognizing that time was not on William's side, might not this have been good reason to adopt the tactics that the Duke of Wellington would perfect in Spain: choosing a favourable piece of ground and then waiting for the enemy to attack – as attack they must?

To this, though, there may have been a twist. According to several of the medieval commentators, and also the tapestry, when Harold had been in Normandy two years before, he'd sworn some sort of oath to William over sacred relics. The Norman apologists are adamant that it was an oath recognizing William's claim to the throne. Others are silent on the matter or impute trickery – claiming that, for instance, Harold gave a pledge of allegiance over a covered reliquary, which William only revealed to him afterwards by dramatically removing the covering. When Edward the Confessor died, William put his claim to the Pope, Alexander II, who gave his blessing to the invasion.* On coming ashore, Duke William was therefore able to unfurl his papal banner, which to any uneasy conscience would have been demoralizing to say the least, especially as William also carried an edict from Alexander to the independent-minded Old English clergy requiring them to submit to the new regime. We must assume that Harold learned of this on arrival in London on or about 6 October. According to the *Carmen de Hastingae Proelio* ('Song of the Battle

---

* Pope Alexander II was the first to be elected (in 1061) by the college of cardinals rather than by the Holy Roman Emperor and the Roman metropolitan church. His election was contested by the German court, but eventually the emperor gave way. It is interesting to speculate on whether the emperor's candidate would have backed William.

of Hastings'),* generally recognized to be the earliest chronicle of the battle, both leaders sent monks as envoys to parley with the enemy. If William's envoys stressed their papal sanction and Harold knew he had indeed sworn an oath, even if tricked into it (medieval piety wasn't famous for allowing latitude), he would at this point have begun entertaining a doubt as to which of them could rightly claim divine providence, the protective care of God. That said, in 1062 when he invaded neighbouring Maine, William had justified his action by claiming that the late Count of Maine had pledged his province to him if he died without heirs – the first of three occasions on which he would use the same excuse. If Harold had no doubts, he would be able to submit confidently to that providence. If he did hold genuine doubts, as a devout man (at least ostensibly) he would likewise have been inclined to submit to trial by combat. In either case he would have to take personal command in the field. But besides being influenced in that decision, did Harold entertain a doubt that gnawed at his self-belief – that divine providence would not be with him? Did he also extend that doubt to his own subjects, fearing they too would question his legitimacy, and therefore that he must prove it not just in trial by combat but *quickly*? We can never know, but the curiously passive defensive battle he would fight at Hastings, seemingly so out of character, suggests it's worth a thought. The Duke of Wellington, before sailing to Spain to fight Napoleon, speculated that 'the continental armies were more than half beaten before the battle was begun – I, at least, will not be frightened beforehand'. That tells us nothing about Harold's state of mind before Hastings, of course, but it does tell us that the general's state of mind is crucial.†

---

* Attributed to Bishop Guy d'Amiens, uncle of Count Guy de Ponthieu, vassal of Duke William.

† There are also accounts that William sent envoys to Caldbec the day before with the message that Harold had been excommunicated, and those who stood with

Whatever the case, according to the *Anglo-Saxon Chronicle* ('E') Harold left London with his housecarls and brothers Gyrth and Leofwine – probably on 11 October – and arrived at the rendezvous for the gathering *fyrd*, the 'Hoar [grey] Apple Tree' on Caldbec Hill, seven miles north-west of Hastings, on 13 October. The fact that the rendezvous was so specific suggests a high level of contingency planning during the summer months of the watch on the *Sueth-Sae*.

As for whose army had the numerical advantage, it's not possible to say with anything like certainty, although of course the chroniclers have made their own assertions. The Anglo-Norman Wace, who according to the most recent and most thorough examination is probably the most reliable on this as well as on the number of William's ships, says that the two armies were of much the same size, and modern estimates put this at between 5,000 and 7,000 men.* And this makes sense, as the battle couldn't have lasted so long, even with the Saxon advantage of the higher ground, if one side had been significantly larger than the other. That said, the composition of the two sides was very different. The Saxons consisted purely of 'infantry' – housecarls, *thegns*, the select fyrdsmen and local men of the great *fyrd* (this latter is clear in the tapestry's depiction of so many men armed with little more than clubs, or stones tied to sticks). Harold had no archers to speak of; just a single bow is shown in the tapestry. Perhaps those who'd survived Stamford Bridge had simply

---

him – false, of course, an unwarranted elaboration of the papal blessing, but unnerving perhaps. The story is not inconsistent with military practice – Harold too might have sent envoys, ostensibly to deliver an ultimatum, but in fact to spy out the army. William would certainly have been keen to know whether Harold himself was in the field, and seeing his standards at Caldbec would have reassured him that he would have his decisive battle.

* Marc Morris, *The Norman Conquest* (London, 2012).

not been able to keep up in the forced march south. He'd probably lost a great many housecarls at Stamford Bridge, too, so that there couldn't have been many more than a thousand of Harold's and his brothers' household troops combined – perhaps just half that number. They were undoubtedly tired after the exertions of the past month, though they'd the victory to buoy them up. The Icelandic chronicler Snorri Sturluson, writing a hundred and fifty years later, said of them at Stamford Bridge that they'd been 'so valiant that one of them was better than two of [Hardrada's] best men'.

Duke William's army was organized in three 'divisions', the largest being his own Normans, the other two being the Bretons and the Franco-Flemish, who were in essence mercenaries. Modern estimates suggest 3,000 mounted knights, most of them Normans, in chain armour with swords and lances, 1,000 archers, including crossbowmen, and the rest *pedites*. Their morale must have been high: against the weather odds, they'd crossed the Channel and landed unopposed. They'd fortified their bridgehead and laid in supplies by pillaging. They could expect fortunes if they succeeded, or remission of sins and admittance to heaven if they failed. This was an offer that had always brought men flocking to a martial adventure, for Duke William had promised them the riches of England – gold and silver for the humble foot soldiers, land for the knights – and he'd assured them (falsely, despite the papal sanction for the mission) that the Pope had guaranteed salvation for those slain in the cause. Besides, as most of them must have realized, there could be no retreat.

With strategic surprise impossible, there still remained tactical surprise to aim for – on both sides. Harold had moved quickly once he'd taken the decision to fight without delay. He appears to have passed the night of 13 October on Caldbec Hill resting while men of the more westerly of the Wessex *fyrd* joined him throughout the hours of darkness. To make a night attack on the Norman camp at Hastings 7 miles distant would have taken careful preparation, and even so, surprise would have been difficult to achieve if Harold had approached in daylight and William had taken the usual precautions of a mounted 'screen' to warn of any such move. And fighting in darkness – there was less than half a moon that night – is a desperate business. For one thing, control is next to impossible. Far better to use the darkness to get into position for an attack at dawn. And here a half moon would have favoured Harold, for it would have been just enough to march by, but too little for the Normans to see by. The English could have set out at midnight – leaving fires blazing on Caldbec Hill to maintain appearances – and been in position a little short of the Norman camp by four o'clock. There they could have rested for an hour or so and then, at 5.45, break of day,* they could have risen, formed ranks and attacked.

Harold chose not to. Why, as ever, we don't know. Perhaps on seeing the hill again, and the country to its front, he thought it a stronger position than he had before. Perhaps his men – his house-carls in particular, the backbone of the army – were just too tired. Perhaps the men of the Wessex *fyrd* were rather too late arriving that afternoon and evening, and likewise needing rest. But if he'd already decided to fight a defensive battle, would he not have taken precautions against cavalry? He'd seen its capability two years before when in Normandy. Sharpened stakes, famously used by the Greeks and Romans, could easily have been improvised to give at least his flanks more protection. Perhaps he too, like William when he landed, had decided first to gather his army and only then to judge what was best to do.

It is well that he didn't attempt a dawn attack, for William, learn-ing of his approach, kept his men under arms all night. Indeed, it seems he'd decided that if Harold did not attack during the night he

---

* 14 October by the old Julian calendar is 20 October by the modern Gregorian, when the sun rises at about 6.30 GMT.

himself would steal a march on him by striking out for Caldbec Hill at first light. After all, his army – so many cavalry and archers – was just as suited to mounting the attack (arguably even more so) than waiting for it. Whose army was the more tired next morning therefore is a moot point. Maistre Wace says that 'the English passed the night without sleep, in drinking and singing'. Perhaps some did – it plays to national archetype – just as some Normans, again according to Wace, spent theirs in prayer and confession.

We know for certain that soon after sunrise William was on the move. We can also assume that at sunrise Harold's army was standing to arms, either to take up a defensive position or, if he was confident he'd now assembled enough men, to march against the Norman camp.

Very soon, however, Harold must have learned of William's approach; but even then, although surprise would no longer be his, he could hardly have been too disconcerted. Gaining surprise could only ever have been a bonus, and he must have known that William would have his scouts and spies. Indeed, Harold may have welcomed the news. He could now fight on ground truly of his own choosing.

There is dispute as to what exactly was the ground he chose, but the weight of literary evidence and tradition – for there's no archaeological evidence of anything whatever – is that it was a ridge half a mile or so below Caldbec.* Why he should have given up Caldbec, whose slopes are steeper, we cannot know, except that there may have been too much ground cover. The lower ridge – Battle Hill, as it's now called – even in 1066 before its medieval terracing was no great obstacle to movement. Its slope was about 1 in 15 in the centre (roughly 7 per cent – not excessive for horses, or even for men in mail) and even less on the right flank. In many ways it resembled the ridge at Mont St Jean, where 750 years later the Duke of Wellington

---

* According to tradition, Battle Abbey was built on the spot where Harold fell.

would stubbornly hold his ground against Napoleon and the flower of the French army. It had just enough 'capability', though, as Lancelot Brown, the great landscape architect of the eighteenth century, used to say of a piece of country that he thought he could adapt to his patron's purpose. 'Ground' is the first factor in a modern military appreciation, and the first paragraph in operational orders. It would have been so too in 1066.

The Duke of Wellington spent many weeks before Waterloo riding the ground, looking for where he might deploy if the French came this way or that, and there's no reason to suppose that Harold, as an experienced soldier, would have done otherwise during the months of watching for invasion. And he would have seen that the lower ridge had capability for a defensive battle. Its flattish top of open heathland, some 700 yards long and 200 deep, before the steep rise to Caldbec Hill, was an ideal spot on which to form the 'shield wall', and would have partially concealed those drawn up behind, making it difficult for William's archers to judge the fall of arrows. The flanks were by no means unassailable, but the marshy ground at the foot of the slopes would have been a hindrance to mass movement, and the frontage of attack narrow. Envelopment would have been near to impossible. William would have little option but a frontal assault.

This in itself would not be easy. The ridge, like that at Mont St Jean, stood square astride the direct road to the enemy's ultimate objective – in Napoleon's case, Brussels; in William's, London. But whereas Napoleon's troops had a relatively short and shallow climb, Battle Hill stood 60 feet above the lowest point of the road, and twice that in the marshiest parts of the valley, with an approach of between 450 and 500 coverless yards. It made for excellent observation; and if Harold had had archers (and William could not have known that he hadn't) this would have made for a considerable killing field.

So here Harold formed up his army, placing his faith in the lie of the land, the solidity of his shield wall and in particular the blooded

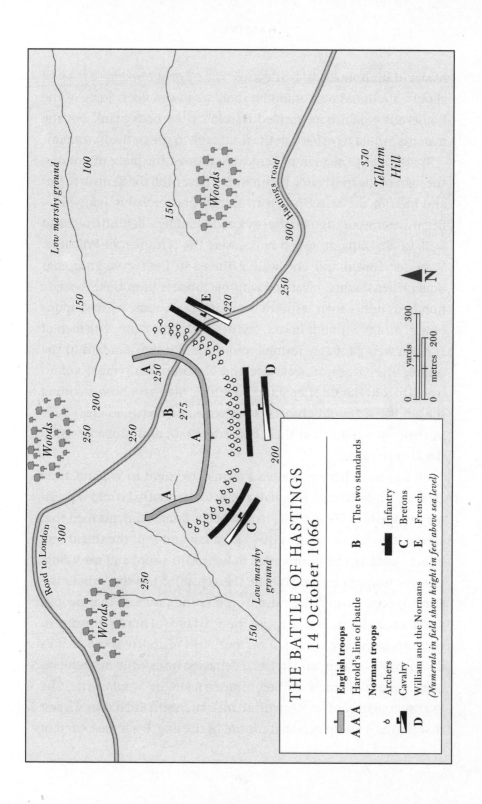

THE BATTLE OF HASTINGS
14 October 1066

English troops

A A A   Harold's line of battle   B   The two standards

Norman troops

⋏   Archers   C   Infantry

▬▬   Cavalry   C   Bretons

D   William and the Normans   E   French

(Numerals in field show height in feet above sea level)

Road to London
300

Woods
250

Woods
250   200

250

250

A
250

A

B
275

A

C

200

D

Woods
150

Low marshy ground
100

150

E
220

300
Hastings road

250

370
Telham
Hill

Low marshy
ground

150

N

yards   300
0

metres   200
0

blades of his housecarls' battle-axes. The ridge allowed for a front of about a thousand men standing shoulder to shoulder. Some of the housecarls would have formed Harold's close bodyguard, but the majority would have been in the front rank to stiffen the fyrdsmen.

Traditionally the men of Kent were allowed the place of honour, the right of the front rank; here it would have been the Kentish *thegns* and men of the select *fyrd* with shields and probably hauberks – defensive armour to guard the neck and shoulders. Behind the shield wall, in anything up to ten ranks, were the fyrdsmen of Wiltshire, Somerset, Devon and Cornwall, gathered in their shire groupings under their sheriffs, mustered with neighbours from their separate hundreds under their respective hundredmen, some with weapons of war, others with bill-hooks, scythes, forks and clubs. The men of London were probably formed round the Wyvern standard in the centre. The Danes of Yorkshire and Northumbria, who'd volunteered to join Harold after Stamford Bridge, may have been guarding the left flank. Harold's brothers Leofwine and Gyrth, as great lords in their own right, had their housecarls too, and probably stood flanking the king.

All this must have presented a formidable sight to William as he came up on to Telham Hill, half a mile to the south. Harold was evidently sure of it. He rode the length of the line, telling his men that all would be well as long as they stood fast and kept the shield wall intact. And then he dismounted to fight with sword and axe alongside his housecarls, probably at the centre of the line where the London road crossed the ridge. For, says the *Carmen*, 'that people, unskilled in the art of War, spurn the assistance of horses: trusting to their strength they stand fast on foot'. This of course is the victor's disdain of his enemy, and in fact it detracted from William's achievement, for as William of Poitiers (himself a knight) would write, 'the English fought confidently with all their strength'. But it does suggest that Harold gave up personal control of the line. For a start, on foot he would not have been able to see much of it. Had he remained in the saddle, although he would have been more vulnerable to the archers, he would also have seen more and been able to make his presence felt anywhere in seconds. But he'd given his orders for the shield wall to stand fast, and so now perhaps he committed the battle to divine providence.

William, meanwhile, was drawing up his troops at the foot of the ridge, and rather more is known about their dispositions than those of the English. On the left were his mercenaries from Brittany, Anjou and Maine under Alain le Roux – 'the Red(-haired)'.* In the centre was the main body of Normans under William himself and his half-brother Bishop Odo, while on the right stood a combined French and Flemish mercenary force under Count Eustace of Boulogne. Each division was formed of archers to the front, foot soldiers in the second line and, behind them, mounted knights.

'At the third hour', say the chroniclers (nine o'clock, though it was probably nearer ten, for the rear of a column of 7,000 men doesn't reach a point at anything like the same time as the front), the battle commenced with volleys of Norman arrows. Almost certainly the English line would have dropped to the knee, locked shields and bowed their helmeted heads in defence. The archers, around a thousand of them, were shooting uphill at a line 700 yards long and at a range of between one and two hundred yards. Each man would have carried a quiver of two dozen or so arrows, but even if each loosed half his sheaf the effect would not necessarily have been too destructive if

---

* There is confusion as to his name. It is sometimes given as Alain 'Fergant' (in Breton 'Younger', in French 'Iron Glove'), but the Alain 'Fergant' who was later Duke of Brittany, and William's son-in-law, was an infant at the time of Hastings. It is not impossible that both the Christian name and the soubriquet were shared by two men. The Alain who led the Breton division at Hastings was subsequently given large estates near York and made Earl of Richmond.

the fall of arrows couldn't be observed, and indeed it seems that most of the arrows passed over the heads of the front rank or were caught on their shields. The English, says the *Carmen*, were 'rooted to the ground'. Indeed, 'Just as a wild boar, wearied by the hounds and at bay, protects itself with its tusks and with foaming jaws refuses to submit to the weapons, fearing neither the enemy nor the spears that threaten death, so the English phalanx fights on unafraid.' That said – and handsomely by the author of the *Carmen* – it could only be a matter of time (and resupply of arrows) before the archers found their mark and began serious attrition. Without any of his own to reply, or cavalry to disperse them, Harold had no counter. The archers could stand all day where they were and plague the line with iron-headed arrows that could burst the mail rings of a hauberk. This, however, was unlikely to decide the battle, except in favour of Harold if the shield wall was maintained. William decided therefore that it was time to close with the enemy.

It is strange, though, that he then sent in his *pedites* – his 'helmeted soldiers' (*Carmen*) – rather than his cavalry to break the shield wall. Perhaps it was because he'd drawn up the army with the infantry in front of the mounted knights. Some chroniclers say that he'd intended doing the opposite, but that on coming into Santlache* valley he concluded that he hadn't the time.

The foot soldiers therefore began their advance up the slope to 'the harsh bray of trumpets' (Poitiers), and in return the defiant roar of the housecarls and fyrdsmen, who banged their shields and cried 'Ut! Ut!' ('Out!').

Heading uphill, towards half a mile of well-armed Englishmen ready to defend their country, and a great noise the like of which they'd never heard before, must have been an unnerving experience

---

* 'Sandy Stream', which the Norman chroniclers, unwittingly or not, turned punningly into 'Senlac' ('Blood lake').

even for men promised gold or a free pass into heaven. Yet a mile away no one would have heard a sound. For that was the nature of medieval battle: it was nasty, brutish, usually short and, above all, compact.

And having trudged up 'land too rough to be tilled' (*Carmen*), William's *pedites* were met with 'a fusillade of javelins and missiles of various kinds, murderous axes and stones tied to sticks'. Like the poor bloody infantry of the Western Front, few seem to have got to the enemy's line – or if they did, made any impression on it.

Then it was the turn of the cavalry – or strictly speaking, the mounted knights, for even though they'd trained in their *conrois* and their movement was concerted, they fought as individuals. They too received what must have seemed a surprisingly ferocious reception, probably meeting for the first time the battle-axe, which 'easily penetrated shields and other protections', says Poitiers. The English line 'strongly held or drove back those who dared attack them with drawn swords ... They even wounded those who flung javelins at them from a distance.'

The Bayeux Tapestry shows a cart carrying arrows. This may suggest that additional arrows were taken to the battlefield, in which case the archers would once again have been able to come forward and begin volleying when both the *pedites* and knights had been repulsed. Maistre Wace says that arrows rained down on the English (which implied they'd been loosed almost vertically, the archers having found their aim by now): 'All feared to open their eyes or leave their faces unguarded.' Thus the sequence of attacks could begin again, and what must have been little more than a bloody, hacking brawl continued intermittently for some hours, the archers meanwhile taking opportunity shots from increasingly closer range.

At some stage, however, probably early afternoon, the battle seemed to have reached its culminating point. As defined some eight hundred years later by the Prussian general Carl von Clausewitz in his great work of military theory *Vom Kriege* ('On War'), in the attack the culminating point is that moment when the attacking force can no longer continue its advance, because of the opposing force, supply problems or the need for rest. Clearly the attacker must seek to achieve his objectives before the culminating point is reached, while the defender, on the other hand, must somehow try to bring the attacking force to its culminating point before it achieves its objectives. Exactly what happened at Hastings and why is related differently by the two major sources, the *Carmen* and Poitiers. According to Poitiers, the former knight, it began with a serious reverse in which the battle could then have gone either way. Some of the Breton knights on the left turned tail and ran back down the hill. Flight is infectious, and so it was here, fuelled by a rumour running through the entire Norman line that William had been killed: 'almost the whole of the duke's battle line [gave] way', at which point men on the right of the English line gave chase. The day was saved, however, by William himself, who raised his visor and galloped to the fleeing troops, shouting: 'Look at me! I am alive, and with God's help I will conquer!' Thus rallied, they turned on the pursuers and cut them down.

The *Carmen* has it differently. The Normans (Bretons) on the left did not break, but feigned retreat. The English pursued them and the Normans turned on them as planned, but then found themselves outfought and began to flee for real – 'Thus a flight which had started as a sham became one dictated by the enemy's strength' – at which point William weighed in to the rescue.*

Poitiers then suggests there was a second feigned flight, also turned to advantage. Who knows? But at this point the Duke of Wellington's famous remark when approached by someone who wished to

---

* The Bayeux Tapestry shows William's brother, Bishop Odo, weighing in too, with the superscription, *Hic Odo episcopus baculum tenens confortat pueros* ('Here Bishop Odo, holding his staff [of office], rallies the lads.')

write an account of Waterloo comes to mind: 'As well write the history of a ball.' We may speculate that if the whole line had charged, the Norman army would have been scattered. However, the ability of the Saxons to withstand cavalry rested on the cohesion of the shield wall. At the foot of the hill, even if they'd overwhelmed the *pedites* and archers, William's knights could have inflicted terrible damage on them. Which is why, presumably, Harold was so determined to stand his ground on the ridge – the English, in the (evidently admiring) words of William of Poitiers, 'standing firmly as if fixed to the ground'. The material point is that the discipline of the shield wall had faltered, and the line now began paying the price.

Losses in the front rank were supposed to be made up by those behind stepping forward. This would have worked to begin with as the better-armed militiamen took the places of the fallen, but the instinct of the housecarls and select fyrdsmen in the front rank would also have been to close up. The line would therefore have contracted, and the flanks thereby become exposed. 'Up to now,' says Poitiers, 'the enemy line had been bristling with weapons and most difficult to encircle,' the inference being that now there were fewer weapons and it was easier to work round the flanks. Sheer numbers – ultimately the key in medieval battles – began to tell. Harold's brothers are thought to have died quite early in the fighting, in which case their housecarls may have quit the field. Certainly they would have suffered a severe blow to their pride and hence morale. The English line grew weaker, says Poitiers, as William's men 'shot arrows, smote and pierced'.

At this stage in the battle, with the English line well and truly on the defensive, housecarls and fyrdsmen alike literally fighting for their lives, the archers would have had a field day. The lower margin of the Bayeux Tapestry at this point is filled with them. Resupplied with arrows, they were probably shooting almost point blank into a huddling crush. 'The dead, by falling, seemed to move more than the living,' says Poitiers. 'It was not possible for the lightly wounded to escape, for they were crushed to death by the serried ranks of their companions.'

And at some point, close to the end of day, in the words of the Bayeux Tapestry, *Harold Rex interfectus est*: King Harold is slain.*

With dusk approaching and the king dead, housecarls and fyrdsmen alike exhausted, and with no hope of respite or relief, the shield wall finally broke. 'Some lay helplessly in their own blood, others who struggled up were too weak to escape,' wrote Orderic Vitalis. 'The passionate wish to escape death gave strength to some. Many left their corpses in deep woods, many who had collapsed on the routes blocked the way of those who came after.'

There was a last stand along an ancient ditch, which the chroniclers dubbed the 'Malfosse', on the reverse slope of Caldbec Hill, where, in the gloom and undergrowth, the pursuing Normans fell 'one on top of the other in a struggling mass of horses and arms'. But, continued Orderic, the battle had been well and truly lost: 'The mangled bodies that had been the flower of the English nobility and youth covered the ground as far as the eye could see.'

---

* At what stage, exactly, Harold was struck down by an arrow is uncertain, though it is unlikely that once the king had been killed the shield wall would have stood for long. Even the story of the arrow is questioned, for recent examination of the Bayeux Tapestry has suggested that the original stitching placed the arrow above the figure of Harold's head, the eye becoming its lodging only during nineteenth-century restoration work. Indeed, the figure assumed to represent Harold is itself questioned, for he holds a spear; Harold the king would have carried a sword – and Harold the Saxon warrior an axe (which the falling warrior to the right of the figure with the arrow in the eye carries, under the actual words 'interfectus est'). The story is hallowed by centuries of telling, however. What is certain is that neither Harold nor his two brothers left the field alive.

4

DEEP SIGHED THE ABBOT*

He is dead, and all the Godwinssons, and England lost.

Charles Kingsley, *Hereward, The Last of the English*

What happens when a battle ends can say as much about the strategy of both sides as what happens before it starts. Legend has it that Harold's common-law wife, Edith Swan-neck, was afterwards

---

* Deep sighed the abbot when the news
  Reached Waltham's courts that day,
  That piteously on Hastings' field
  King Harold lifeless lay.   .

Two monks, Asgod and Ailric named,
Dispatched he to the plain,
That they might seek King Harold's corpse,
At Hastings 'mongst the slain . . .

Heinrich Heine, *Schlachtfeld bei Hastings* ('The Battlefield at Hastings'), 1851, trans. the Hon. Julian Fane, 1854.

brought to the field by William to identify her husband, which she did from marks that 'only a lover might know'. Legend also has it that she took the body to Waltham Abbey, which Harold had founded, for burial, though other versions have William refusing a proper interment because Harold was an 'oath-breaker'. The tapestry is remarkably silent on the matter. Looking at the situation from William's point of view the day after the battle, however, it's not difficult to conclude that he was unsure what sort of victory he'd achieved. It was certainly complete in the sense that he'd killed his strategic opponent – what would in modern parlance be called decapitation strategy – and destroyed the major part of his army, but William could have no clear idea what would follow. Was another, much larger, English army already converging on Sussex (when he himself had lost many men, and had no more immediately at hand)? When the news of Harold's death reached London, would the Witan immediately elect a new king? Releasing Harold's body for stately burial might reinforce resistance, not quash it, for in Anglo-Saxon England, death in battle was a noble thing. Harold had faced his fate rather than run for his life (or perhaps, as the later French proverb would have it, *reculer pour mieux sauter*: literally, to draw back in order to jump better). There was, after all, Edgar Aetheling; and if he were elected king there would be a strong regent appointed. Did William see himself now as king by conquest – the epithet by which he would soon come to be known – or as the rightful ruler of *his* people? The two called for different approaches, and if he saw himself as the latter, his security would depend on 'his' people's acceptance of his claim. Either way, he would have to proceed cautiously. And that was the irony: William's need for a quick, decisive victory had been greater than Harold's.

In fact, two months would pass before William entered London. First he went east, to Dover, 'which had been reported impregnable and held by a large force'. But, continues William of Poitiers,

'The English, stricken with fear at his approach had confidence neither in their ramparts nor in the numbers of their troops.' Doubtless they'd heard of the outcome of the battle at Hastings, and of the fate of Romney, where Normans who'd been blown off course in the crossing had landed and been killed. The town was almost certainly torched and a good many of its citizens put to the sword.

And indeed Dover almost went the same way. 'While the inhabitants were preparing to surrender unconditionally,' wrote Poitiers, 'our men, greedy for booty, set the castle on fire and the great part of it was soon enveloped in flames.' The word 'castle' in this much-used translation* is a rendering of the Latin *castrum*, used by the Romans to describe a military camp, from the temporary marching camp to the major fortress of, for example, Hadrian's Wall. It's probable that there was a *castrum* at Dover before the Conquest, but recent archaeological evidence suggests that the Normans built an entirely new castle near the Saxon church of St Mary in Castro, which incorporated the old Roman lighthouse. There were at this time no castles in England save a handful built in the previous decade by Norman friends of Edward the Confessor, mainly in the Welsh marches, and these were motte-and-bailey types, with perhaps a little stone. Be that as it may, William of Poitiers goes on to say that Duke William then paid for the repair of the *castrum* and of the property of those who'd been ready to surrender, and that he would have punished the incendiarists had he been able to discover who they were. This, if it's to be believed, suggests a certain willingness to try something of a 'hearts and minds' approach. Poitiers then says that 'having taken possession of the castle, the Duke spent eight days adding new fortifications to it'.

---

* D. C. Douglas and G. W. Greenaway, eds, *English Historical Documents 1042–1189* (London, 1953).

Clearly William saw the town as the future entry point to his kingdom.

Not everyone in his army was able to lend a hand with the construction work, apparently, for there was an outbreak of dysentery. Nevertheless, a short time later he marched for Canterbury, which surrendered without a fight. Other towns along the old Roman road (Watling Street) did the same. By the time he was nearing London, therefore, William might reasonably have expected a similar reception. However, London possessed a great defensive advantage that the towns en route to it did not: the Thames. Most of the old city lay north of the river. And as he neared his would-be capital, William also learned that the Witan had elected Edgar Aetheling king, though he couldn't have known that he hadn't been crowned (and almost certainly never was). While coronation didn't matter ultimately to the English – it merely conferred God's blessing on the man already elected king – it did to the Normans, who of course saw the actual ceremony as conferring kingship. The *Carmen* says that William sent a force of cavalry – by some accounts, 500 – to seize the bridge at Southwark ('London Bridge', details of which at the time there are none), which was then a fortified township. They were met by a force commanded by Ansgar, Sheriff of Middlesex, who'd escaped from Hastings though badly wounded. The English were pushed back, although the Normans could not take the bridge, contenting themselves instead with torching Southwark, doubtless a signal to those north of the river of what to expect if there was continued resistance.

It is probably at this point that William accepted that his entry into London wasn't going to be flower-strewn. He had a choice: either he could make a direct attack from Southwark at once – a formidable undertaking, even if he could take the bridge – or he could continue his indirect approach, marching west to cross the Thames much further upstream. The latter course would take more time, allowing Ansgar and his collaborators to strengthen the defences, but it might work to William's advantage, for if he were to spread terror during his approach march it might undermine resolve in London. Certainly he would have to plunder the countryside as he went in order to keep his troops fed, and the droves of refugees thereby created would spread the word for him. And this he proceeded to do with what looks like increasing vengefulness, the monk John of Worcester writing bleakly that the Normans 'laid waste Sussex, Kent, Hampshire, Middlesex and Hertfordshire, and did not cease from burning townships and slaying men'.* He might have added Oxfordshire, Buckinghamshire and Berkshire too, for it seems that, having been denied crossings at various points, notably Reading, resistance still being determined, William was finally able to gain a bridgehead at Wallingford, just south of Oxford (but at that time in Berkshire), where, as the town's name suggests, the Thames was fordable. Here he built another crude – motte and bailey – castle and waited a while. Perhaps it was here also that Harold's treasury was brought from Winchester by the detachment sent to seize it (at the same time paying due respects to the Confessor's widow, Queen Edith, whose dower the city had been, so that its citizens were therefore spared the usual *hergian* – pillage – in exchange for oaths of loyalty). Here, too, more certainly, William was rewarded with the first significant defection. It was now early December, and according to William of Poitiers, Stigand, the Archbishop of Canterbury, came to do him homage, renouncing Edgar Aetheling. And while this may not have been of the greatest moment to those in London – it was, after all, according to John of Worcester and others, Ealdred the Archbishop of York who'd crowned Harold, and he was one of the leaders of the continuing resistance – it would certainly have been encouragement to William, the first legitimizing of his claim, as it

---

* John was the scribe at Worcester Priory: his *Chronicon ex Chronicis* ('Chronicle of Chronicles') is a history of the world from the Creation to Brother John's death in 1140.

were, by a prince of the church (albeit one whom the Pope had excommunicated for holding bishoprics in plurality).

So now he turned north-east for what he believed to be his rightful capital, probably taking the ancient Icknield Way through the Chilterns to Berkhamsted, some 30 miles north-west of London, where again he made camp and set to building a motte and bailey. We don't know how many men were with William at this point. If we accept the figure of 7,000, maximum, for those who crossed with him from France, there couldn't by this stage have been many more than half of that. It seems unlikely that losses at Hastings would have been much less than 2,000 killed and seriously wounded. He would also, no doubt, have left garrisons in Sussex to protect his ships, and at Dover, intended to be his secure base for communications with Normandy, and also at Wallingford, to secure communications with Dover and the fleet (wherever that was). At Berkhamsted, therefore, he may have had a force of some four to five thousand, possibly considerably fewer. This was still a significant number – Danish raiding armies half the size had exacted a terrible price from England in the preceding centuries – though it could easily have been matched (overmatched, indeed) by the English. But spirits were apparently failing in London, perhaps lowered further by the deepening of winter and the concerns about feeding those still under arms who'd escaped from Hastings, of whom there might have been two thousand and more, along with the additional housecarls and levies brought by the shire officers. News of the terrible wasting of the home counties by the Normans would have been reaching the city for a month and more, and no single strong man had emerged to galvanize the resistance. And then, says John of Worcester, Edwine and Morcar 'withdrew their support and returned home with their army'. The *Anglo-Saxon Chronicle* sums up the situation succinctly: 'Always when some initiative should have been shown, there was delay from day to day, until matters went from bad to worse, as everything did in the end.'

The end was the abject surrender of Edgar Aetheling, who with the magnates of London and a bevy of bishops rode dismally to Berkhamsted in the middle of December to submit. They did so, says the *Chronicle*, 'out of necessity, after most damage had been done', adding that 'it was a great piece of folly that they had not done it earlier'.

Perhaps. But while Harold had acted precipitately by going at once to Hastings, Edgar's resistance party, as the *Chronicle* says, appears to have acted with neither resource nor resolution. Yet they hadn't been compelled to dither. The next five years would prove that there was no lack of resistance in spirit to Norman rule; William would be dragged north, south, east and west by one rebellion after another. Those in Northumbria (which included Yorkshire) were particularly troublesome: here the presence of the last Wessex claimant, the Aetheling, encouraged Anglo-Danish rebellions, including a landing en masse in 1069 by King Sweyn of Denmark's men under command of his two sons. William's ruthless, retributive response would become known as the Harrying of the North. But although the northern rebellions encouraged others in the south and west, there was no *concerted* national rising. Had there been, it's far from certain that William, even with local English support (as in some cases there was), could have prevailed. For England's system of mobilization – the *fyrd* – hadn't been dismantled.

Indeed, in his 1865 novel *Hereward the Wake: Last of the English*, the Reverend Charles Kingsley, Regius Professor of Modern History at Cambridge, makes the point very decidedly. In 1070, Hereward had taken part in – led – a rebellion in the fens of East Anglia. His fate is uncertain, but some sources suggest that he made a peace of some sort with William and returned to his restored lands in Lincolnshire, only to be killed subsequently by Norman knights. Kingsley paints a scene of furious resistance as they break into his manor at Bourne, Hereward killing eleven of them before a lance fells him, then with a final thrust of his shield killing their leader. One who remains standing says: 'That blow will be sung hereafter by minstrel and maiden as the last blow of the last Englishman. Knights, we have slain a better knight than ourselves. If there had been three more such men in this realm, they would have driven us and King William back again into the sea.'

Imagined, fanciful, romantic – of course. But it's unlikely that Professor Kingsley believed he was writing pure fiction.

POSTSCRIPT

The military significance of Hastings has long been debated. For example, according to Sir Charles Oman, the second Chichele Professor of Modern History at Oxford (1905–46) and a pioneering military historian, the battle was 'the last great example of an endeavour to use the old infantry tactics of the Teutonic races against the now fully-developed cavalry of feudalism'; and with the Normans' victory, 'the supremacy of the feudal horseman was finally established'.* And yet, counters Professor Charles Hollister of the University of California, 'in every important battle of the Anglo-Norman age, the bulk of the feudal cavalry dismounted to fight'. At Northallerton in 1138 (when the Scots invaded to take advantage of the war between Stephen and Matilda), the Anglo-Norman knights 'dismounted to a man and fought behind a shield wall such as had been employed earlier by Anglo-Saxon armies'. Indeed, their tactics were 'remarkably similar to those of Harold's troops at Hastings'.† But irrespective of whether the cavalry always or even usually dismounted to fight, Duke William seems to have been impressed with the Saxon infantry, and with the sophisticated, flexible system of mobilization that could bring quickly to the field large numbers of proficient and

---

* Sir Charles Oman, *The Art of War in the Middle Ages*, rev. and ed. John H. Beeler (New York, 1953).

† Hollister, *Anglo-Saxon Military Institutions*.

well-armed men – the select *fyrd* – and when necessary also a great multitude of others who, though poorly armed, could stand their ground. In fact, there was probably no nation in Europe with a better system; and, as Professor Hollister asserts, decently led and under even remotely normal circumstances, 'it could hold its own against any army in Christendom'. The Conqueror says as much by summoning the *fyrd* in 1073 and again in 1079 and transporting it across the Channel to fight in his continental campaigns. He didn't remake the Saxon army in the Norman image; rather, he strengthened his Norman army's weakest arm – infantry. And it may not be too fanciful to trace the English (and in time the British) army's preference for choosing a good defensive position and letting the enemy exhaust himself trying to evict them, back to Hastings. Or rather, back to the Hastings which might – should – have been.

PART TWO

TOWTON

The Battle for the Crown

29 MARCH 1461

Draw, archers, draw your arrows to the head!

Shakespeare, *Richard III*

Towton was the largest, bloodiest battle ever fought on English soil. Comparing the population then and now, the 'butcher's bill' would today equate to some 380,000, the same number as British military deaths in the whole of the Second World War. This alone makes it worth studying. What accounts for those huge numbers of casualties? Was it the ground, the weapons, the tactics, the leadership – the weather; or the condition of England? Towton was to all intents and purposes the pivotal battle of the Wars of the Roses. It was therefore a culmination of strategy and campaigning art – but in a civil war, which has a particular and atavistic character. It was also a battle won against the odds. It turned on the boldness of the Yorkist commander in the prelude to battle, and on the tactical brilliance – the *coup d'œuil* – of one of the senior officers during the opening moves.

Above all, perhaps, Towton demonstrates Montgomery's view that battle boils down to 'a contest between two wills – his [the commander-in-chief's] own and that of the enemy commander. If his heart begins to fail him when the issue hangs in the balance his opponent will probably win.'

1

CASTLE AND SIEGE

Battle *n*. ME. (O) Fr. *bataille* battle (also, fortifying tower) . . .
Shorter Oxford English Dictionary

Once England had been conquered, the Normans began building castles – proper castles. Indeed, building castles, first of wood and then of stone, was part of the process of conquest and pacification. Castle-building was itself an extension of the Norman culture of the high middle ages (from about 1000 to 1250), a time, especially from the mid-twelfth century, marked by economic and territorial expansion on the Continent as a whole, by population and urban growth, the emergence of national identity, and the reordering of both secular and religious institutions. It was the time of the Crusades, of 'Gothic' art and architecture (originally a pejorative term, denoting a departure from classical forms), and of the expansion of education with the foundation of the universities. But in essence continental society still comprised three classes: those who fought, those who prayed, and those who one way or another provided for them. And the foundation of the military class – indeed, of their military thinking – was the castle. Put simply, it was the seat, source and symbol of their power. Members of the military class may have held their land in fealty to a prince, but the castle gave them a certain assured independence – to the extent that in time they would become power-brokers in their own right, and sometimes even direct challengers to the sovereignty of the prince. It followed that to strengthen their castles was the first object of the military class.

And so in the century and a half following the Conquest there were great advances in military architecture. Stone replaced wood, and thickness of wall became the measurement of a *châtelain*'s prestige as much as of his castle's defensive strength. On the other hand, there was no comparable advance in the means of overcoming a castle. Offensive weapons remained much as they had been in Roman times, and siegecraft no more advanced than Joshua's. Across Europe as a whole, field battles were comparatively few and far between (as, indeed, were successful sieges). Campaigning often amounted to little more than trying to destroy an opponent's agriculture, manufacturing and trade, although the rising concept of *chivalry*, with its religious, moral and social code, greatly increased the number of knights; and a knight, of course, needed a military retinue. Thus the proprietors of the castles, in shorthand the barons, built up a considerable trained following, whereas in Anglo-Saxon England only the greater earls had had housecarls. When Henry I died without male heir in 1135, the civil war which ensued between his daughter Matilda, wife of the Holy Roman Emperor, and Count Stephen of Boulogne (whose claim to the throne was a remarkable echo of Duke William's), was made all the worse by the dispersed military potential of the castles and their garrisons.

However, in the late thirteenth century there began something of a revolution in warfare – or perhaps, in truth, a reversion; and it began in England with Edward I, 'Longshanks', 'the Hammer of the

Scots', who reigned from 1272 to 1307. Although there had always been infantry in the conflicts to date, they'd not as a rule been the pivot on which a campaign depended. Now, though, they were to become the deciding factor in battle. In 1265, Prince Edward, as he then was, by a series of well-timed and rapid marches in and about the Vale of Evesham during the fag-end of the so-called 'barons' wars', had kept two enemy armies divided, and then defeated each in turn.* After the death of his father, Henry III, and his own accession to the throne, he tackled the long-standing problem – for the English at least – of the Welsh. It would be a business of some twenty-five years, but when it was done it was the end of Welsh independence, and later rebellions would give little real cause for alarm.

Edward prepared his campaign carefully, and with remarkable strategic foresight. He began conventionally enough by building a network of roads and castles. But whereas the practice of the previous two centuries was then to rely on cavalry operating from the castles – operations restricted perforce to a couple of months in the summer because of the limits of both feudal obligation and logistics (notably food supply for both men and horses) – he recognized that to defeat

---

* After his victory at Lewes in 1264, Simon de Montfort, Earl of Leicester, had controlled the kingdom, with King Henry III and his son Prince Edward 'under his protection'. De Montfort's position was precarious, however. There was a threat of invasion from Flanders, and unrest in the Welsh Marches. Edward escaped, joined up with the Earl of Clare who'd landed with troops from Ireland, built an army in the Marches and seized the strategically important city of Worcester. Meanwhile, de Montfort had begun to assemble his army at Gloucester, the lowest bridging point of the Severn, from where he advanced into Wales to join with Prince Llywelyn and his considerable infantry. Edward then attacked and took Gloucester, threatening to cut off de Montfort west of the Severn. In riposte, de Montfort's son, also called Simon, began to assemble an army in the east. Edward pulled back across the Severn to keep the two armies apart, the younger de Montfort having reached Kenilworth at the end of July. On 4 August the elder de Montfort was comprehensively defeated by Edward at Evesham, killed and his body mutilated – head, hands, feet and testicles cut off. Eventually the younger de Montfort was also brought to heel, and the 'barons' wars' ended.

men waging war from their mountain fastnesses he needed a professional army that could operate on foot throughout the year, and could match the Welsh in their use of the longbow. But again, whereas previous practice would have been to hire mercenaries, Edward instead decided to professionalize the old *fyrd*. For this, of course, he needed money; but he calculated that a smaller, better-equipped and better-trained army was preferable to the mass of the great *fyrd* – as, indeed, the select *fyrd* had demonstrated centuries before. He therefore offered his feudal tenants the option of commuting their military liability for money. This 'scutage' (from the Latin *scutum*, shield, and thence one bearing a shield, i.e. a knight) was a device, a tax, which appears originally to have been created by Henry II a century or so earlier to finance his wars in France. Those not given or declining the option of scutage were to send men who would then be paid after their period of feudal duty service was up.

Edward then divided his infantry into archers and men-at-arms. He was helped in this by an ordinance of his father's, the 'Assize of Arms' of 1242, which required all males aged between fifteen and sixty to keep arms, and for all those who were able (*'qui possunt'*) specifically to keep bows – except those living within the forests, i.e. those tracts of land designated as royal hunting domains.* The English longbow, made of elm or yew, was some 6 feet in length, and its arrow about half that, with a range of about 350 yards.† In practised

---

* Confirmed by Edward's own Statute of Winchester in 1284.

† Clearly the length could not be precisely standardized, and to an extent depended on the stature of its owner. Bows found on the *Mary Rose* (which sank in 1545) ranged from 6ft 2in to 6ft 11in (1.87 to 2.11 metres). There is a record from the reign of Henry VII (1485–1509) of how men and boys were trained to use bows with high draw weights. Bishop Hugh Latimer recalled how his yeoman father 'taught me how to draw, how to lay my body in my bow . . . not to draw with strength of arms as divers other nations do . . . I had my bows bought me according to my age and strength, as I

hands, therefore – and there were many of them – the longbow could shape the battle as never before, harassing an opponent into making an attack, or denying ground without occupying it. Used cleverly in combination with the men-at-arms (usually spearmen) and mounted troops, it could indeed be decisive.*

Examples of commanders who used the longbow in this way are legion in Europe throughout the late middle ages (c.1250–1500): Edward himself at Falkirk against the Scots under William Wallace in 1298 and, most famously and devastatingly, Henry V in 1415 against the French at Agincourt. Henry had sailed for France that year to take back control of some of his lands. After a long but ultimately success-ful siege of Harfleur, he'd had to send many men home who were suffering from dysentery, and then marched with the rest to Calais. The French blocked his route, however, and on 25 October brought him to battle in a recently ploughed field that tapered slightly and was wooded on both sides.

Henry's army was outnumbered some four to one (contemporary

---

increased in them, so my bows were made bigger and bigger. For men shall never shoot well unless they be brought up to it.' Latimer's eighteenth-century biographer, the Rev. William Gilpin, explained 'laying his body into the bow' thus: 'The Englishman did not keep his left hand steady, and draw his bow with his right; but keeping his right at rest upon the nerve [remaining tensed], he pressed the whole weight of his body into the horns of his bow. Hence probably arose the phrase "bending the bow," and the French of "drawing" one.'

* Mounted archers – with of course a much smaller bow, and consequently a shorter range – were famous in biblical times, but their effect was greatest in what might be called biblical landscapes: the trackless semi-deserts of the Middle East, or the steppes of Muscovy and Central Asia. Mounted archers turned back more than one western army in Anatolia during the Crusades, the light horsemen literally running rings round the knightly heavy cavalry. But they never found much favour in the West. Cossack mounted archers buzzed about Napoleon's armies – some of them appeared in Paris in 1814, to the entertainment of all – but they were never thought to be more than a nuisance.

sources say 30,000 French to 8,000 English), and they drove sharpened stakes into the ground to counter the expected attack by mounted knights. At first the French hesitated, and so Henry advanced his line to longbow range, the archers taking the stakes with them and then re-driving them into the ground. The first flight of arrows stung the French into a charge, but that charge was severely blunted by continuous archery, the heavy going and the wooden stakes. The French infantry – the rest of the dismounted nobles, along with the knights and men-at-arms – then advanced but were deluged with arrows, many fired now from the flanks, as they tried to get to grips with the English nobles and men-at-arms who were posted in three gaps in the line of archers' stakes. The advance was funnelled to a standstill by the tapering field and the stakes, resulting in an extraordinary carnage: felled by arrows or toppled in the press of men, most died where they lay, as many suffocated as actually killed fighting. Henry's line held, while his archers continued to pick off the French who followed up the first rank but were impeded by the growing piles of bodies. The battle then turned into rout and indiscriminate slaughter, with the much-vaunted rules of chivalric combat set aside (not that the rules extended to the common fighting man, in any case). It was a victory that proved the superiority of infantry over cavalry, if only they could shape the battlefield to their advantage.

Nowhere did the longbow shape the battlefield more dramatically than at Towton half a century later, less than a dozen miles southwest of Harald Hardrada's victory at Fulford Gate. Not only was the battle of Towton almost certainly the largest and bloodiest battle ever fought on English soil, it was also one of the most extensively chronicled, if not always the most consistently. How that day came to be possibly the most brutal in English history is a study not just in weapons and tactics but in what English society had become. Indeed, it is an object lesson in Sir Michael Howard's assertion that only by studying the combatants' cultures can one come to understand what it was that they fought about and why they fought in the way they did. And the name given by nineteenth-century historians to the peculiar organization of English society at the time – 'bastard feudalism' – is aptly descriptive.

2

BASTARD FEUDALISM

Castles in the air: they are so easy to take refuge in.
And so easy to build too.

Ibsen, *The Master Builder*

England just before the Conquest had been both prosperous and, on the whole, peaceful. After the Conquest a good deal of England – the north, principally – had been laid waste at William's command, though by the turn of the century it had largely recovered. It was no longer, however, a kingdom of prevalent peace. Pre-Conquest England had been a place of agriculture, with a high degree of agrarian organization. As the high middle ages advanced it was increasingly a country organized for war. It became, in the words of that angular but acute historian of monarchy, David Starkey, 'a war state [which] could only be ruled successfully by a warrior monarch'.* For not only

---

* Introduction to George Goodwin, *Fatal Colours* (London, 2011).

had the Normanization of England to be consolidated and relations with its neighbours – Wales, Ireland, Scotland – settled; the English king was now of course a continental monarch too, and with that came continental wars of succession and territorial ambition. The English war machine was fed by a plentiful supply of capable troops raised by the occupants of the castles, assisted by Edward I's innovation of paid service. The system was in fact perfected – if that's the right word – by his grandson, Edward III, whose unprecedentedly long reign stretched from 1327 to 1377. His aim was to recreate the continental empire lost by that worst of all English kings, John (and to an extent by his own father, Edward II); and so began what might be called the first phase of the Hundred Years' War, the series of campaigns waged in Europe from 1337 to 1453 between the English crown and the House of Valois over the sovereignty of France.

In the fifteenth century, therefore, English society was centred more intensely on the landowner and his household than it had been before the Conquest. That household – the extended family and servants – could now number hundreds. The greatest of the landowners would also attract into their circle the lesser ones, the minor nobility and gentry, who in turn would have their own followers. These groupings were often formalized by the adoption of a great noble's badge – worn by the household and servants on their everyday clothes or their 'livery' (uniform), a word deriving from the Old French *livrée*, delivered, in the sense of food or clothing provided to servants – or on a gold chain round the neck of a satellite lord. The greater landowners would however increase their followings by retaining other men with a money fee, often formalized by written contract or 'indenture',* that committed them to attend and ride

---

* The contract was written up in duplicate, the copy immediately following the original on the same piece of parchment. An indented line was then drawn between the two and the parchment cut along that line, the copy being given to the retained man.

with their lord whenever required, suitably armed and equipped. Thus the old feudal system which flowed 'top down' from the crown was progressively distorted by defensive baronial alliances, giving rise to the system that historians have come to call 'bastard feudalism'. The essence of the original feudal system imposed by Duke William was that tenants of manors or other substantial units of land had obligations to their lords, commonly including military service. Under bastard feudalism the bond between a man and his lord was not tenurial – relating to the holding of land – but financial; and it was not hereditary, but personal. This system, which – properly managed by a strong king – had its advantages in both war and peace (not least in 'law and order', connecting the crown to the regions through a franchise of the king's peace), seemed also, however, to have its own adverse momentum. By the mid-fifteenth century, the numbers recruited by the great lords were huge. The 'Black Book' of Edward IV (1461–70 and 1471–83) lists the maximum number of retainers permitted to each rank of society – an earl being the lowest rank allowed to exceed one hundred. In practice, however, these levels were far exceeded. The greatest lords had several thousand soldiers each, not least so they could fulfil their obligation to the king while still having plenty in reserve for their own purposes. Many of these additionals were 'off the books', because neither 'feed men' nor 'maintenance men' were under formal contract.*

Any later dispute over terms of service could then be examined on comparison of the two copies if they made a perfect match along the indented line.

* The term 'feed men' (or feedmen) is sometimes misunderstood, not unreasonably as a result of the spelling. They were fee'd retainers, i.e. those 'apart from the household' who were paid a fee for fealty and service, rather than those 'of the household' who were given food and clothing. Similarly, 'maintenance' was nothing to do with victualling but entailed commitment to some powerful neighbour or guardian who would 'maintain' a man's cause (whatever the cause was), to avoid his having to seek redress on his own through the expensive and uncertain remedies of the law courts – in

In essence, then, the great lords had private armies.

A militarized state with distributed centres of fighting power, which could only be ruled successfully by a warrior monarch, was clearly going to be troubled when the monarch didn't live up to expectations in the eyes of one faction or another. Especially so when there was also a doubt about lineage, and almost inevitably when the monarch was an infant. And in the absence of war abroad, 'bastard feudalism' was almost bound to turn in on itself.

In the late fourteenth century, two rival factions within the House of Plantagenet had emerged: the House of York and the House of Lancaster. Both houses claimed the throne through descent from the sons of Edward III, but as the Lancastrians had occupied the throne from 1399, the Yorkists might never have pressed their claim had it not been for the country's descent into near-anarchy in the mid-fifteenth century. For the death of Henry V, arguably England's greatest monarch (reigned 1413–22), was followed by the long and factious minority of Henry VI, who inherited the throne at the age of nine months.

Henry VI's council of regency had been dominated by Lancastrian magnates, and when Henry finally achieved his majority he soon proved ineffective – and, worse, subject to bouts of madness; he was also dominated by his ambitious queen, Margaret of Anjou, who was nine years his senior. In 1453 he lapsed very decidedly into insanity, and his cousin Richard, third Duke of York, by now the head of a considerable baronial league and by strict primogeniture in possession of a better right to the throne than the king himself, was made protector of the realm by his supporters. Most prominent of these was his nephew the Earl of Warwick – 'Warwick the kingmaker' – who'd amassed many hundreds of followers among the gentry across half the counties of England. When Henry appeared to recover two years

---

exchange, of course, for military fealty, in the course of which he would probably wear his guardian's livery.

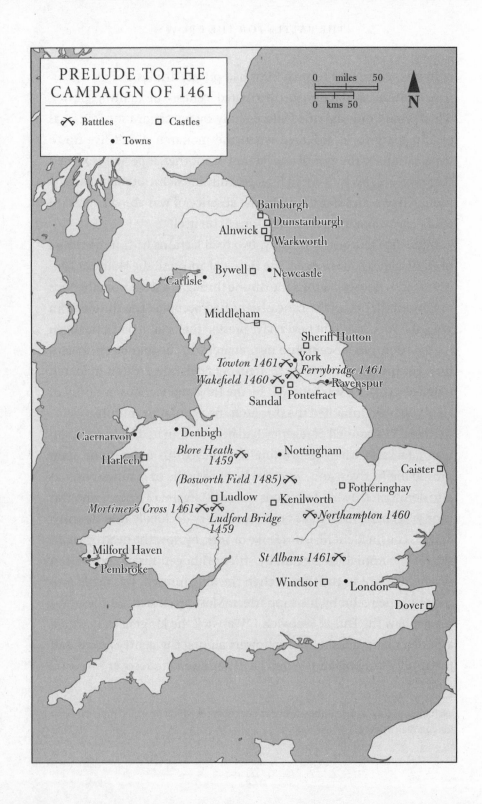

PRELUDE TO THE
CAMPAIGN OF 1461

⚔ Battles   ☐ Castles
    ● Towns

0   miles   50
0   kms   50

N

Bamburgh
Dunstanburgh
Alnwick   Warkworth

Bywell   Newcastle
Carlisle

Middleham

Sheriff Hutton
York
Towton 1461   Ferrybridge 1461
Wakefield 1460   Ravenspur
Sandal   Pontefract

Caernarvon   Denbigh
Blore Heath   Nottingham
Harlech   1459
(Bosworth Field 1485)
Ludlow   Kenilworth
Mortimer's Cross 1461   Caister
Ludford Bridge   Fotheringhay
1459   Northampton 1460

Milford Haven   St Albans 1461
Pembroke
Windsor   London

Dover

later, he at once tried to re-establish the authority of the queen's – the 'Lancastrian' – party, forcing Richard of York to take up arms. A small-scale battle took place at St Albans in May 1455. There were only about 5,000 combatants in all, and remarkably few casualties, though several of them were senior Lancastrian figures. The prize, however, was Henry himself, whom York took back to London in 'protective custody', parliament formally reappointing York as protector a few months later. Four years of uneasy truce followed;* then, in 1459, on discovering that the queen's party was preparing to stage a comeback, Richard of York took up arms again.

The problem with 'bastard feudalism' – or rather, with its dispersal of military force – was that its constituent parts could be vulnerable before they were able to concentrate. And those parts could change their minds about whom to join up with. In 1459 both the king and the queen were in Warwickshire, in the heart of England, where assembling dispersed forces – and recruiting further numbers – was much easier. On the other hand, the Yorkists were much more widely separated. The duke himself was at his fortress in Ludlow near the Welsh border; Warwick was in Calais, of which he was captain (in effect, governor); and Warwick's father the Earl of Salisbury was in his fastness of Middleham in the Yorkshire Dales.

York's plan of campaign was admirably straightforward: the three major constituents would combine at Ludlow; they would then march east to Kenilworth, in whose great castle the royal court had taken residence, and there, as at St Albans, they would capture and reassert control over the king. Predictably, however, the first clash of arms took place during the assembly phase, on 23 September at Blore Heath on the Cheshire–Staffordshire border, where a Lancastrian

---

* Henry's religiosity prompted him to arrange the 'Loveday' of 1458 in St Paul's Cathedral (also known as the Annunciation Loveday, as it took place on the Feast of the Annunciation, 25 March), a ritualistic attempt at reconciliation between warring factions.

force of twice the size (10,000) tried to ambush Salisbury's. An ineffectual archery duel, the Yorkists keeping their distance, and two failed cavalry charges ended in the rout of the Lancastrian army and the death of its commander, the experienced 5th Baron Audley. During the battle, 500 Lancastrian troops changed sides.

Salisbury pressed on the remaining 50 miles to Ludlow, deftly evading two more Lancastrian forces. Warwick, too, made the rendezvous with his troops after a close shave in the county of his title, and in early October the unified Yorkist army set out for Kenilworth. North of Worcester, however, they sighted the unified Lancastrian army, which was far stronger than their own.

If the physical element of Lancastrian fighting power was greater, the moral element was greater still. For York now learned that the royal standard was raised opposite him – the king himself was in the field. Making battle against Lancastrian forces was one thing; making battle against the king in person was a very different matter. Yes, Henry had been at St Albans, but there for some reason his standard hadn't been raised.

At this point Richard of York's nerve failed him. He retired with his army to Worcester to consider his options.

In truth he hadn't got many. He sent an emissary to the king swearing an oath of loyalty. Henry ignored it and advanced on Worcester, whereupon York retreated south to Tewkesbury. The king then offered dubious terms. York rejected them, crossed the Severn and took his army back to Ludlow. Here he set about constructing a defensive position at Ludford Bridge on the River Teme, which he fortified with cannon, still an unusual instrument of war except at sieges. As the forward detachments of the Lancastrian army closed on the river towards dusk on 12 October, a thunderous volley of shot met them, but over their heads.

Yorkist morale was low, however, as among any troops who retreat without a fight. Outnumbered, and with the royal standard in sight, their prospect in battle was indeed bleak. After dark, one of their ablest commanders, Warwick's deputy Andrew Trollope, crossed the lines with 500 seasoned troops from the Calais garrison and pledged himself to the king.

York, too, was on the move that night – but heading west, along with Salisbury and Warwick, abandoning the army to its fate.

Unsurprisingly, the following morning the king's army crossed the bridge without opposition, the leaderless Yorkist troops kneeling in submission before Henry, who promptly pardoned them.

Ludlow itself paid the price, however, and dire it was too. William Gregory describes the rape and pillage, a very definite signal to future would-be rebels:

> The misrule of the King's gallants at Ludlow, when they had drunk enough of the wine that was in the taverns and other places, they full ungodly smote out the heads of the pipes and hogs heads of wine, that men went wet shod in wine, and then they robbed the town and bore away bedding, cloth and other goods and defiled many women.*

His description is borne out by other more or less contemporary accounts. Ludlow, says the *Cronycullys of Englonde*,† 'was robbed to the bare walls'.

---

* William Gregory was a London skinner who became mayor of the city. The quotation is from his *Historical Collections of a Citizen of London in the Fifteenth Century*, ed. James Gairdner, Camden Record Society, Old Series, vol. 17 (London, 1876). By way of illustration – neither England nor its language was now Anglo-Saxon – the actual Middle English runs: 'The mysrewle of the kyngys galentys at Ludlowe, whenn they hadde drokyn i-nowe of wyne that was in tavernys and in othyr placys, they fulle ungoodely smote owte the heddys of the pypys and hoggys hedys of wyne, that men wente wete-schode in wyne, and thenn they robbyd the towne, and bare a-waye beddynge, clothe, and othyr stuffe, and defoulyd many wymmen.'

† Given the title *A Short English Chronicle* by the historian James Gairdner when he published it as part of his *Three English Chronicles* collection (London, 1880).

York's flight may have been a tactical humiliation, but it would prove a strategic windfall. He at once sailed for Ireland, where he was still lieutenant and retained the backing of the Irish parliament, which at once offered him money and men. Warwick, too, sailed for his offshore fastness – Calais, kept for him by his exceptional deputy, Salisbury's brother William Neville, Lord Fauconberg. Not only was Warwick a considerable soldier, he was no less formidable a general at sea (if little more than a pirate much of the time). His ships controlled the English Channel, which gave him great leverage with the English wool merchants of London and Calais, the latter promptly providing him with a loan of £18,000, an astonishing sum.* This dominance of the Channel also gave him 'control of the narrative', his ships spreading the word around southern England – and Kent in particular, whose wealth relied to a high degree on continental trade – emphasizing his loyalty to the king while denouncing Henry's evil counsellors. Further, it kept communications open with Ireland, whither he sailed in March 1460 to discuss strategy with York, before returning to Calais in May.

And there was a pressing need to discuss strategy, for the situation, bad enough already, had taken a turn for the worse in December 1459 when the 'parliament of devils' in Coventry passed bills of attainder whereby York's and Warwick's lives and property were made forfeit, along with Salisbury's. Only a successful invasion of England could now restore their fortunes.

They were certainly not wanting in ways and means, and their ends were at least now crystal clear. And there was always the prospect of Lancastrian mistakes to exploit. In January Warwick's ships took advantage of their mastery of the Channel in a daring raid on Sandwich, capturing the Lancastrian fleet that was preparing to

---

* In 1520, the eleventh year of Henry VIII's rein, the total annual income of the crown was estimated at £100,000.

invade Calais while its commander was still in his bed. A second raid, in early June, overwhelmed another invasion fleet, and this time the landing party, under Fauconberg, stayed to establish a bridgehead for Warwick's own invasion. A few weeks later Warwick joined him with 2,000 more troops of the Calais garrison. They moved so fast that Canterbury, a dozen miles away, was in their hands without a fight that same day.

3

TREASONS, STRATAGEMS
AND SPOILS

To win by Strategy is no less the role of a general than to win by arms.

Julius Caesar

Warwick had prepared the ground well. Already admired for his
earlier naval exploits (almost those of a proto-Francis Drake), he had
taken care to spread favourable propaganda, declaring his intention
'to place himself at the head of the true commons in defence of the
common weal', especially against maladministration of the law and
burdensome taxation, and to exercise 'good lordship'; thus he and
his allies would remove the bad lords while remaining 'true subjects
of the King'. All this resonated with the men who'd marched to London with Jack Cade in the famous rebellion a decade before. Recruits
from Kent and Sussex flocked to Warwick's banner, and they were
no rabble. With the end of the Hundred Years' War, thousands of
men-at-arms and archers had returned from France. Many of these
veterans – sometimes whole companies – had been recruited by the

richer English and Welsh nobles and gentry; and while for the most part it was the Lancastrians who'd benefited to date, there would have been plenty of seasoned soldiers for the Yorkists too in these southern counties.

London opened its gates to Warwick on 2 July. Or rather, the merchants did. The commander of the royal garrison in the Tower, Lord Scales, kept his gates firmly closed, and primed the cannon on the battlements. Warwick ignored him, and instead convoked an assembly of bishops in St Paul's. Taking the moral – or, at least, the spiritual – high ground would do him no harm at all. Indeed, it was the same tactic that Duke William had used before Hastings. Men liked to know whose side God was on. And Warwick could go one better than William and his papal banner. For with him at St Paul's was Francesco Coppini, the papal legate. As a bishop of the church, Coppini was of course concerned for the lives of men, but he also had family and political reasons for backing the Yorkists. The day after the bishops had met, he posted at St Paul's Cross, an open-air pulpit in the grounds of the cathedral, a copy of the missive he'd sent to the king, who was now at Northampton, warning of the consequences (implicitly, excommunication) if slaughter ensued from not heeding Warwick's just demands. When Fauconberg's advance guard left that same day for Northampton, it was therefore with the reassurance of divine providence.

That reassurance must have been doubly welcome, too, for the weather now turned to heavy rain. Even so, the main body of the Yorkist army, headed by a host of impressive titles, including the Duke of Norfolk, set out on 6 July, accompanied by the legate and seven bishops, including the primate of all England himself, Thomas Bourchier. The intention was to have these eminent clerics approach the king in person to negotiate a peaceful settlement. For Henry, if nothing else, was a famously pious man.

However, the commander of the Lancastrian army, the Duke of Buckingham, who'd also been in command at Ludford Bridge, would brook no compromise. On 9 July, when the ecclesiastical delegates approached the Lancastrian camp, they were turned away without ceremony. Even Warwick's herald was rebuffed, contrary to the usual customs. The king was in the field with his standard raised, and although the Yorkists were numerically superior, the Lancastrians occupied a strong position.*

Or rather, they appeared to, for they'd chosen to fight with their backs to the River Nene along the north edge of the deer park of Delapré Abbey just to the south of the town. It was certainly an attractive position for the defenders. The park was roughly square, each side nearly a mile, bordered by a ditch on the inner side and a fence 10 feet high to keep the deer in and the poachers out, and the Lancastrians were able to mount several artillery pieces along their fortified line. Gunpowder had first been used by the English at Crécy, more than a century before, and possibly as early as the 1320s in battle with the Scots, but cannon were still primitive weapons – cumbersome, slow to load, prone to misfire, erratic in aim and limited in effect against troops in the open. For all that, however, the noise of discharge could at least be unnerving to assaulting troops and encouraging to the defenders. In any case, next morning it was still raining, and the gunners couldn't keep their powder dry. The advantage was at once upended, silent cannon now encouraging to the Yorkists and demoralizing for the Lancastrians.

Worse, perhaps – and certainly when the tide of battle changed – was the river to their rear. There has always been debate among fighting men as to which side of a river gives the best defence. Is it better to try to stop the enemy from closing up to the river, as he's forced to concentrate his forces on the crossing place, and thereby renders himself vulnerable? For if he turns the tables, there's no

---

* The figures are uncertain, but recent calculations put the respective strengths at 10,000–15,000 Yorkists and 6,000–8,000 Lancastrians.

retreat across a river without risking serious loss. Or is it better to allow him to try to cross, which he'll not be able to do on a broad front, thereby allowing the defender to concentrate his forces to pinch out the crossings on the 'home' bank? So much depends of course on the ground, and also the enemy's intention. For example, does he *need* to cross here?

Warwick didn't need to cross the Nene. The objective wasn't Northampton; it was the defeat of the king's forces. But the Nene at the Lancastrians' back also meant that they couldn't easily be encircled, or even heavily outflanked. The position the Duke of Buckingham had chosen on the king's behalf would force Warwick into a frontal attack and confine him to the deer park. But that meant there'd be precious little room for manoeuvre if the fortified line were breached. And the only bridge across the river lay outside the defended area, covered only by Buckingham's cavalry.

The rain, however, wasn't entirely to the Lancastrians' disadvantage. It would mean heavy going for the foot soldiers in the attack – and it would have to be *dismounted* attack, for cavalry could do nothing except perhaps to scout the flanks outside the park – and make the ditch and embanked fence even more difficult to cross.

Rather like the French at Waterloo, on another wet battlefield morning, the Yorkist army took until midday on the 10th to form up, while the 'scourers', the light cavalry, of the two sides skirmished with each other. The Yorkist horse, led by Lord John Scrope of Bolton, got the better of their opponents, crossed the Nene and entered the town, and by some accounts promptly set fire to it – something that must have taken a certain effort, given the weather.

Once the foot soldiers were drawn up ready in their three columns, Warwick rode among them with words of inspiration. Again he told them that they were fighting not against the king but to overthrow the king's corrupt advisers. For all the inspiring words, though, and the silence of the cannon, the rain can't have filled the ranks with joy. But worse, it was soon a rain of arrows – perhaps a hundred thousand during the time it took the columns to close with the entrenched Lancastrians, who for the most part were shielded from the Yorkists' archery. The effect must have been like raking machine-gun fire on the Western Front.

However, the outcome of the battle was not going to rest on a duel of archers or hand-to-hand fighting at the ramparts. Warwick had prepared the metaphorical ground even better than Buckingham had prepared the actual, for the right of the Lancastrian line was held by the 43-year-old Lord Grey of Ruthin, and Lord Grey had been suborned by Warwick. For Grey was in a property dispute with the Lancastrian grandee Henry Holland, third Duke of Exeter, and Warwick had promised him that the land – and more – would be his if he turned his coat. As the Earl of March's column on the Yorkist left reached the ditch, instead of the expected reception – arrows, swords and pikes – they were met literally with helping hands. With the Lancastrian right flank now turned in both senses of the word, and with no room to manoeuvre, the line was soon was rolled up – in half an hour, by all accounts. Henry's troops fled for the river, and it certainly wasn't a time to be wearing high-priced plate armour. Many of them drowned. The king's four lieutenants – Buckingham, the Earl of Shrewsbury, and Lords Egremont and Beaumont – died fighting to defend their lord, who'd remained in the royal tent. Henry himself was lucky to survive in the heat of the pursuit. He was saved by a Yorkist archer – by tradition, one Henry Montfort – who realized just in time who he was. When Warwick and the 18-year-old Earl of March (Richard of York's son and heir, Edward) found him, they at once knelt and swore their allegiance. It played perfectly to the Warwick 'narrative': loyalty to the king, death to his evil counsellors. But the king would now return to London under escort. He was again a prisoner.

The casualties hadn't been as high as they might have been: Ruthin had seen to that. But they're hard to establish definitively, not least because the Lancastrian dead were denied Christian burial, Coppini having supposedly excommunicated them (though he later denied it). Most of them were probably killed after Ruthin's defection. But the rain of arrows must have taken a heavy toll on the Yorkists in dead and wounded, though there was a good deal of cover in the deer park. The Battlefields Trust puts the total number killed at just over three thousand, 'mostly being Lancastrians killed in the rout'.* Armies at this time weren't much disposed to give quarter unless for good reason or, as at Ludford Bridge, at the express wish of the commander. And the 'parliament of devils' certainly hadn't made for a spirit of magnanimity.

When Warwick returned to London he promptly dealt with the defenders of the Tower, who'd held out against the investing troops during his foray north. They were quickly overcome; seven were hanged, drawn and quartered, as traitors. Lord Scales was granted safe conduct, perhaps on account of his previous good service in the wars with France, but was killed by Thames watermen as he tried to leave the City. His body – 'naked as a worm', in Chaucer's striking image – was dumped in the porch of St Mary Overy across the river (now Southwark Cathedral). The civil war was becoming thoroughly uncivil.†

---

* The Battlefields Trust charity was founded in 1993 to work for the protection, promotion and interpretation of Britain's battlefields.

† In *War: How Conflict Shaped Us* (London, 2020), Professor Margaret MacMillan writes: 'Civil wars so often take on the character and cruelty of a crusade because they are about the nature of society itself. The other side is seen as having betrayed the community by refusing to agree to shared values and a common vision and so extremes of violence and cruelty become permissible, even necessary, to restore the damaged polity. When peoples who come from what has been the same family turn on each other, what was once love or at least tolerance becomes hatred, even to the extent of each wanting to annihilate the other. Each side in a Civil War is struggling for legitimacy and dominance within the space that was once shared. An external enemy is a clear but understandable threat; a Civil War is rather fuelled by anger and hurt at the incomprehensible betrayal of the other side.'

Northampton was a turning point for the Yorkists. As soon as Duke Richard learned of the king's capture he returned from Ireland, and in October, after a good deal of legal consideration, Henry was obliged to grant him the right of succession, thereby disinheriting his own son. On 25 October, parliament ratified the decision in an Act of Settlement (the 'Act of Accord'), which included a provision that neither Richard nor Henry – nor indeed anyone – should hasten the succession by the sword.

Pious hope. The king might make his orders in council – a council cowed by Warwick – and parliament might pass its acts; but Queen Margaret would have none of it. She at once began raising a new army in Scotland and the north, and, with Buckingham gone, appointing younger and more capable commanders. The civil war would continue, and with even greater vengefulness.

It was now well past the campaigning season, but in December, and for reasons not entirely clear, the Duke of York felt compelled to go north. The queen's new army was still far from ready, but there may have been enough troops belonging to Lancastrian supporters in Yorkshire to make Richard fear that his enemies might waste his estates there, and those of his loyal retainers. Or perhaps, like Harold after his hasty coronation on the day of the Confessor's funeral, he felt the need to go north to be sure the Lancastrian grandees acknowledged the Act of Accord. With the queen still in Scotland, there was, after all, a reasonable chance of persuading them with whom the future lay. Whichever the case, he set off on 9 December, but with just a few thousand men (some accounts say merely hundreds), the necessary money perhaps not yet raised, while Edward his son was at the old family seat of Ludlow mustering more troops. Warwick, now appointed lord treasurer, stayed in London to keep an eye on both the king and the expropriation of Lancastrian revenues.

The weather, as might be expected, was foul, so much so that York soon decided to send back the artillery train. Nevertheless, on 15

December his army reached Newark, a key town on the Great North Road, the crossing point of the Trent and a Yorkist stronghold. Next day, according to the contemporary chronicler William of Worcester,

> the Duke of York, with the Earl of Salisbury and many thousand armed men, were going from London to York . . . when a portion of his men, the van, as is supposed, or perhaps the scouts . . . were cut off by the people of the Duke of Somerset, Edmund Beaufort at Worksop.*

There are no other accounts of the episode, and it would appear to have been but a clash of scouts, no more. Worksop then (as now) having a charter market every Wednesday, the van may have come into town the previous day (Tuesday 16th), hoping to seize food from the merchants as they gathered. Beyond William's few words, nothing more is known, but clearly the Lancastrians left with a bloody nose, as York was able to continue his march north, reaching Sandal Castle near Wakefield on the 21st. William of Worcester says his destination had originally been the city bearing his name, but having learned it was firmly in Lancastrian hands, and with Lancastrian troops ranging as far south as Worksop, he decided on Sandal instead – a formidable fortress, if not a large one.† Whatever the case, here again there are echoes of Hastings, when Harold was lured to

---

* *Annales rerum Anglicarum*, published with his *Letters and Papers Illustrative of the Wars of the English in France during the Reign of Henry VI*, ed. Joseph Stevenson (London, 1864).

† The castle could probably have housed about 500 men, but not the numbers that York had with him, and certainly not those which Edward, Earl of March, was bringing from the Welsh Marches. Provisioning these numbers in winter would have presented a major problem, especially with the surrounding estates threatened by the gathering Lancastrian army at Pontefract, 10 miles to the east. Adjoining the castle earthworks to the south were 30 acres of stoutly fenced deer park, where Yorkist troops probably hunted for the pot.

battle by William's ravaging of his estates: now Richard of York, perhaps also chagrined by his abandoning of Ludlow the year before, seems to have been lured likewise by threat of the same.

Either way, Legate Coppini would later write of what followed as 'a rash advance'. It seems also that York hadn't quite grasped the change in the political and military weather. The Duke of Somerset was no Buckingham, a statesman–soldier of many years' experience and a certain civility. At nineteen, Somerset had fought at St Albans and seen his father killed – butchered indeed. Now at twenty-four he was full of youthful desire for retribution, and done with any notions of chivalry in war. One of those chivalric customs was the truce at the time of major religious festivals, and York appears to have believed a Christmas truce was in force, which would have extended at least to the feast of the Epiphany on 6 January. This would help to explain why he was content to billet his army in the villages around Sandal (some historians say they camped just outside the castle; but keeping several thousand troops under canvas in the depths of winter isn't the act of a seasoned soldier), and also, apparently, to leave the 10 miles between Sandal and Pontefract, where he knew there was a Lancastrian force gathering, without adequate scouts. For on 28 December, to his complete surprise, Somerset's forces began to appear before Sandal Castle.

The events at Wakefield are, as usual, far from clear – unlike the result. Historians have given various figures for the two sides, of which York's 5,000–6,000 against Somerset's 17,000–18,000 seem plausible.* It appears, however, that York can't have realized he was so greatly outnumbered, for the country was wooded and concealment therefore easy – though Shakespeare, in *Henry VI Part III*, has it differently:

---

* These figures are well argued for in Philip Haigh's *The Battle of Wakefield 30th December 1460* (Stroud, 1996).

(Enter a Messenger)

YORK: But, stay: what news? Why comest thou in such post?

MESSENGER: The queen with all the northern earls and lords
Intend here to besiege you in your castle:
She is hard by with twenty thousand men;
And therefore fortify your hold, my lord.*

Queen Margaret was, of course, still in Scotland, and by all accounts Somerset didn't have a siege train. York had sent word to Ludlow for reinforcements, so there was the option of sitting tight and forcing the Lancastrians into a humiliating withdrawal, for camping before the walls of a castle in midwinter without artillery was a wretched prospect. Or if they didn't withdraw there was the other prospect: defeat by Edward and his new-raised men from the Marches. But Sandal Castle was now crowded with troops forced in from their outlying billets, and rations and shelter would have been limited. A long siege wasn't an inviting prospect for the Yorkists either.

The Duke of York held a council of war the following day at which his senior commanders, all experienced soldiers, notably the Earl of Salisbury, urged him to hold fast and await the reinforcements. For giving battle in medieval times was no less precarious than in modern, and probably a great deal more. If it wasn't strictly necessary to engage with the enemy, then it was necessary not to.

Legend has it – and it may be no more than legend – that Somerset sent York insulting messages to provoke a sally, saying that he was too cowardly to come out of his castle and give battle to an army 'led' by a woman. Shakespeare takes this up, obliquely, a few lines later with a reference to the innate inferiority of such an army:

---

* Act I, scene ii.

(Enter John Mortimer and Hugh Mortimer)

YORK: Sir John and Sir Hugh Mortimer, mine uncles,
You are come to Sandal in a happy hour;
The army of the queen mean to besiege us.

JOHN MORTIMER: She shall not need; we'll meet her in the field.

YORK: What, with five thousand men?

RICHARD: Ay, with five hundred, father, for a need:
A woman's general; what should we fear?

The scene is fanciful, of course – Richard, his youngest son, later King Richard III, was only eight at the time and not at Sandal – but it testifies to the discussion in the council of war. But Shakespeare's depiction of a cautious York belies the reality, for on 30 December, despite the advice of his principal officers, he led his troops out of the castle. By some accounts it was to rescue his foragers, but more probably it was to defend – or display – what one historian has called his 'overbearing sense of honour and rectitude'.*

But as the rainbow mnemonic has it, Richard of York gave battle in vain. The Lancastrians were taken by surprise initially, but then rallied, with troops rushing to the fight from three directions, crucially those of the 25-year-old John Clifford – ninth Baron Clifford, ninth Lord of Skipton – whose father too had been killed at St Albans. It may have been a clever ruse by Somerset, a lure; and some of the Lancastrians (led by Lord John Neville, of a collateral branch of Warwick's family) may have been Yorkist turncoats. Whatever the case, there could have been little military art in such a battle, and by several credible accounts it was over in not much more than half an hour – as

---

* Starkey, introduction to Goodwin, *Fatal Colours*.

to be expected when a small force closes with one three times as numerous in the open. Most of it was probably mere butchery.

Some 3,000 Yorkists may have died that morning, a good many of them while trying to escape across the River Calder (once again demonstrating the perils of having a river lying across the line of retreat); the rest were taken prisoner – whatever that entailed. One of the prisoners was the Earl of Salisbury, who was taken to Pontefract ('Pomfret') Castle and promptly beheaded. Most of the other Yorkist leaders were killed on the field – Sir Thomas Harrington, Sir David Hall, Sir Hugh Hastings, Sir Thomas Neville and the two Mortimers.

Most prominent of all those put to death was the Duke of York himself. Shakespeare, though, not unreasonably wanting more drama for the end of a key character than a mere death in an armoured brawl, has him subjected to a mocking coronation with a paper crown by Queen Margaret, and presented by Lord Clifford with a handkerchief soaked in the blood of his second son, Edmund, Earl of Rutland, before being executed. Young Rutland – at seventeen, old enough to fight but young enough for the Victorian artist Charles Leslie to portray him as a defenceless child – had escaped with his chaplain–tutor to Wakefield but was captured by Clifford outside the chantry chapel on the bridge over the Calder. Indeed, he may well have taken sanctuary in the chapel – which, heavily restored, still stands – and been dragged out, for Clifford was bent on vengeance. In short, Shakespeare probably got what happened next about right:

CLIFFORD: Chaplain, away! thy priesthood saves thy life.
As for the brat of this accursed duke,
Whose father slew my father, he shall die.*

---

* Act I, scene iii.

And it was certainly true that Duke Richard's head, and several others, including Salisbury's and the youthful Rutland's, were taken to York and displayed on the Micklegate, as Shakespeare had it, 'that York might overlook York'. Except that, as a rule, impaled heads looked *out* of a city, for the delight or caution of those entering; but, again, Shakespeare's wit is preferable. And the mocking paper crown on Richard of York's impaled head is well attested to.

Decapitation strategy was all very well, and it must have appeared so to Queen Margaret and her faction at this point, but the Yorkist party would at once grow another head. The Duke of York's eldest surviving son, Edward, Earl of March, would now take up the Yorkist cause, with the help of course of his older cousin Warwick, the 'kingmaker'. And with this succession would come the end of all moderation, such as there had been: indeed, not just an end to chivalry, but the coming of a new element in the dynastic struggle – a sort of xenophobia. For while Warwick and March were now dominating the recruiting in Wales, parts of the midlands, East Anglia and the south (by commissions of array, which at times were little more than press gangs*), the army gathering to Queen Margaret's standard was now predominantly a northern one, including a large number of Scots promised good pay or plunder in lieu. The Wars of the Roses were in no way a war of east against west, Yorkshire against Lancashire. This was north versus south.

---

* A commission of array was a written grant of authority from the king to named individuals (commissioners) to muster all able-bodied men within a particular town or shire for military service, usually to resist foreign invasion or quell internal rebellion. Under Edward I's Statute of Winchester (1284), all men between the ages of sixteen and sixty who were fit to bear arms could be summoned annually for forty days' service. Twice a year, royal commissioners, usually members of the gentry, were authorized to inspect and report on the military readiness of the county or town in their charge. In times of emergency, the commissioners then mustered the levies for service with the royal (retained) army.

Warwick, the master strategian, would play on this division remorselessly, and his propaganda would have its effect. In a letter to his brother just three weeks after Wakefield, Clement Paston, of the famous epistolary Pastons of Norfolk, wrote that in London 'every man is willing to go with my Lords here and I hope God shall help them, for the people in the north rob and steal and are set to pillage all this country and give away men's goods and livelihoods'.

Henceforth, the war, the battles, were clearly going to take on the worst nature of a civil conflict – a war of tribal survival, atavistic and total. Shakespeare perfectly captures the frame of mind in Clifford's final words to Rutland on Wakefield Bridge:

> Had I thy brethren here, their lives and thine
> Were not revenge sufficient for me;
> No, if I digg'd up thy forefathers' graves
> And hung their rotten coffins up in chains,
> It could not slake mine ire, nor ease my heart.
> The sight of any of the house of York
> Is as a fury to torment my soul;
> And till I root out their accursed line
> And leave not one alive, I live in hell.

This 'leave not one alive', communicated to the foot soldiers of both sides, together with the 'north–south' narrative, is central to understanding how the campaign of Candlemas to Palm Sunday – from the battle of Mortimer's Cross to Towton – would unfold, and with what result.

4

CANDLEMAS TO PALM SUNDAY

Ye gods, what dastards would our host command!
Swept to the war, the lumber of the land.

Homer, *The Iliad*

If there are arguments today about where the north begins, there
were none in January 1461. The border was the River Trent. It was not
only the demarcation line between the lands held – in large part
owned – by Yorkist and Lancastrian supporters, it was the most promising defensible line. It was an odd border, though, for to the east of
Newark, its lowest bridging point, the Trent ran almost due north
until emptying into the Humber. It thus formed a border, via Lincolnshire, with East Anglia too.

The army that now crossed the Trent in late January with Margaret
at its head was indeed made up of Paston's 'people in the north' –
north, northern . . . Norsemen? – and many a freebooter and border
reiver who lived for plunder: 'a whirlwind from the north . . . a plague
of locusts covering the surface of the earth', says the contemporary

chronicle of the Abbey of Croyland (or Crowland) in Lincolnshire. Fifteen thousand strong, perhaps many more, they met no resistance at first, for Warwick was in London arraying all the troops he could, while Edward, Earl of March, was at Ludlow still. As they marched south they sacked the towns of Grantham, Stamford, Peterborough, Huntingdon and Royston.* On 10 February Warwick left London for St Albans with 10,000 men to halt the advance, but many thought the Yorkist cause done for, not least the papal legate Coppini, who left London the same day to hazard the Channel crossing for Flanders.

Seven days later – Shrove Tuesday – he appeared to be proved right. For Warwick, outnumbered, outflanked and frankly outgeneralled by Andrew Trollope, who'd changed sides at Ludford Bridge and was also probably responsible for the easy victory at Wakefield, was soundly beaten. By evening – which, mercifully for Warwick, came soon on a short winter's day – some 4,000 Yorkists lay dead or dying in the streets and trenches, and Warwick was in full retreat: not towards London, though, but west. And, worse still, behind him at St Albans he left the captive king. Poor bewildered Henry is supposed to have spent the battle sitting under a tree, singing. His contribution to the cause came instead the following day, in knighting Trollope. 'My Lord, I have not deserved this,' Sir Andrew is supposed to have said, 'for I slew no more than fifteen men . . . I stood still in one place and they came to me . . . but they stayed with me . . .'

An exaggeration perhaps, but even if he'd killed 'only' half the number it reveals something of the face of battle at this time. Trollope was fighting on foot in full armour and would have had his retainers about him. It would have taken another in full armour, with *his* retainers, to have any chance of felling him. The 'fifteen' who fell to his blade or pole-axe or to those of his retainers (the

---

* 'laying waste all the towns and villages that stood along their way': John Benet, *Chronicle*, English trans. with new introduction, ed. Alison Hanham (London, 2016).

total count would have been his) were probably not so favoured. This contrast between the protected and the unprotected becomes particularly significant when accounting for the huge casualties at Towton.

Why Warwick left Henry behind isn't clear. Perhaps he hadn't intended to. The king had been under the guard and protection of the 69-year-old Baron Bonville and the 65-year-old Sir Thomas Kyriell, veterans of the Hundred Years' War. As night fell they escorted the king, under promise of amnesty, to the tent of Lord Clifford. The queen, however, repudiated the amnesty – we don't know how keenly Henry pleaded for them; he was a pious man, but Margaret was fearsome – and their heads joined the tally of Lancastrian retribution, adding in turn to the score to be settled by the Yorkists. That is, if ever they were to be in a position to do so. For London was now Margaret's for the taking – the richest city in Christendom, said Coppini.*

But Margaret hesitated. London had defences of its own; and besides, letting loose a victorious army in her would-be capital would not be edifying. And she wasn't strong enough to over-awe the city and arrange a more orderly occupation. So instead she withdrew a little way north and west to Dunstable to wait for Jasper Tudor, Earl of Pembroke, to join her from Wales with his 6,000-strong force of Welsh and Irish levies and French mercenaries. It would prove a fatal hesitation, however, because just over a fortnight earlier, on 2 February – Candlemas – Pembroke had been soundly beaten by March at Mortimer's Cross south-west of Ludlow. It was a close-fought battle, the sides evenly matched in numbers, but one in which March showed both tactical skill and personal bravery. The

---

* As ever, there was a personal angle to the blood-letting. One of Margaret's commanders was the Earl of Devon, whose family had a long feud with Bonville's. Civil war was the perfect opportunity for settling such feuds – for the time being at least.

Lancastrians lost a third of their force, while Yorkist losses were relatively few. Captured Lancastrian leaders, including Pembroke's father, Owen Tudor, paid with the now customary price – their heads. March then took his troops east, meeting up with Warwick in Gloucestershire, where the two decided to make at once for the relief of London. They were spared the fight, however, for on 20 February, the very day Margaret was pulling back to Dunstable, she got word of Pembroke's defeat, and lost her nerve.

Or perhaps prudence prevailed? Even if she'd been able to occupy London, with or without a fight, her army might not have been able to resist a combined assault by Warwick's and March's forces. Especially if a large part of hers had descended into rape and pillage, as the burghers of London had expected and she no doubt had feared. Either way, she now turned back north, leaving London open to March and his cousin. Mortimer's Cross, a clash of a few thousand in the marshy meadows of the River Lugg, had proved a victory of the first strategic importance. And Warwick's strategic brilliance was in realizing the potential of a tactical success.

Much has been written about Margaret's decision not to close on London. She wasn't short of experienced advisers, and some historians have suggested that she herself would have been familiar with the same writings on warfare as they. Chief of these – besides the Bible, whose Old Testament is an incidental manual on strategy and tactics – was *Epitoma Rei Militaris* (sometimes *De Re Militari*, 'On Military Matters') by the fourth-century writer Publius Flavius Vegetius Renatus. Or if her Latin was not up to that, there was a derivative work by the remarkable Christine de Pisan, almost a contemporary, a favourite of the court of Charles VI of France (r.1380–1422) – her *Livre des fais d'armes et de chevalerie* (Book of Feats of Arms and of Chivalry).*

---

* Sir John Talbot, first Earl of Shrewsbury, is said to have presented Margaret with a compendium including Pisan's writing as a wedding present.

The Roman Vegetius is famous for his caution: 'A battle is commonly decided in two or three hours, after which no further hopes are left for the worsted army. Every plan, therefore, is to be considered, every expedient tried and every method taken before matters are brought to this last extremity.'

Vegetius didn't of course advise absolutely against battle; he observed that 'good officers never engage in general actions *unless induced by opportunity* [emphasis added]' or if, of course, 'obliged by necessity'.* Instead, they preferred 'the employment of stratagem and finesse to destroy the enemy as much as possible in detail and intimidate them without exposing [their] own forces'. He concluded simply that 'it is much better to overcome the enemy by famine, surprise or terror than by general actions'. And, indeed, he added a great deal about the imposition of famine on the enemy, and its avoidance for one's own troops.

Whatever Margaret's source of strategic advice, her decision now was thoroughly Vegetian. She would retreat north to her 'comfort zone' to draw March and Warwick out of theirs. And not just to the Duchy of Lancaster's former midlands centre of power – Leicestershire and Warwickshire, and the great fortress of Kenilworth – but north of the Trent. Indeed, *well* north of the Trent: to York, the second city of England and the old capital of Northumbria, the kingdom that had resisted Athelstan's campaign of unification the longest, where Richard of York's head still topped the Micklegate (and where also she could receive supplies and reinforcements through Hull). For she knew that March, or King Edward IV as he was soon to be proclaimed in Westminster Hall, would have to bring her forces to the battlefield and, like Duke William of Normandy at Hastings, settle the matter once and for all by combat. Edward's 'Witan' – the Yorkist lords, the Archbishop of

---

* Christopher Allmand, *The 'De Re Militari' of Vegetius* (Cambridge, 2011).

Canterbury and the Bishops of Salisbury and Exeter – may have given him the royal sceptre and the other symbols of sovereignty, as the Witan had done for Harold, but they couldn't give him the holy unction and crown – yet. For the anointed king would be in York, and to resolve this inconvenience the provisional king would, in Vegetius's words, be 'obliged by necessity' to fight. And if Margaret were to give battle on Henry's behalf, it would be on ground of her choosing.

Understanding this, Edward was determined to fight with the largest possible army. On 5 March, the day after his proclamation as king, he despatched commissions of array for thirty-two counties, all but one of which were south or east of the Trent. The exception was Northumberland, the seat of his implacable enemies the Percys, clearly targeted more in defiance than expectation.

As with Harold's march to meet Hardrada, the mustering continued throughout the Yorkist army's progress north. By the time they crossed the Trent, unopposed, in the third week of March, it had grown to at least 20,000, possibly even twice that, as allied lords and their considerable numbers of retainers, feed men and maintenance men joined en route, and the commissioners of array brought in their levies. Fauconberg was again in command of the advance guard of some 5,000, Edward himself and this time Warwick were present in person with the main body, and following them, though not yet in close contact, was the earl marshal, the Duke of Norfolk, with at least a further 5,000. Ill-health had delayed his start and slowed his advance – as had the laggardliness of the East Anglian gentry in committing themselves to the Yorkist cause.

These numbers were impressive, however, even the lower estimate, especially as it was still winter and food stocks were dwindling. But Edward had taken care to muster a large supply train before leaving London, as well as making arrangements for requisitioning on the march, as opposed to the Lancastrians' plundering, of which Warwick had made good use in his propaganda. One chronicler remarked on the great number of waggons parked in the fields outside the city, and it seems the commissaries had ranged wide to fill them. The jurats of Lydd on the Kent coast record payment 'for vitelle sent to London, to the journey of York, £3. 11s. 9d'.* And as more than one historian has remarked, life for geese in southern England suddenly got colder, too, for by royal command three primary feathers from every goose wing were plucked and sent to the fletchers at the Tower of London, the arsenal of England, to make the several hundred thousand arrows that Edward's archers would need.

Margaret's army was formidable too, though. It certainly outnumbered the potential Yorkist force: at least 30,000, and according to some historians double that. These figures shouldn't surprise. Three-quarters of the peerage and gentry of England and Wales had become embroiled in the disputes, local and national, that had coalesced into what only later became known as the Wars of the Roses.† They themselves had as much to gain from a decisive victory in battle as the principals, and equally as much to lose from defeat: death either during the conflict or afterwards, and the disinheritance of their families. They therefore had every incentive to exploit the full potential of 'bastard feudalism', and they brought vast retinues to the field. Most of the peerage, however, still remained loyal to the king *de jure* – Henry – and to the House of Lancaster.

Not only did Margaret have the numerical advantage, then, she now had the advantage of location. Although she'd had the long trek

---

* Jean de Waurin (*c.*1400–*c.*1473), chronicler, quoted in Anthony Goodman, *The Wars of the Roses* (London, 1990).

† It's sometimes claimed that the phrase 'Wars of the Roses' came into popular use in the nineteenth century after publication of Sir Walter Scott's *Anne of Geierstein* (1829), in allusion to the scene in *Henry VI Part 1*, in Temple Church gardens, in which nobles pick red or white roses to show their loyalty to the House of Lancaster or York. In fact, the term was in common use long before that date.

north to York, once there, deep in Lancastrian territory, her army had good shelter and plentiful supply. This was fine agricultural country, both arable and pasture. Even towards the end of winter, York's cellars and granaries wouldn't have been empty, and more could be brought through Hull, too, via the Humber and Ouse. Indeed, Warwick tried hard to halt or intercept supplies reaching Hull from King's Lynn. Normally, all things being equal, the advantage lay with the attacker, who could choose his time and means. But Edward hadn't much freedom of action, while Margaret's army could conserve its strength and wait until the Yorkists, after a tiring march of 200 miles, showed themselves. He'd have to bring her to battle in the open, and he could only do that by threatening York. Margaret, therefore, could follow a dual strategy: either denying him passage of the River Aire, which ran roughly west–east some 15 miles south of York, in the hope that his army, starved of rations, would begin to disintegrate (one of the reasons for the desertions at St Albans); or, if he forced the Aire, which would be costly anyway, she could destroy the army on ground of her own choosing. The first would follow the precepts of Vegetius – to overcome the enemy by famine – while the second would wrest back the initiative from Edward as the attacker by forcing him to make his assault where the advantage lay with the defence.

In the weeks before Napoleon crossed the border in June 1815, the Duke of Wellington made a thorough reconnaissance of the potential French axes of advance and chose a number of places where he could give battle on his own terms, as indeed Harold would have done in the months of watching the coast before Duke William landed. The ridge at Mont St Jean – Waterloo – wasn't chosen hastily; and nor was that at Hastings. The Duke of Somerset, Margaret's commander now, would have selected several places too, the most likely of which was Towton, for he'd have appreciated that crossing the Aire in late winter or early spring, a river of considerable strength, possibly in spate, wasn't something that Edward could easily improvise, especially when opposed, and there were few all-weather bridges. Indeed, the lowest bridging point of the Aire, which rises in the Pennines, lay south-west of York, at Ferrybridge on the Great North Road. And between Ferrybridge and the Aire's confluence with the Ouse 20 miles east were impassable marshes. At this time the road was carried across the river by a three-arched stone bridge, 15 feet 6 inches wide, good enough for an army to cross in all weathers.* There was a second crossing 3 miles west as the crow flies, at the old Roman settlement of Castleford at the confluence of the Aire and Calder, where besides the ford of the name when the river was low enough, there was a timber bridge. West of Castleford was a large belt of marsh, and no practicable crossing point till Leeds, almost in the foothills of the Pennines, which would have meant a considerable diversion. The strategic importance of Castleford was huge, therefore, as it had been since Roman times when York was the military capital of Britain, headquarters of the famous Ninth Legion. But while Castleford had been the lowest bridging point on the Aire in Roman times, with the building of the stone bridge Ferrybridge was the more important now, as an all-weather crossing and a slightly shorter route to York. The great Norman castle at Pontefract guarded both crossings, 2 miles or so to their south-east and south-west respectively. Whichever crossing point the Yorkists chose, except the much longer route via Leeds, it was at Towton that the roads to York converged.

Margaret – or more probably Somerset – chose not to garrison Pontefract, however. Instead she kept her army north of the river, warm

---

* The width is known because it is recorded that in 1765 the old bridge was widened by 10 feet, before being rebuilt entirely in 1804. There seems no reason to doubt that this was the original bridge built in the early fourteenth century, consisting of three arches, seven pillars and a chantry chapel at one end, and therefore the one that stood in 1461. Certainly it could not have been less substantial. See, *inter alia*, David Featherstone Harrison, *The Bridges of Medieval England: Transport and Society, 400–1800* (Oxford, 2004).

and dry. As soon as she had word of Edward's approach she could send detachments to destroy the arches at Ferrybridge and the wooden structure at Castleford, and move the bulk of the army to Tadcaster (where King Harold had spent the night before Stamford Bridge) to be ready to support the watch on the Aire. Or perhaps to take the commanding ground at Towton, let the Yorkists cross and force them to fight with the Aire at their backs, barring their flight south. It would be risky, but if battle went her way it would be a complete and probably final victory.

The weather was still cold, and the men of the forward detachments needed shelter, but there was little to be had on the north side of the river at either Castleford or Ferrybridge. So the force guarding the latter crossing, under the command of Lord Clifford of Skipton – the man whose sudden appearance at Wakefield had had such dramatic effect and whose murder of the young Edmund of Rutland on Wakefield bridge had intensified the war's savagery – seems to have camped at Sherburn-in-Elmet, a village 5 miles to the north of Ferrybridge. The whereabouts of that guarding Castleford, if indeed there was a separate detachment, isn't known.

Margaret, then, had the numerical advantage, and also the advantage of choosing the ground; Edward, to some extent at least, had the advantage of choosing when to attack. He could void some of Margaret's advantage by taking the crossings by surprise. But to do so he'd have to close very fast once his presence was discovered.

His army was certainly marching apace. Edward and Warwick, with the main body, reached Pontefract some time on 27 March. What exactly happened then, in what order and why, depends as ever on which source is believed, although several support one another and some are patently more plausible than others. What's beyond doubt is the outcome. Somerset, naturally, had scouts south of the river, and possibly Clifford did too, but these may not have discovered the arrival of the Yorkists in strength, for when Warwick's deputy, Lord

FitzWalter, was sent towards dusk (some time after seven o'clock) with his 'foreprickers' to seize the stone bridge, he took it with barely a skirmish. It had been partly destroyed, however, the roadway in the centre breached and preparations made to bring down the rest, possibly by gunpowder. But the spandrel walls (the longitudinal stiffenings above the arch), 2 feet wide, remained in place to allow the pickets to cross. FitzWalter also appears to have had 'engineers' with him, and although by now it was almost dark, they at once began widening and strengthening the crossing with timber.

Unfortunately this brilliant coup wasn't followed up quickly enough. With the alarm raised, Clifford and his 'Flower of Craven' – 500 mounted retainers and feed men (and many a border reiver) – made a fast march from Sherburn and counter-attacked in the early hours, taking the Yorkists completely by surprise. FitzWalter and Warwick's half-brother were killed in the fighting, and by dawn the bridge was back in Lancastrian hands.

As soon as Edward heard, he and Warwick rushed the 2 miles to Ferrybridge with more men. But Clifford, reinforced by archers who'd hurried from Sherburn, some perhaps on horseback, was able to hold them off. The Yorkists had only a narrow defile by which to cross, while he could extend his archers along the bank to enfilade them – fire the length of their line – as they made the attempt. More reinforcements arrived from Sherburn, and possibly even Tadcaster, and casualties began to mount. According to Jean de Waurin, the fighting at the bridge cost the Yorkists 3,000 dead and wounded, a good many drowned in the icy water of the Aire.

Meanwhile, the crossing at Castleford had been taken without even a skirmish. Again, the details aren't clear, but at some stage – and it's difficult to believe that it wasn't the evening before, at the same time that FitzWalter took Ferrybridge (for why delay?) – Fauconberg arrived with mounted troops to find no Lancastrians there. Doubtless he sent word back at once to Edward and then secured a

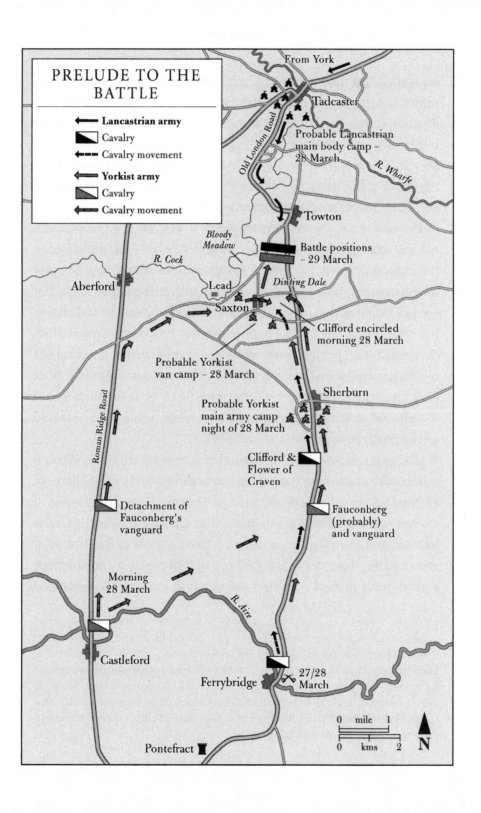

PRELUDE TO THE BATTLE

Lancastrian army
Cavalry
Cavalry movement

Yorkist army
Cavalry
Cavalry movement

From York

Tadcaster

Old London Road

Probable Lancastrian
main body camp –
28 March

R. Wharfe

Towton

R. Cock

Bloody
Meadow

Battle positions
– 29 March

Aberford

Lead

Dinting Dale

Saxton

Clifford encircled
morning 28 March

Probable Yorkist
van camp – 28 March

Sherburn

Probable Yorkist
main army camp
night of 28 March

Roman Ridge Road

Clifford &
Flower of
Craven

Detachment of
Fauconberg's
vanguard

Fauconberg
(probably)
and vanguard

Morning
28 March

R. Aire

Castleford

Ferrybridge

27/28
March

Pontefract

0   mile   1

0   kms   2

N

bridgehead for the night. Although there was a full moon, there was probably little to gain by probing further, but as an experienced soldier he'd have sent patrols out as soon as it was light to discover where the enemy was – and, almost as important, where he wasn't. He may therefore have learned of the battle at Ferrybridge by his own reconnaissance rather than by message from Edward, but either way, he decided on an immediate flank attack.*

This would have been useful enough, but Fauconberg saw a chance to recapture the bridge and also to destroy Clifford's mounted force – the 'Flower of Craven' – comprehensively. Fauconberg could hardly have had many more men than Clifford, and quite possibly fewer, but he decided nevertheless to divide his force. One group would charge the defenders at the bridge, forcing them to bolt north towards Tadcaster, and then pursue them, while the other would advance up the old Roman ridge-road from Castleford which ran parallel to that from Ferrybridge for 8 miles, and at some stage turn east to cut their line of withdrawal. Fauconberg's estates lay in north Yorkshire, and he would undoubtedly have known the roads well.

In short, the ploy was spectacularly successful. At Hook Moor, 6 miles north of the ford, the parallel party turned east for the village of Saxton, and caught Clifford's men in Dinting Dale. The 'Flower of Craven' were quickly overwhelmed, with Clifford killed early in the fighting and the rest given no quarter. Besides those at the Aire, Margaret had now lost 500 well-armed and well-horsed men, and perhaps a good many archers – though not nearly as many as Warwick had

---

* Some sources say it wasn't until daylight, i.e. *after* the Lancastrian counter-attack, that Fauconberg was sent to Castleford, but it seems inconceivable that between them, Edward, Warwick and Fauconberg would have left the only other crossing unexplored for so long – not least as it was a potential route for a Lancastrian raid or, worse, an assault against his main body at Pontefract. That said, it seems inconceivable too that Somerset should have left the crossing without any guard. Perhaps Clifford was meant to cover both and was slow off the mark.

likely lost to gain the crossing; and Somerset would now have to fight a general action rather than holding the Yorkists at arm's length, wearing down their strength in attempts to cross the river and letting 'starvation' help as well.* Yes, the Aire would be at the Yorkists' backs, and he could still choose the ground; but to be forced into battle wasn't what he'd have wanted, while on the other hand, a general action was all that Edward could reasonably have hoped for. Even with the loss of Clifford's 'flowers', however, the Lancastrians still had the numerical advantage, and they could choose the ground. And Somerset chose the plateau of Towton, the highest point between Ferrybridge and York.

---

* There has long been speculation as to why Clifford had no support. The 'Flower of Craven' may well have been the finest fellows, but 500 – or even five times that number – was hardly a strong covering force. Jean de Waurin remarks that 'the Earl of Northumberland . . . failed to attack soon enough' (*Recueil des croniques et anchiennes istories de la Grant Bretaigne*). This is variously taken as referring to the attack at Castleford or at Towton itself, and there has been speculation that such was his personal enmity with Clifford that he deliberately held back at the Aire and was glad of the outcome at Dinting Dale. This, with its consequential abetting of the enemy, seems extreme, but it does raise the possibility that Somerset intended there to be a bigger forward fight. Perhaps there was confusion, a slow coming of Northumberland's men from York; such things happen still.

5

A FIELD OF BATTLE*

The coup d'œil is a gift of God and cannot be acquired.

Jean Charles Le Chevalier Folard,
Esprit du Chevalier Folard

Edward's engineers must have worked miracles at Ferrybridge, for that night the army slept at Sherburn, with its vanguard under Fauconberg, perhaps consisting only of horsemen, 2 miles further north at the village of Saxton. Margaret's army undoubtedly had the better of things at Tadcaster, a market town for two centuries, for it was another cold night. They'd have had a strong screen of horsemen keeping the ridge at Towton that afternoon, and no doubt the odd escapee from the execution at Dinting Dale would have kept the pickets alert. With just 2½ miles down a good road to their battle positions, however, it's unlikely the main force at Tadcaster would have

---

* 'Act II Scene iii: A Field of Battle between Towton and Saxton, in Yorkshire. Alarum: Excursions. Enter WARWICK': Shakespeare, *King Henry VI, Part 3,* scene rubric.

been much disturbed once it was clear that the Yorkists were encamping at Sherburn. Spending the night in the open on the highest ground for miles without shelter would not have been good preparation for battle. The Duke of Wellington's men did so before Waterloo, but although it rained a good deal, it was summer – and they had no choice, for Napoleon's men were already on the ridge opposite.

Despite the deteriorating weather and lack of shelter, though, Yorkist spirits must have been high. While the Lancastrians' king remained in York (where he could do least harm), *their* king was with them in the field, and in personal command. He'd fought on foot at Ferrybridge and they'd gained the crossing. They'd no doubt learned too of Fauconberg's despatch of the 'Flower of Craven', and now they were but a dozen miles from the walls of York. There was just the little question of Margaret's army, which would undoubtedly try to halt their advance on the city, probably in front of Tadcaster, for once across the Wharfe by the town's bridge, the road to York was straight and level. Both sides knew therefore that there'd be a major battle next day, but only the Lancastrians could know exactly where.

One part of Edward's army was rather more in the dark, though. The Duke of Norfolk and his 5,000 still hadn't caught up with the main body; but fortuitously, the delay at Ferrybridge had meant he'd closed the gap considerably, and – the law of unintended consequences – this would prove decisive in the coming battle. Nevertheless, although he and Edward must have been in some sort of contact that night, Norfolk and his host were probably still south of the Aire, at Pontefract.

If they were at Pontefract they were indeed fortunate, with a little shelter and warmth, and perhaps even hot food. Edward's men weren't so lucky. By the modern calendar it was the night of 9–10 April,* but it

---

* In 1752, to align England with continental practice, the Gregorian calendar was substituted by Act of Parliament for the Julian calendar, which meant an advance of eleven days.

was still a cold one, the ground frozen. However good the campfires, dawn at about five-fifteen must have been welcome. But the sky was leaden, there was a biting wind from the south-west, and with the acute weather eye of medieval man, both sides must have known that it wouldn't be long before snow fell.

Somerset, or whoever had made the decision, had chosen his ground well. This was – still is – open, undulating farmland, a standard medieval mix of pasture and arable. In the west, to the right and rear of the ridge (some thousand yards long) which the Lancastrian army would occupy, was coppiced woodland. From this highest point of the northern part of the plateau just south of Towton village the ground falls away south for some 400 yards, to 'North Acres' and Towton Dale, before rising gently again. The right of the battlefield as the Lancastrians saw it (the west), was marked by the Cock Beck. This snakes north, perhaps surprisingly, and eventually turns east to empty into the Wharfe just south of Tadcaster; and its eastern bend just north of Towton formed the northern bound of the battlefield. The Cock Beck was no river – a beck in northern English is a stream – but in spring it was no trickle either. The right of the Lancastrian line, which extended just west of the old Roman road from Castleford to Tadcaster, was protected not just by the beck but also by the steep wooded drop to it, and the marshes beyond. But, and as if by Lancastrian design, just south of the ridge, the beck snakes sharply west again to form a sort of 'sack' of meadowland on the left flank of the line that the Yorkists would have to form in order to assault the ridge. And at the western, 'closed', end of the sack was a wood that offered perfect concealment for men on horse or foot. To the east of the Lancastrian line was more marsh, giving a measure of protection, but here the approaches were more open, with several small woods which might offer some concealment to men advancing, or alternatively present obstacles to their movement. In sum, the ground offered the numerically inferior Yorkists little room for manoeuvre, unless by the boldest strike at the rear with cavalry in a similar move to Fauconberg's the day before. This would mean heading west from Sherburn to the old Roman road again, following it north to where it turns slightly east for Tadcaster, then riding cross-country for the bridge over the Cock Beck just north of Towton (if it hadn't been destroyed) or chancing the stream. It would have been one of the great enveloping moves of history had it taken place, but for whatever reason it didn't. Perhaps the ground was unfamiliar, or the troops couldn't be spared, or Fauconberg, perhaps the only one who could have pulled it off, was needed to command the Yorkist van, the great body of archers who would try to even up the odds before the men-at-arms began their hacking. So instead the battle would be fought in the manner of old, the sides squaring up to each other in a contest of will, skill and numbers.

Breakfasting, armouring and mustering would all have taken time. It was Palm Sunday, too – celebrating Jesus of Nazareth's humble entry on a donkey into Jerusalem to observe the Passover, the first day of Holy Week, which would end with His crucifixion on Good Friday – and there would have been a good deal of religious ceremony in both camps, the chaplains saying mass, hearing confessions, pronouncing general absolution. But by nine o'clock the Lancastrians were arrayed in their divisions on the ridge – 30,000 of them at least, probably many more. Those who'd not seen the ground before must have been reassured. They were first to the field, their position dominated the valley, and to close with them – which the Yorkists must do, while they themselves need only hold their ground – the assaulting troops would have a long trudge up the exposed slope. But the cold, southerly wind in their faces may just have troubled some of the archers, for loosing arrows into the wind would cost them range and therefore their advantage of the ridge. They may or may not have known of the cavalry secretly taking post in the woods at the bottom of the slope to their right. Only one source – Waurin – mentions them, but Somerset

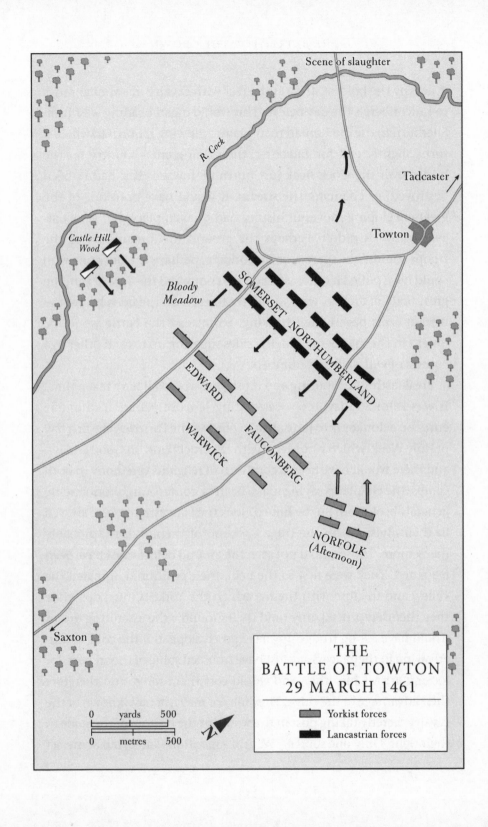

Scene of slaughter

R. Cock

Tadcaster

Castle Hill
Wood

Towton

Bloody
Meadow

SOMERSET

NORTHUMBERLAND

EDWARD

FAUCONBERG

WARWICK

NORFOLK
(Afternoon)

Saxton

0   yards   500

0   metres   500

N

THE
BATTLE OF TOWTON
29 MARCH 1461

Yorkist forces

Lancastrian forces

was too good a soldier to miss such an opportunity for ambush, and circumstantial evidence suggests he didn't.

Not long after nine, Edward and his army, having advanced unseen from Sherburn, broached the ridge of the southern slope and immediately began the customary cheering of their leader, to be met by counter-cheering from the much greater number of Lancastrians. And almost at once, it started to snow – blustery showers making it suddenly difficult to see.

Nothing is known for sure about the detailed dispositions, but it seems that both sides had adopted the conventional arrangement of vanward (or forward), mainward and rearward divisions. We do know that Fauconberg commanded the Yorkist van, so we can suppose that Edward, in all his six feet and more of impressive youthful stature, commanded the mainward division, with Warwick either at his side or commanding the rearward – the latter, probably, as he'd received a leg wound at Ferrybridge; and, in truth, his record in offensive battle, as opposed to his strategic acumen, wasn't that distinguished.

Somerset, of course, was in command of the entire Lancastrian army, and specifically of the mainward, along with the Earl of Northumberland and Sir Andrew Trollope, the slayer of fifteen at St Albans, while the Duke of Exeter led the rearward. In addition to the rearward division on both sides, there was also the rear*guard* which consisted largely of mounted men – 'prickers' – who as well as guarding the rear kept, as their name suggests, the faint-hearted from bolting. Above all, though, their job was to wait for the word to let loose and harry the broken ranks of the enemy as they made away, turning retreat into rout. Especially this day, with the words 'no quarter' passed along the ranks.

Snow squalls were no conditions in which to stand and wait. Medieval man may have been more used to life out of doors, but while armour was good protection against wind and weather, it was not a good insulator. Equally, *unarmoured* muscles lose heat and contract, thus reducing their range of movement, and were not going to be helpful in a contest that would boil down to brute strength. Nor were frozen fingers any good to an archer.

Fauconberg certainly didn't intend losing time hanging about. Down the slope he led his van of 10,000 archers in their spaced ranks, the 'herse' (harrow) formation that had served so well at Agincourt. Ordinarily they'd need to close to within at most 300 yards, and then, in an equal archery duel, trust to their greater accuracy and rate of fire. Fauconberg, however, small of stature and in his late fifties but a veteran of many a fight, at once saw his advantage. Vegetius had said it: 'In drawing up an army in order of battle, three things are to be considered: the sun, the dust and the wind.' And the wind was with Fauconberg. It would *not* be an equal duel. The (much) later chronicler Edward Hall relates:

> The lord Fauconberg, which led the forward of Edward's battle, being a man of great policy and having much experience of martial fields, caused every archer under his standard to shoot one flight and then made them stand still. The northern men, feeling the shoot, but by reason of the snow, not perfectly viewing the distance between them and their enemies like hardy men shot their sheath arrows as fast as they might, but all their shot was lost and their labour in vain for they came not near the southern men by forty tailors yards.*

With the snow driving at them, the Lancastrians may not even have seen the first flight of arrows. If so, the shock must have been very great. It certainly can't have helped the reply; they may not have

---

* Edward Hall, *Hall's Chronicle containing the history of England during the reign of Henry the Fourth and the succeeding monarchs, to the end of the reign of Henry the Eighth* (London, 1809). A tailor's yard is 37 inches, rather than 36 – clearly a poetic distinction in this context.

been able to see their own fall of shot, and even if they had, there was little they could do to correct it, for it seems that Fauconberg had judged the distance perfectly and they were simply outranged. Somerset's men loosed off volley after useless volley until their sheaths were empty – perhaps a quarter of a million arrows, and maybe even more – and all to no effect. Hall recounts what happened next, yet another masterly move by Fauconberg:

> When their shot was almost spent the Lord Fauconberg marched forward with his archers, who not only shot their own sheaves, but also gathered the arrows of their enemies and let a great part fly against their own masters, and another part they let stand on the ground which sore annoyed the legs of the owners when battle was joined.

Indeed, by some accounts it was Fauconberg himself who ordered them to leave the arrows embedded in the ground to hamper the Lancastrian advance, as he knew it must now come. Shooting at up to twelve arrows a minute with the skill that came with so many years' training – 'All servants and labourers are to have bows, and to practise with them on Sundays and holidays' (Act of Richard II, 1388) – could have sent as many as 120,000 into the air in any one minute, and at least 30,000 at once. The massed longbow was quite simply a medieval machine gun. And with a resupply of arrows from the waggons to their rear, or those lying at their feet, Fauconberg's archers could have stood their ground with impunity and begun to devastate Somerset's mainward, for the 'bodkin' arrowhead could penetrate chainmail and sometimes even plate armour. In all, the duel could not have lasted even ten minutes. But those minutes would prove decisive, for to evade destruction, the Lancastrian men-at-arms had to give up their ground and advance through their own line of archers, standing or dead, towards adversaries seen only fleetingly in the flurries of snow.

All was by no means lost, though. Their archers may have done next to no damage, and could do little now even if they advanced, for they'd loosed off all their arrows, but the Lancastrians still outnumbered the Yorkist main and rear. Nevertheless, while the cheering was still loud – 'King Henry!' – as they descended the slope, some of them at least would have been all too aware of the maxim that he who quits his chosen ground first usually loses the battle. For the shape of the battlefield was now very different from the one that Somerset had planned.

Meanwhile in the Yorkist lines, as Fauconberg's archers prepared to withdraw to the rear, there was a brief 'Shakespearian moment'. Edward rode along the ranks and, according to Waurin, 'where all the nobles were', reminded them that they had made him king, that others would usurp their rights, but that if any wished now to leave the field they should do so:

> So that all of them hearing this good request by the young king shouted in unison that they would follow him until death if need be. Hearing this good support, the king thanked them and he jumped down from his horse and told them, sword in hand, that he would live or die with them in order to give them courage.

Perhaps they needed no heroic encouragement, but it's hard not to speculate on the effect of personal leadership at such a moment. The Yorkists were outnumbered, Norfolk and his men were nowhere to be seen still, and the royal standard was flying in the Lancastrian line. Not that many could have seen it in that weather, or even recognized it perhaps, but it counted for something. That said, to men about to put the rival claims to the test, the symbolic presence of the semi-imbecile Henry could hardly compare with the real and impressive presence of Edward. And Edward's maternal uncle, Fauconberg, had just pulled off a tactical masterstroke, slaughtering so many with so little cost and forcing the Lancastrians to quit their ground. His archers, bows levelled, now loosed their last arrows at about 30 yards against the approaching men-at-arms, before slipping back to the rear, where they could once again shoot at longer range, bows at high angle, against the Lancastrian rearward division.

Ideally, the Yorkist line would have stood a little way up the slope to have the benefit of momentum as they clashed, but there's no evidence one way or the other. What seems to have happened is that as the Lancastrian mainward advanced, Northumberland's men on the left fell behind, perhaps slowed by the thousands of embedded arrows, or perhaps just failing to hear the initial order to advance. The Lancastrian right and centre collided with the Yorkist line and perhaps pushed it back a little, while in turn the Yorkist right surged forward rather than waiting to engage the lagging Northumberland left, and the battle line became reoriented more south-west to north-east than the original east–west.*

It was now the exhausting business of muscle and steel, with here and there a 'hand cannon' brought by foreign fireworkers to add noise and smoke – and not much else: these were crude weapons, more dangerous to their handlers and those nearby than to the enemy, judging from the fragments of barrel explosions found lately on the battlefield. For how long this metalled melee continued, no one really knows. There were men enough on both sides for some to take a rest from the hacking – even to take a gulp at fortifying wine – and then rejoin the combat. They fought in lines, but these consisted

---

* It's sometimes suggested that at this stage Somerset's cavalry, under Sir Andrew Trollope, charged and broke their counterparts – who were possibly guarding the Yorkist left flank – who fled the field, disordering their own baggage train in the process. This is doubtful; the sources aren't reliable and it makes no sense in what is generally acknowledged to be the outline of the battle. Trollope himself was anyway killed during the hand-to-hand fighting on foot, as was his son.

more of small 'combat teams' centred on their lord than men drilled to fight as a single rank. The regimented line would have to wait for the musket and pike, and for permanent companies – or, at least, companies embodied for long enough to train as a unit. And so the melee continued, with men slipping and sliding in snow turning to slush underfoot. Simply to lose one's balance and fall would be enough if there were a pole-axe close. Shakespeare has Henry – who in reality was sequestered in York – take himself aside on the battle-field to muse on the ebb and flow of the fighting, in words that reflect his decidedly non-martial qualities:

> This battle fares like to the morning's war,
> When dying clouds contend with growing light,
> What time the Shepherd, blowing of his nails,
> Can neither call it perfect day or night.
> Now sways it this way, like a mighty sea
> Forced by the tide to combat with the wind;
> Now sways it that way, like the selfsame sea
> Forced to retire by fury of the wind:
> Sometime the flood prevails, and then the wind;
> Now one the better, then another best;
> Both tugging to be victors breast to breast;
> Yet neither conqueror nor conquered:
> So is the equal poise of this fell war.

Nor was it necessarily safer to be the lord at the centre of his combat team, for it was he who was meant to be on the offensive, his retainers guarding his flanks and back; and, practised though he probably was, so too was his opponent, and luck always played its part. The Earl of Northumberland, forty years old and as experienced as any man in fighting – if only with his neighbours, fellow lords and Scots – was mortally wounded in the hand-to-hand struggle and was dragged to the rear by his retainers.* With one of its captains *hors de combat*, this would have been an anxious moment for the integrity of the line, though it did hold, for numbers in a brawl will always tell, and the Lancastrians, especially with their greater total of nobles and their retinues, could feed fresh troops into the front rank at a greater rate than the Yorkists. In his work of 1513, *Anglica Historia*, the Italian priest and papal diplomat Polydore Vergil, who'd spent most of his working life in England, probably best sums up the scene at the foot of the slopes: 'So great was the slaughter . . . that the very dead carcasses hindered them that fought.'

Certainly on the Yorkist left at one point the battle was clearly going ill for Edward. *Hall's Chronicle*, despite its author's Lancastrian sympathies, describes how he 'so courageously comforted his men, refreshing the weary, and helping the wounded', which suggests they were in sore need of it. And what with the early falling back – or failure to keep up as they advanced – of the Lancastrian left, and the greater weight and push on their right, the lines by then may have pivoted by as much as 45 degrees. To the side with the greater number of men – the Lancastrian – there was now the distinct possibility of breaking the other's left flank.

Perhaps it was now, therefore, that the Lancastrian jack-in-the-box was sprung, if indeed it ever was. Only Waurin mentions it – the charge, the appearance at least, of two hundred 'spears' (not necessarily, but in this case almost certainly, horsed) from the closed end of the sack formed by the loop of the Cock Beck. However, whereas Somerset's original intention must have been to attack the Yorkist rear or perhaps the left flank of the rearward as they ascended the northern slope, the advance of the Lancastrian line down into Towton Dale, and the pushing back of the Yorkist line, meant that the

---

* Northumberland may have been carried alive to York, dying there rather than on the field. The evidence is disputed.

spears had far less shock effect, appearing more as new troops joining the fray than as a surprise attack. Be that as it may, for the Yorkists the trend of the hand-to-hand fighting was steadily retrograde, and soon they found themselves fighting almost at the top of the southern slope. If the Lancastrians could just push them over the ridge, their own momentum would increase and the Yorkist line must at some stage break. And then it would be helter-skelter flight and pursuit.

In fact, the line buckled but it didn't break. And then in the early afternoon the scales tipped dramatically back. The Duke of Norfolk's division appeared at last on the road from Ferrybridge. Surprisingly, it's not known for sure whether Norfolk was actually with them; nor by whom and how they were fed in to the battle. Perhaps the 'afore-riders' made contact with the Yorkist rearguard and learned what was happening, or saw for themselves from atop the southern slope. Somewhere around Saxton, however, the Norfolk lords and retinues must have paused to dismount or put on armour, and the rest make ready, for instead of forming a line and ascending the reverse slope to come up in rear of Edward's line as a reserve, they pressed on up the York road and wheeled left, taking the Lancastrians in the flank.

The battle had already lasted four or five hours – a long time by medieval standards. Exactly when and what was its culminating point – that point in time when the attacking force can no longer continue its advance for whatever reason (supply, strength of opposition, exhaustion . . .) is impossible to say. Perhaps it was a general loss of impetus in the Lancastrian fighting line, despite the numerical advantage. Perhaps, though, the point was reached in the minds of the Lancastrian rearward when they saw Norfolk entering the field? Large numbers of fresh troops appearing on the flank: who knew how many more? Perhaps suddenly they didn't like what they saw, and thought that if they didn't turn away now they'd never break clean? Vergil suggests it was Somerset himself who was first to turn: 'He with a few horsemen removing a little out of that place, expected the event of the fight, but behold, suddenly his soldiers gave back, which when he saw this he fled also.'

The problem now for the Lancastrians in flight was the ground. 'Their' battlefield had been pulled horribly out of shape. Where once the northern ridge had been their advantage, and the Cock Beck their flank defence, both were now sealing their fate. To the rear was the snowy, slippery hill, and beyond that the beck, spanned by just a single bridge. And even if they'd been able to get across the beck, there was then the Wharfe between them and York, with its single bridge at Tadcaster. To their left as they fled was the beck again, here with no bridge at all; and to their right were Norfolk and the enveloping Yorkist flank. Fleeing men have no right of survival to fight another day, but the Yorkist cavalry went after them not just out of military necessity but literally with a vengeance: for Wakefield, St Albans, Ferrybridge and many an earlier fight – all scores to be settled. The particular, ferocious dynamic of civil war (then and now). Shakespeare has Henry bewailing the day thus:

> Oh piteous spectacle! Oh bloody times!
> While lions war and battle for their dens,
> Poor harmless lambs abide their enmity.
> Weep, wretched man, I'll aid thee tear for tear;
> And let our hearts and eyes, like civil war,
> Be blind with tears, and break o'ercharged with grief.

Few probably tried to surrender, for Edward's command was that none was to be spared, not the lowliest bodyman. And the more the press of fleeing men, funnelled towards the Cock Beck, the easier was the slaughter. Some drowned in the swollen stream with the weight of their armour. Some drowned with the weight of their soaked jacks, the wool-padded vests that gave a degree of protection against glancing blows and spent arrows. Some drowned underfoot

of those who somehow managed to stay upright. There was soon a bridge of bodies, and the open end of the sack in Towton Dale would for ever be known as 'Bloody Meadow'. The heralds, whose job it was after battle to identify the fallen nobles and count the dead – not for humanitarian reasons, but for intelligence and treasure – would have their work cut out.

POSTSCRIPT

Although twentieth-century revisionism pushed the casualty figures at Towton downwards, as too the actual numbers of men in the field, recent reassessments of the documentary evidence and new archaeological work have veered towards the original, higher numbers.* Some of the earlier revisionists questioned the figure of 28,000 deaths, 20,000 of them Lancastrian, simply on the grounds of 'consequence', arguing along the lines that if a third of the army were destroyed it would be too grievous a blow for them to continue the war. But that was indeed what the Lancastrians were dealt: a blow that left them unable to muster a field army for another three years. Besides, it should be no surprise that upwards of 60,000 men fighting at close quarters for hours on end, and then the homicidal rout, with the Lancastrians pursued and harried all the way to York, could produce a butcher's bill of 20,000 – or even the 28,000 of contemporary chroniclers. The battle was an emphatic Yorkist victory. Henry VI and Queen Margaret, with Edward, Prince of Wales, and Somerset, fled to Scotland—

---

* See e.g. George Goodwin, 'The Battle of Towton', in *History Today*, vol. 61, no. 5, May 2011.

PRINCE EDWARD: Fly, father, fly! For all your friends are fled,
And Warwick rages like a chafed bull:
Away! For death doth hold us in pursuit.*

—where James III gave them shelter. And then, according to the Croyland Chronicle,

King Edward, after the festivities of Easter, which he celebrated with great splendour at York, having placed garrisons throughout the whole country in whom he could fully rely, returned, as conqueror, to London. Here he immediately assembled the Parliament, and was crowned at Westminster by the venerable father Thomas, archbishop of Canterbury, and solemnly graced with the diadem of sovereignty.

For Henry had first abdicated the throne by fleeing, and Edward, who'd been proclaimed king before marching north, had proved he was the strongest man in England. He'd eliminated the Lancastrian threat.

However, the House of Lancaster was not entirely done. Nine years later they would return and briefly restore Henry to the throne, although the following year, 1471, as if in some bizarre liturgy of war, Towton having been fought on Palm Sunday, Edward inflicted another crushing defeat on the Lancastrians, this time at Barnet just north of London, on Easter Day.

When Edward died unexpectedly in 1483, aged just forty, he left two young sons who would be deposed (and possibly murdered – 'the princes in the Tower') by his brother Richard, Duke of Gloucester, later Richard III. Richard was then defeated at the Battle of Bosworth Field two years later – famously, according to Shakespeare, for want

---

* *Henry VI, Part 3*, Act II, scene v.

of a horse. That was the last battle of the Wars of the Roses, and the end of the Yorkist ascendancy. Edward's legacy was secured through his daughter Elizabeth of York, who the following year married the new Lancastrian (in truth, Tudor) King Henry VII. The long dynastic struggle was at last over, marked symbolically by Henry's adopting a rose badge conjoining the white of York with the red of Lancaster – the Tudor, or Union, rose.

PART THREE

WATERLOO

The Battle for Europe

18 JUNE 1815

A battle of the first rank won by a captain of the second.

Victor Hugo, *Les Misérables*

The Battle of Waterloo is a work of art with tension and drama with its unceasing change from hope to fear and back again, change which suddenly dissolves into a moment of extreme catastrophe, a model tragedy because the fate of Europe was determined within this individual fate.

Stefan Zweig

In that quote from his celebrated work of 1927, *Sternstunden der Menschheit* (literally, 'Stellar Moments of Humankind', published in English as *Decisive Moments in History*), Stefan Zweig perfectly captures why Waterloo is both important *and* endlessly fascinating. But why did the battle – one of the great defensive engagements of history – shape up as it did? The victory was the Duke of Wellington's, and also in considerable measure the Prussian Field Marshal Blücher's. Why did Wellington fight as he did that day; how and why did the battle meet his expectations; and how did Blücher influence them?

To understand those hows and whys, it's necessary to begin at the beginning of Britain's continental war with Napoleon Bonaparte – indeed, even earlier. For Wellington was in the end the heir to the British army's century and a half of hard-won experience of war, and the beneficiary of two decades of his own.

1

PRELUDE: THE SPANISH ULCER

It is certainly astonishing that the enemy [the French] have been able to remain in this country so long; and it is an extraordinary instance of what a French army can do.

Sir Arthur Wellesley (Duke of Wellington), December 1810

In later years the Duke of Wellington would tell the Marchioness of Salisbury that by the end of the Peninsular War he'd beaten the army into such good shape that 'I could have done anything with that army it was in such perfect order'.

He'd certainly restored the British army's reputation, which after twenty years of war didn't stand very high in the estimation of the major continental powers; or indeed with the public at home. It was undoubtedly over-centralized – far too reliant on Wellington's personal direction of almost every detail – but without doubt it could fight. So well, indeed, that Colonel – later, Marshal of France – Thomas Bugeaud observed simply: 'The British infantry is the most dangerous in Europe.' Though the compliment was made somewhat backhanded by his adding: 'Fortunately it is not numerous.'

One of the reasons why it was so dangerous was what would today be called 'fire control'. This was a peculiarly British technique – the regimental equivalent of a naval broadside (also a British innovation) – although one originating with the Dutch (some would argue the Swedes), which the English army had adopted and adapted when serving alongside William of Orange's regiments against the French in the late seventeenth century. With the coming of William to the English throne, jointly with his wife Mary, in 1688, the adoption of Dutch methods gained pace. The man who would become Duke of Marlborough, and in 1689 was commander-in-chief in Flanders, wrote to the secretary at war William Blathwayt to 'desire that you will know the King's pleasure whether he will have the Regiments of Foot learn the Duch [sic] exercise, or else to continue the English, for if he will I must have it translated into English'. What he meant was the standardization of volley fire. Hitherto, the practice had generally been for each rank (perhaps two companies in line – up to 200 men) to fire as a single entity, with the rank behind firing the next volley while the first rank reloaded, and so on. Since this involved 'dressing' (the realignment of the rank about to fire after it had stepped forward of the previous front rank) there was inevitably a hiatus between volleys. In Marlborough's 'Duch system', however, the companies were subdivided into 'platoons', each firing independently, so that a rolling fire could be kept up. And with that also, the foot drill of the army was sharpened up considerably, both to maintain the tempo of fire and to enable it to be redirected quickly. All this was made possible by the adoption of the flintlock musket – in due course the 'Brown Bess' – shorter and lighter than the former matchlock (and so not needing a 'rest' on which to lay the barrel to take aim), and with a socket bayonet which did away with the need of protective pikemen. The flintlock's calibre was also smaller than the matchlock's and the ball therefore lighter, while no less lethal, allowing the infantry-man to carry more rounds. The new weapon simply permitted a greater rate of fire.* At Edgehill (1642), the first battle of the English Civil War, it had been one round in two minutes; now it was three or even four a minute in the best-drilled regiments. Musketry was now therefore a decisive force on the battlefield, where before it had been more often than not a hazard, an irritant, and secondary to the *arme blanche*, as the knightly sword and lance or the 'puissant pike' were known. The British infantry became hugely adept at this system of fire control: time after time their disciplined volleys won the day in Marlborough's battles. And they'd continue the ascend-ancy in the later continental wars of the eighteenth century – and after that, most spectacularly of all, at the hands of that master of the tactical battle, the Duke of Wellington. Tight fire control is still today a hallmark of the British infantry. Its deep-seated importance in the collective subconscious of the army is demonstrated in the annual Queen's birthday parade on Horse Guards ('Trooping the Colour'), for the drill evolutions through which the Foot Guards are put in that magnificent hour – sharp, precise, emphatic – are the relict of the battlefield drill that got the serried ranks of infantry-men to deliver volleys in whichever direction was needed in the shortest possible time. No other troops in the world save those of

---

* Its 'stopping power' against unarmoured targets was more or less assured up to 200 yards, but its accuracy even in the best of hands wasn't much better than fifty, which is why volley, rather than individual, fire was so important. The British Baker rifle (more correctly, rifled musket) of the Napoleonic Wars was much more accurate: the 'rifleman' was expected to hit his target at 200 yards – but it took twice as long to load. It was a weapon for skirmishing with, in advance of the main volleying line, or to cover its withdrawal. It was said, not entirely fancifully, that the first and last shots fired in any action during the Peninsular War were fired by a rifleman (often of the 95th Regiment, later 'The Rifle Brigade').

the old Commonwealth look like the British on parade, for their drill comes from a different period and purpose.*

However, armies can lose their edge. After the spectacular successes of the Seven Years' War (1756–63) – again (principally) against the French, on the Continent and in North America – the army, or rather, the nation, suffered its first and perhaps only strategic defeat: in the American Revolutionary War. On 19 October 1781 at Yorktown, Virginia, after six years' desultory fighting, Major-General the Lord Cornwallis surrendered his army to General George Washington. Cornwallis was outnumbered three to one (almost half the opposing troops were French, France having entered the war after the British defeat at Saratoga in 1777 – a backwoods battle with profound strategic consequences), and reinforcements from New York couldn't be brought by ship because the French navy controlled Hampton Roads. Bitter skirmishing continued for another eighteen months, but after Yorktown the war was lost. In September 1783 Britain recognized the reality, conceded independence to the Continental (American) Congress and negotiated a peace with France and her allies.

The consequences of the American war for the army were profound. Never again would Britannia *not* rule the waves: in Whitehall all thoughts of the red coat were eclipsed by those of the blue. The Royal Navy would be the prime strategic instrument; the army would furnish a few essential garrisons, the flotsam and jetsam, almost, of global sea power. So thoroughgoing was this strategic vision that within two decades the navy would be consuming two-thirds of Britain's gross domestic product, while the army would wither and almost die. Soon indeed, as the nineteenth-century historian Macaulay put it,

---

* The 'goose-stepping' of some armies makes a political point, while the more languid pace of those in the Napoleonic heritage – the French and Italian notably (and even to an extent the US) – are more the relict of the old drill which moved large numbers of conscripts about the battlefield in column.

The English Army, under Pitt [the Younger, prime minister from 1783], was the laughing stock of all Europe. It could not boast of one single brilliant exploit. It had never shown itself on the continent but to be beaten, chased, forced to re-embark, or forced to capitulate. To take some sugar island in the West Indies, to scatter some mob of half-naked Irish peasants, such were the most splendid victories won by British troops under Pitt's auspices.*

Macaulay was writing of the French revolutionary wars, of course. In February 1793 the Committee of Public Safety, the executive government of Revolutionary France, had declared war on every power in Europe except Russia. This time the issue was neither dynastic nor commercial, but ideological: the fight against it was a fight for the survival of Britain's constitutional monarchy, and to most, therefore, for the survival of Britishness.

At first it looked as if the Revolution's resources would be as infinite as its goals, for the Committee of Public Safety passed a measure authorizing a *levée en masse*, and France soon had 850,000 men in its army. But because the Royal Navy, 'the wooden walls', had been so determinedly strengthened after the American defeat, that vast army of Frenchmen would not be able to come to England by sea. On the other hand, because the British army had been so comprehensively run down, Britain wouldn't actually be able to take Paris, the only certain way of defeating France. The strategy would have to be indirect, therefore: the Royal Navy would squeeze the enemy commercially, seize its colonial wealth – principally the sugar islands of the West Indies – and use those gains to subsidize the continental powers traditionally able to field large armies. It would be Russia, Prussia and Austria that would do the 'heavy

---

* *Macaulay's Essay on William Pitt the Younger*, ed. William Leask (London, 1918).

lifting' in battle with the massive, vigorous new armies of *La République*.*

So for ten years the British army had little to do except, as Macaulay put it, take some sugar island, courtesy of the Royal Navy, or 'scatter some mob of half-naked Irish peasants' who made trouble for absentee landlords – or, in 1798, rose more ominously in support of a half-cock French landing. Occasionally the army might try some 'descent and alarm' in a diversionary attack, usually in the Low Countries, but the legatees of Marlborough's great victories would soon be, in Macaulay's words, 'beaten, chased, forced to re-embark, or forced to capitulate'. It was, as the former secretary at war, Henry Fox, scoffed, like 'breaking windows with guineas'.

Fortunately, by the time Napoleon Bonaparte seized power in 1804, the army hadn't entirely lost its spirit and its officers of capability. Indeed, it had even begun innovating, with specially trained light infantry – and riflemen, troops equipped with the rifled musket, whose range and accuracy was much greater than the Brown Bess and who operated in loose skirmishing formation, as individuals, rather than in the 'industrial' ranks of those armed with the smooth-bore musket. But it was still not large, and could hardly be risked in the great field battles of continental Europe. Then, in July 1807, flushed with his success in forcing the Russians to make peace, Napoleon turned his attention back towards Britain. This time, however, his strategy would be economic, having been dissuaded from direct attack two years earlier at Trafalgar, and to do this he had to deal as well with Sweden and Portugal, the two nations that remained

---

* At the beginning of the French Revolutionary Wars, the British army numbered barely 40,000 men. By the end of the war(s) with France, the numbers had increased to a level not seen since Marlborough's day. At its peak in 1813, the regular army stood at a quarter of a million, though (as in Marlborough's day too) not all of them were British nationals.

allied with or friendly to Britain. The tsar agreed that Russia would deal with Sweden, while France (allied with Spain since 1796) would deal with Portugal. Napoleon called on the Portuguese to close their ports (including those in their colonies, notably Brazil) to the British, to complete his so-called Continental System, for while the Royal Navy was commanding the oceans there was no other way to force a peace than by striking at trade. When the Portuguese refused, Napoleon ordered General Jean-Andoche Junot with a force of 30,000 to march through Spain into Portugal. The Portuguese royal family was evacuated to Brazil in British warships, and Junot arrived in Lisbon in November.

The French also occupied parts of northern Spain, and in March the following year, 1808, the Spanish minister Manuel de Godoy persuaded the king, Charles IV, to do what the Portuguese royal family had done and relocate to South America. However, before Charles could do so Napoleon sent General Joachim Murat to occupy Madrid, and placed his own brother Joseph on the throne. Not surprisingly, the Spanish were enraged. On 2 May Madrid rose against the invader – Goya's 1814 painting of the execution of partisans the following day, *El tres de mayo de 1808 en Madrid*, bears witness to the violence – and the battle for Spanish independence began.

Britain at last had her chance to enter the war on land in strategically favourable conditions, unlike her earlier faltering attempts in Flanders and Italy. For in the Iberian Peninsula the French were operating on long, exterior lines of communication, while British troops would be campaigning in a part of Europe whose lengthy coastline was tailor-made for the exercise of naval strength. And the difficult country of the interior, its scale and its climate, somehow seemed to favour the temperament and experience of British soldiers, especially their commanders, who'd fought in India: the Peninsula was like India, but nearer home.

Major-General Sir Arthur Wellesley and a force of some 10,000

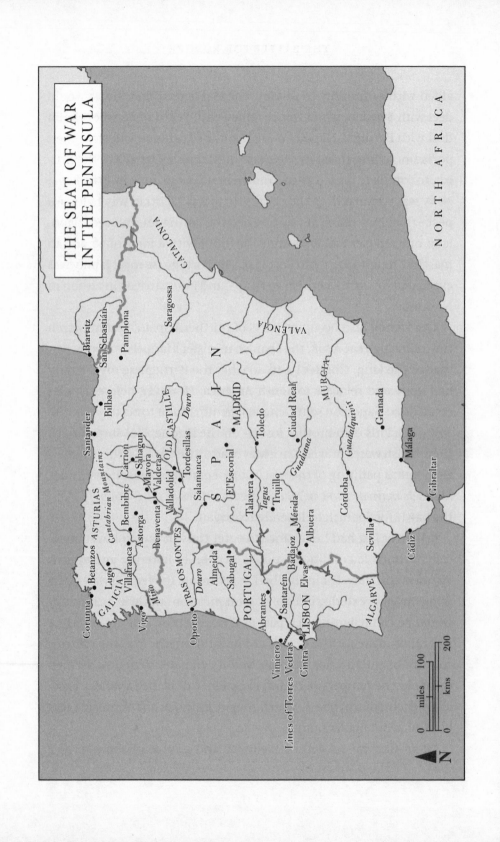

THE SEAT OF WAR
IN THE PENINSULA

NORTH AFRICA

N

0   miles   100
0   200
0   kms

CATALONIA

Biarritz
San Sebastián
Pamplona
Saragossa

Santander
Bilbao

VALENCIA

S   P   A   I   N

Douro
OLD CASTILLE
MADRID
Toledo
Ciudad Real
MURCIA

ASTURIAS
Corunna
Betanzos
Cantabrian Mountains
Lugo
GALICIA
Villafranca
Bembibre
Astorga
Sahagun
Carrion
Mayora
Valderas
Benaventa
Valladolid
Tordesillas
Salamanca
El Escorial
Talavera
Trujillo
Tagus
Guadiana
Mérida
Albuera
Córdoba
Granada
Guadalquivir
Málaga

Vigo
Miño

Oporto
Douro
TRAS OS MONTES
Almeida
Sabugal
PORTUGAL
Abrantes
Santarém
Badajoz
Elvas
Sevilla
Gibraltar
Cádiz
ALGARVE

Vimiero
Lines of Torres Vedras
Cintra
LISBON

landed in Portugal three months later and had some quick successes, regaining Lisbon and forcing the capitulation of the French in Portugal. Unfortunately, under the terms of the famous Convention of Cintra – negotiated by Wellesley's recently arrived superiors – the French were allowed to leave with their arms, and in British ships. All that might be said about these extraordinary surrender terms is that the British hadn't had much practice of late at taking a French surrender.

As soon as the news reached London there was an outcry, and Wellesley and his superiors were recalled for a court of inquiry. Sir John Moore – a hugely respected soldier, but politically a Whig and therefore always suspect in the eyes of the Tory administration – was now sent to take command of the army, which was soon to be augmented to 42,000 men. However, the foreign secretary, George Canning, warned him that his army was 'not merely a considerable part of the dispensable force of this country. It is in fact *the* British army . . . Another army it has not to send.' It was certainly the largest army that Britain had sent abroad since the Duke of Marlborough's day (not counting augmentation by German mercenaries), and Moore's orders were 'to cooperate with the Spanish armies in the expulsion of the French from that Kingdom'.

So, with about 30,000 men he made at once for Madrid; but the French were there in vastly greater numbers than anyone had thought, and the Spanish armies weren't in much position to cooperate; so Moore turned north. At Christmas 1808, on the River Esla in León, with the snow lying deep, he learned that Napoleon himself had taken personal command of the army and was marching with far superior forces to cut him off. He decided therefore to run for the coast – and Napoleon, learning of this, thinking his mission accomplished, went home.

So began the famous retreat to Corunna, in which the army was brilliantly covered by the cavalry under Lord Uxbridge, later the

Marquess of Anglesey, enabling the infantry to break clean from their pursuers and then get across the mountains of Galicia in good enough order to fight a general action at Corunna on 16 January, which stopped the French in their tracks and allowed the Royal Navy to evacuate the army.

But at Corunna, Moore was fatally wounded; and so Wellesley, by now exonerated, was sent back to Portugal to take command. By July he'd advanced as far as Talavera, about 80 miles south-west of Madrid, and together with the Spanish gained a useful victory; but with other French armies closing in on him, he was compelled to retreat. Thereafter, for the best part of a year the army watched and waited near the border, while to the rear, in great secrecy, he had the defensive lines of Torres Vedras built, a chain of strongpoints in the mountainous terrain east of Lisbon sited by him personally. When the French renewed their offensive the following year, Wellesley's Anglo-Portuguese forces, greatly outnumbered, were gradually pushed back towards Lisbon, though inflicting a severe check on their pursuers at Bussaco Ridge in late September 1809. When the French finally came up to the lines in December and laid siege, they starved and froze – not least because Wellesley had ordered a scorched earth policy for 50 miles in front of the lines.

For the next two years the battles were inconclusive, but 300,000 French troops had by now been sucked into Spain, of whom only 70,000 could be spared to confront Wellington: the remainder were pinned down by the Spanish armies and the guerrilla war – hence Napoleon's rueful 'my Spanish ulcer'. During this time too the Portuguese army was re-formed, re-equipped and retrained under Wellesley's deputy, General William Beresford, and with British officers seconded as advisers it had come to be a formidable force, much admired by the rank and file of the British army.

So, by January 1812, Wellesley, now the Viscount Wellington – soon to be Earl and then Marquess – was ready to take the offensive again. The key border fortresses of Ciudad Rodrigo and Badajoz fell to him by early April. And in late July he won a crushing victory at Salamanca, whence he pressed on to Madrid, and from there north to Burgos; but he was forced back to the border again by superior numbers, to winter in the fortresses he'd captured in the spring.

During that winter, though, events were moving in his favour. Napoleon's invasion of Russia in June 1812 had ended in disaster, and by March 1813 French armies in eastern Europe were falling back, tempting Prussia to rejoin the war against France. Napoleon could no longer spare any reinforcements for the Peninsula.

The French commanders in Spain, Joseph Napoleon and Jean-Baptiste Jourdan, were now increasingly pinned down by allied regulars and guerrilla forces. In May 1813 Wellington returned to the offensive, striking northwards towards Burgos again – something over halfway between Madrid and the coast – without allowing the French armies the chance to concentrate. From Burgos, he outflanked Joseph Napoleon by wheeling through the mountains to the north, and then east, forcing him to take up a defensive position in the valley of the Zadorra river, and then on 21 June routed him in the pivotal battle of Vitoria.

Vitoria sealed Napoleon's fate. News of Wellington's victory not only rallied the new Russo-Prussian alliance after their defeats at Lützen and Bautzen, but also helped persuade Austria to rejoin the war.

By mid-July 1813, Wellington had reached the Pyrenees. Joseph Napoleon and Jourdan had been replaced by Marshal Jean-de-Dieu Soult, who launched a counter-offensive, but Wellington quickly regained the upper hand, and on 7 October crossed the Bidassoa into the south-west corner of France – the first coalition troops to set foot on French soil.

On 10 November Wellington broke the French defences on the line of the Nivelle river, and there was a month's sharp fighting before the allied army forced Soult back to the outskirts of Bayonne. Meanwhile the continental allies were closing on France from the east after a notable victory at Leipzig in October, and Wellington's army went into winter quarters, re-emerging at the end of February 1814 to defeat Soult again, at Orthez. The continental allies entered Paris on 31 March and Napoleon abdicated, but the last battle of the Peninsular War, at Toulouse, was not fought until 10 April, the news of the abdication only reaching Wellington two days later.

'I could have done anything with that army it was in such perfect order.' Indeed, the Peninsular War was perhaps *the* formative experience for the British army. By the end it had become as efficient as any on the Continent – in its own very British way: cautious, persistent, choosy of ground. And the army's success was largely of Wellington's making. Sir Arthur Wellesley, created Duke of Wellington at the end of hostilities, hadn't had a day's true leave since landing in Portugal in 1809, and his daily work rate – at his desk or in the saddle – had been prodigious. It was necessary, he said, that a general be able to trace a biscuit from Lisbon all the way to the army in the field. This was the way that war was made – in truth, had always been made (when made well) – and he'd learned first how *not* to do it by observing the army in Flanders in the 1790s, and then *how* to do it, hands-on, in India. The Duke of Marlborough had learned it through a longer process of experience in Flanders, and through a practical intuition, a doctrine of common sense, which Wellington shared. Both commanders, in their own fashion, had evolved a way of making war that perfectly suited the nation's character and the realities of its politics and economy.

2

WATERLOO:
THE 'NEAR-RUN THING'*

[T]he men in the front of a stricken formation cannot run away until those behind them have opened the road.

John Keegan, *The Face of Battle*

The 1815 campaign was an affair of a few days only before its climax at Waterloo. Forced to abdicate the previous year as the armies of Britain, Austria, Prussia and Russia began closing on Paris, and consigned to exile on the island of Elba, Napoleon escaped at the end of February and arrived in his old capital on 20 March – the costliest flight

---

* 'It has been a damned nice thing – the nearest run thing you ever saw in your life.' Remark by the duke to Thomas Creevey in Brussels shortly after the battle ('nice' in the older sense of 'uncertain, delicately balanced'), quoted in *Creevey Papers* (collected and published in 1903 by Sir Herbert Maxwell). The phrase 'a damned nice thing' has sometimes been rendered as 'a near-run thing' or even – by this author indeed – as 'a close-run thing'.

from exile until Lenin slipped out of Switzerland a century later. Louis XVIII, whom the allies had restored to the French throne, was already an unpopular king and soon fled to the former Austrian Netherlands (Belgium), which was now united with the Dutch crown. Napoleon at once began resurrecting the Grande Armée, while the allies at the Congress of Vienna agreed to do what they'd done the year before and converge on Paris, although this time a British army would be approaching from the north rather than from over the Pyrenees. An Anglo-Dutch army would assemble in Belgium, based on a nucleus of British troops already in the Low Countries, where they'd be joined by 100,000 Prussians. A huge Austrian army of 200,000 would enter France through Alsace-Lorraine, followed by the Russians in roughly the same strength later in the summer.

Napoleon couldn't hope to counter these numbers if they combined. He therefore decided on an immediate offensive against the Anglo-Dutch and Prussian forces: if he could destroy them, or even just deliver a sufficient blow, it might deter the Austrians and Russians from risking a similar fate. And it would buy him time to raise more troops and to put the eastern fortresses on to a strong footing.

Immediately, the Duke of Wellington took command of the Anglo-Dutch army and began talks with the Prussians under their doughty old commander Prince Gephard von Blücher. Wellington was well used to dealing with allies – notably the Spanish, who hadn't always been the easiest of partners – and he perfectly understood the Marlburian maxim that in coalition warfare the first imperative was to keep the coalition together. Wellington and Blücher saw eye to eye over the need for a defensive strategy, although Blücher's chief of staff, Gneisenau, distrusted the duke: British armies in Flanders had run for the sea too often. The allies were, in fact, too weak to risk an offensive, especially since the reliability of the Dutch–Belgian element was questionable and half the British regiments were inexperienced. The army that, only a year before, Wellington 'could have done anything with . . . it was in such perfect order', as he later boasted to Lady Salisbury, had for the most part been dispersed. A good many of his veteran Peninsular troops had been sent to North America for the 'War of 1812' – that eruption of festering sores, grievances and unfinished business from the Revolution whose outbreak still defies all good sense, and whose conduct is unworthy of study. It was poor, nasty, brutish and, mercifully, short. It did, however, detain a large part of the British army and some of its most experienced commanders. And it clearly discomposed Wellington, who in early May, six weeks after Napoleon had entered Paris, complained that 'I have got an infamous army, very weak and ill equipped, and a very inexperienced Staff. In my opinion they are doing nothing in England. They have not raised a man; they have not called out the militia either in England or Ireland.'

So, not only did a defensive strategy best suit Wellington's instincts; it played to the British army's strengths – or rather, such strengths as Wellington hoped they still possessed. He and they – some of them at least – had taken the offensive often enough in Spain, and there'd been some impressive actions; but just as often it had been their resolute defence that broke the French, their disciplined volleying. Wellington had perfected the art of choosing a piece of ground which would give shelter from the enemy's artillery (which was always superior to his) and offer concealment for a major part of his force, enabling him to confuse the enemy and then surprise him with their sudden appearance; and always good fields of fire to allow him to exploit his strongest card – the lethal volleying of his infantry.

In turn, Napoleon knew he wasn't strong enough to fight both Wellington and Blücher in the same battle. He would therefore have to deal with them in turn, making sure they couldn't combine. This – dealing with two armies – he'd done often enough before. Success consisted in hitting one of them so hard that it had to withdraw to recover, at which point he would turn to the other and destroy it utterly, and then, if necessary, if it hadn't already fled, return to the first to complete its destruction. The trick was never allowing one of them to render support to the other in the process.

Wellington and Blücher understood this perfectly, and were determined to remain in close mutual support. The flaw in allied cooperation lay, however, in their respective lines of communication: if these gave way in the face of a huge French offensive the two armies would naturally begin to diverge, for the British supply lines ran north-west to the Channel ports, while the Prussians' ran east to the Rhineland.

It was indeed this fault-line, the boundary between the two armies, that Napoleon intended exploiting.

Wellington had another factor with which to grapple in his calculations: the French axis of advance on Brussels (their presumed objective – beyond, that is, breaking apart the armies) might be from the south through Charleroi, or from the south-west through Mons or even Tournai. An offensive from the south-west would threaten his lines of communication, and he would have to dispose a considerable force to guard them. He couldn't deploy the army forward on the border until he knew Napoleon's real axis of advance, for there'd not be time to switch positions. And besides, the problems of billeting and supply, particularly fodder for the cavalry and artillery, obliged him to disperse his troops more than he'd have liked. But he was confident that he would have sound intelligence of French moves, for he'd always had supremely good intelligence in the Peninsula (once he'd got himself organized after Torres Vedras). He'd had tactical intelligence from his own 'exploring officers' and strategic intelligence on capability, such as French troop strengths in southern France and throughout Spain, and on strategic intentions, from the network of civilian agents organized by British diplomats in Lisbon and the provisional Spanish capital, Cadiz. And he now had his trusted spies in Paris and elsewhere. If he'd had greater confidence in his cavalry he might have arranged some reconnaissance with the Prussians across the French border: that would at least have spared him the tactical surprise of Napoleon's appearance with all his men – to the complete amazement of both himself and Blücher – before Charleroi on 15 June. Wellington was not exaggerating when he exclaimed: 'Napoleon has humbugged me, by God!'

Intelligence can be simply lacking – crucially lacking – or it can be downright faulty. So much so that Clausewitz, reflecting on the wars with revolutionary France a decade after Waterloo, was sceptical about relying on it: other than broad background intelligence on the country in which the army was to fight, 'the only situation a commander can know fully is his own: his opponent's he can only know from unreliable intelligence'; more intelligence, he argued, would make commanders 'more, not less, uncertain'.

To a degree, he has a point: there is such a thing as 'analysis paralysis' – of which there were clearly examples in the planning for the invasion of Normandy in 1944.* That said, the sum total of experience supports the opinion of the Duke of Marlborough, arguably Britain's greatest general: 'No war can ever be conducted without good and early intelligence.'

On 16 June the French inflicted a sharp reverse on the unsupported Prussians at Ligny, Blücher himself being unhorsed and almost killed. Racing south from Brussels, gathering up the army as he went, Wellington managed to fight an action on the extreme right (west) of the battle area at Quatre Bras. Had Marshal Ney – *le brave des braves*, as Napoleon had dubbed him – whose job it was to deal with any appearance of the Anglo-Dutch, pressed his attack with more vigour, Wellington might have been forced from the ground. By nightfall, however, he was still in possession of the

---

* See Part Four, 'Sword Beach', below.

crossroads that gives its name to the village and the battle. There is probably some truth in the idea that Ney didn't press the attack because he knew Wellington's trick of keeping the main part of his force concealed, and was wary of being wrong-footed (he'd seen the British army at Bussaco and Torres Vedras). Such is the 'virtuous circle' of good tactics.

Whatever its cause, Ney's apparent timidity allowed some semblance of cooperation between the allies at a crucial moment. Despite Gneisenau's urging that the Prussians withdraw east, in the belief that Wellington had failed to show sufficient resolve in supporting them, Blücher promised to fall back north instead, and to continue the fight. For his part, Wellington would withdraw to the ridge of Mont St Jean before the village of Waterloo on the southern edge of the Forest of Soignes and astride the Charleroi–Brussels high road, and there give battle when Napoleon switched his main effort – as both he and Blücher knew he must.

Next day, the 17th, in heavy rain, the Prussians began to withdraw as agreed. Emmanuel de Grouchy – who'd commanded Napoleon's escort on the retreat from Moscow, and had now been made a marshal – at once advanced to harry them. However, by one of those misreadings of the situation usually ascribed to 'the fog of war', he sent back a report to Napoleon that Blücher was withdrawing east rather than north. He had, in fact, mistaken the supply train for elements of the army itself. Thus confirmed in his good opinion of his own strategic skill, believing the Prussians to have been knocked out of the contest, Napoleon now turned with a vengeance on the Anglo-Dutch.

Wellington's withdrawal to Mont St Jean went well, however: just as Lord Paget and his cavalry had covered Sir John Moore's escape from east of the Esla river, allowing the infantry to gain a head start for Corunna, so now would the Earl of Uxbridge – as Paget had become – cover the infantry back from Quatre Bras.* The wet and weary regiments of foot which tramped to their watery bivouacs on the ridge that night, joining those whom Wellington had ordered up directly, had much to thank Uxbridge's cavalry for, though they'd not actually seen anything of them – appreciating only the absence of French *cuirassiers* harassing them on the march back.

Waterloo today – despite the huge memorial mound of which the duke complained in later years – is remarkably similar to what it was that day in 1815. Ascending the mound gives a fine panorama of the whole battlefield, but the relevant prospect on Sunday, 18 June was at head height and from the saddle. And to see today the ground as an infantryman atop the ridge would have, and as Wellington had during his reconnaissances in the months before the battle, is to see at once the position's 'capability', as 'Capability' Brown liked to put it – its potential, in this case for lethal purpose. The ridge, just short of 3 miles long, isn't high, but there's a pronounced slope, which was rather more pronounced 200 years ago. It wasn't so much an obstacle to the French advance as an elevation which gave the defenders a slight psychological advantage and, more importantly, Wellington the opportunity to work his favoured tactical trick of concealment behind the crest.

The ridge by itself, unlike that at Bussaco which at its highest rose some 1,800 feet, was unlikely to stop the Grande Armée in its tracks, however. The flanks were also more vulnerable here (although at Bussaco Wellington's 25,000 Anglo-Portuguese army had been able

---

* Paget hadn't served with Wellington in the Peninsula, having eloped with the wife of the duke's younger brother. Stapleton Cotton (first Viscount Combermere) had been his cavalry commander, more than adequate but generally thought to lack 'cavalry genius'. Uxbridge took command in Belgium reportedly at the insistence of the Prince Regent – the greatest contribution to history of that sad monarch.

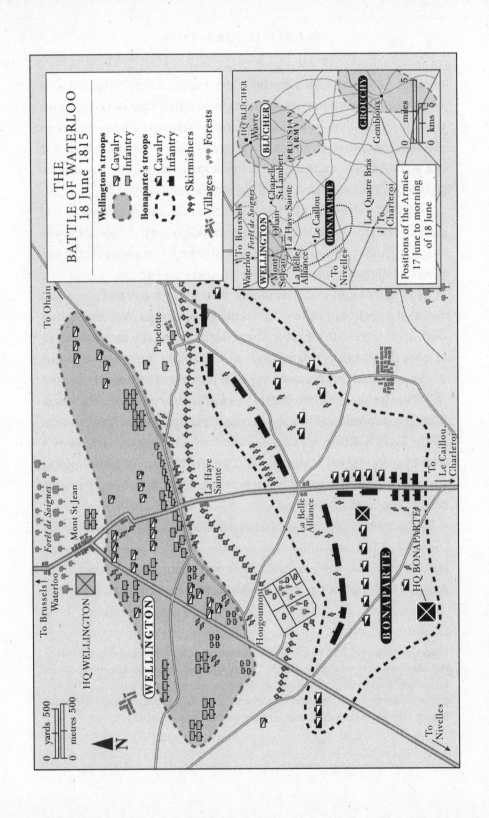

THE
BATTLE OF WATERLOO
18 June 1815

Wellington's troops
  Cavalry
  Infantry

Bonaparte's troops
  Cavalry
  Infantry

Skirmishers

Villages   Forests

Positions of the Armies
17 June to morning
of 18 June

GROUCHY

BLÜCHER   HQ BLÜCHER
           Wavre

           Chapelle
           St Lambert
To Brussels
Waterloo Forêt de Soignes
WELLINGTON Ohain   La Haye Sainte
            Mont   Le Caillou
            St Jean
            La Belle   BONAPARTE
            Alliance
To   Les Quatre Bras
Nivelles   To
            Charleroi   Charleroi   Gembloux
            PRUSSIAN ARMY

0 miles 5
0 kms 5

To Ohain

Papelotte

To Brussels
Waterloo

HQ WELLINGTON

WELLINGTON

Forêt de Soignes
Mont St Jean

La Haye
Sainte

La Belle
Alliance

Hougoumont

BONAPARTE

HQ BONAPARTE

To Le Caillou,
Charleroi

To
Nivelles

0 yards 500
0 metres 500

N

to repulse twice that number of French, ultimately they'd had to withdraw after an outflanking move by Marshal Massena). But three man-made features on the forward slope or in the shallow valley at the foot of the ridge opposite might, if held, break up an offensive by the whole French line. They would give the position some depth, which along with reserves is the first requirement of 'balance', the *key* attribute, tactical and strategic. And here indeed lay the genius of the position – *if* they could be held (long enough).

First of these were the hamlets of Papelotte, Frichermont and La Haye, all clustered at the foot of the slope on the left flank, and Braine l'Alleud on the extended right flank. Garrisoned by the Dutch and Belgians – a gamble, some must have thought, the loyalty of Belgium, annexed by France in 1794 and then in 1814 forced into union with the Protestant Dutch, being particularly suspect – these villages gave a solid pinning to both ends of the position, and since Wellington had no idea how steady his allies might be in the open, the solid cover of masonry would have given him some assurance that they would stand and fight. It was, after all, their country.

The second of these features was the chateau of Hougoumont at the foot of the slope on the right inner flank. This might act as a rock breaking up the waves of an attack on that flank. It was exposed, however, out on a limb and likely to be surrounded, and once under attack would be difficult to support; and so Wellington would put several companies of the Guards into Hougoumont, with some German riflemen and Dutch light infantry – 1,500 men in all.

Finally, in the centre, halfway down the slope on the high road, was the little farm of La Haye Sainte. This might have the same effect as Hougoumont in breaking up an attack on the centre if it could be held. And it might be useful cover to the French if they could take it. Wellington therefore placed a battalion of some of his trustiest troops, the King's German Legion (about 400 men), inside the walled farmyard, with companies of the 95th Rifles in some sandpits across the road.

This left him with just enough infantry to occupy two-thirds of the ridge itself, but none to keep in true reserve. His red-coated (i.e. British) infantry and the rest of the KGL he placed in the centre and right of the line, where he expected the main weight of the attack to fall, with his untried Dutch–Belgians, and Hanoverians,* on the left.

For a reserve he'd rely on his cavalry, about whose habit of 'galloping at everything' in the Peninsula he'd regularly complained. It was undoubtedly true, but they'd done a great deal more too; and besides, the French had become very wary of them as a result. Nevertheless he intended giving them strict instructions not to leave their positions without his express orders. In conventional fashion, therefore, he posted two brigades of light cavalry on the left (east) flank – the flank on which he could hope for the Prussians to come to his support, but also the flank that might be threatened by the French who'd pursued them after Ligny – and a third on the inner right; and he placed his heavy cavalry (two brigades – some 2,000 horses), of which very few had been in the Peninsula, in the centre.

Then he had to decide on how to deploy his artillery. Napoleon himself had been an artillery officer. Indeed he'd made his name with a famous 'whiff of grapeshot',† and he said that 'it is with artillery that

---

* The troops of the kingdom of Hanover (or Brunswickers, as they're sometimes known), which had recently been restored to George III after occupation by the French for the better part of fifteen years (Britain and Hanover having been in personal union since the accession of George I), were to Wellington's mind untried, although their allegiance wasn't as suspect as that of the Belgians. The KGL were Hanoverians, too, of course, but as fugitives after Napoleon overran the kingdom in 1803 they'd been willingly incorporated into the British army – and had been British to all intents and purposes for a decade and more.

† In October 1795 he'd helped quell a royalist rising against the Convention in Paris by firing grapeshot – round shots, of much smaller calibre than the usual single projectile, packed in a canvas bag and separated from the gunpowder charge by metal wadding. Grape was intended primarily to inflict structural damage, especially aboard ship. The field artillery ammunition was more usually 'canister' (or 'case') shot, which

war is made'. He tended to concentrate his artillery against a particular portion of the enemy for devastating effect before then sending his infantry or cavalry to exploit the devastation. Wellington, on the other hand, especially in defence, was keener to give his infantry intimate support, and so on the ridge at Mont St Jean he spread his artillery along the line, sometimes just a pair of guns in each position.

The ground and the possible strength and direction of a French advance had first determined the broad shape of the battle to come – a confrontation that in many ways Harold Godwineson's and Duke William of Normandy's armies would have understood, and those of the Wars of the Roses. But gunpowder and regular troops transformed the old clash of arms and greatly enlarged the battlefield, not least its depth. Archers had extended it by several hundred yards, then cannon by a mile. And although the bayonet killed in the same way as the sword, the axe or the pike, the musket could shatter an infantry attack before it got close enough to use cold steel. As for how the battle itself would actually go, that of course was determined by Wellington's deployment of the army. Interestingly, Uxbridge, his nominal second-in-command – 'nominal', for Wellington hardly ever made use of one – asked the night before what were his chief's plans. Wellington replied, with some asperity, that since it was Napoleon who'd be attacking, and the 'Emperor' had not vouchsafed his plans to him, how might he know what he'd do once battle was joined? But then he added, more emolliently, 'There is one thing certain, however, Uxbridge, that is, that whatever happens you and I will do our duty.' It was gallant, but hardly helpful.

---

consisted of much smaller projectiles, about the size of a musket ball – a devastating anti-personnel weapon. At the 'Insurrection of Vendémiaire' (Vendémiaire being the first month of autumn in the Revolutionary calendar), as it became known, Napoleon almost certainly used canister, but Thomas Carlyle's famous phrase worked better with 'grapeshot'.

But Wellington certainly *had* had some idea of the possibilities open to Napoleon, which was of course why he made his dispositions on the ridge of Mont St Jean as he did. And he'd made them in detail, assisted by the 37-year-old Colonel William Howe de Lancey. De Lancey had been on his staff throughout the Peninsular War, and supervised the dispositions while Wellington recovered after his 'humbugging' and got himself to Quatre Bras. Wellington had decided exactly which troops to place in Hougoumont, La Haye Sainte and the villages to left and right of the line. He himself had decided which brigades were to go where, and it is not impossible to believe also that he'd directed the divisional and brigade commanders just where and how to dispose their regiments. And he'd played to a T the different national characteristics and regimental capabilities. Indeed, when Baron Müffling, Blücher's liaison officer, had asked if 1,500 men were really enough to hold Hougoumont, Wellington replied, 'Ah, you don't know Macdonnell. I've thrown Macdonnell into it.' He meant Lieutenant-Colonel James Macdonnell, commanding officer of the Coldstream Guards. This was the level of decision-making to which Wellington applied himself. He and de Lancey shaped the battlefield to play to the strengths of his 'infamous army', and to his own: concealing his hand, not being drawn, obliging the enemy to come on to the immovable red ranks of musketry and in formations that meant they couldn't deploy their own firepower to effect; standing his ground and letting the enemy exhaust themselves until the Prussians, coming on to the French right flank, showed them the game was up.

Did the battle go as Wellington envisaged?

There are probably more accounts of Waterloo than of any other battle, and Wellington was always sceptical of attempts to render them. 'The history of a battle is not unlike the history of a ball,' he wrote afterwards. 'Some individuals may recollect all the little events of which the great result is the battle won or lost, but no individual can recollect the order in which, or the exact moment at which, they occurred, which makes all the difference as to their value or importance.'* Even the best attempts to weave together the many individual recollections of both sides – some individual actions so well attested to that they can be taken as fact – can only ever be an approximation. Yet an overall common narrative of the order of events can emerge, even if cause and effect ultimately remain speculative. Then again, place and 'atmosphere' are another matter. And no one has conveyed those better than Thomas Hardy in his epic verse drama *The Dynasts* (1904), in which he pictures the ridge of Mont St Jean, and that opposite on which the French were camped, the night before the battle:

CHORUS OF THE PITIES: . . . And what of these who to-night have come?

CHORUS OF THE YEARS: The young sleep sound; but the weather awakes
In the veterans, pains from the past that numb;
Old stabs of Ind, old Peninsular aches,
Old Friedland chills, haunt their moist mud bed,
Cramps from Austerlitz; till their slumber breaks.

CHORUS OF SINISTER SPIRITS: And each soul shivers as sinks his head
On the loam he's to lease with the other dead
From to-morrow's mist-fall till
Time be sped!

(The fires of the English go out, and silence prevails, save for the soft hiss of the rain that falls impartially on both the sleeping armies.)

---

* Letter to John Croker, 8 Aug. 1815, in *Selections from the Dispatches and General Orders of Field Marshal The Duke of Wellington*, ed. Lieutenant-Colonel John Gurwood (London, 1842).

Hardy uses the term 'English' as it was used loosely at that time: there were Scots, Irish and Welsh regiments the length of the ridge, and half the allied army had German or Dutch or French (Walloon) as their first and perhaps only language.

There was no patrolling during the night, and little movement at Mont St Jean other than ammunition waggons and the odd commissary's sparse load of rations, nor any forward movement by the French, exhausted as they were by the battles at Ligny and Quatre Bras and the following marches. Only sentries keeping sodden watch.

Then, as trumpets and bugles sound reveille, Hardy describes the scene in his 'stage directions':

THE FIELD OF WATERLOO

An aerial view of the battlefield at the time of sunrise is disclosed . . .

The sky is still overcast, and rain still falls. A green expanse, almost unbroken, of rye, wheat, and clover, in oblong and irregular patches undivided by fences, covers the undulating ground, which sinks into a shallow valley between the French and English positions. The road from Brussels to Charleroi runs like a spit through both positions, passing at the back of the English into the leafy forest of Soignes.

The latter are turning out from their bivouacs. They move stiffly from their wet rest, and hurry to and fro like ants in an ant-hill. The tens of thousands of moving specks are largely of a brick-red colour, but the foreign contingent is darker.

Breakfasts are cooked over smoky fires of green wood. Innumerable groups, many in their shirt-sleeves, clean their rusty firelocks, drawing or exploding the charges, scrape the mud from themselves, and pipeclay from their cross-belts the red dye washed off their jackets by the rain.

At six o'clock, they parade, spread out, and take up their positions in the line of battle, the front of which extends in a wavy riband three miles long, with three projecting bunches at Hougoumont, La Haye Sainte, and La Haye.

Looking across to the French positions we observe that after advancing in dark streams from where they have passed the night they, too, deploy and wheel into their fighting places – figures with red epaulettes and hairy knapsacks, their arms glittering like a display of cutlery at a hill-side fair.

They assume three concentric lines of crescent shape, that converge on the English midst, with great blocks of the Imperial Guard at the back of them. The rattle of their drums, their fanfarades, and their bands playing 'Veillons au salut de l'Empire' contrast with the quiet reigning on the English side.

A knot of figures, comprising WELLINGTON with a suite of general and other staff-officers, ride backwards and forwards in front of the English lines, where each regimental colour floats in the hands of the junior ensign. The DUKE himself, now a man of forty-six, is on his bay charger Copenhagen, in light pantaloons, a small plumeless hat, and a blue cloak, which shows its white lining when blown back.

On the French side, too, a detached group creeps along the front in preliminary survey. NAPOLEON – also forty-six – in a grey overcoat, is mounted on his white Arab Marengo, and accompanied by SOULT, NEY, JEROME, DROUOT, and other marshals. The figures of aides move to and fro like shuttle-cocks between the group and distant points in the field. The sun has begun to gleam.

The rain had stopped, and the sun had indeed begun to dry out the armies, if not the ground. The French seemed in no hurry to attack, though, troops forming up on the ridge opposite Mont St Jean as if for a review. Indeed, the bands played and Napoleon rode the length of the line raising cheers. There has always been speculation that he delayed the opening of the battle so that his artillery could have greater effect: the drier the ground, the greater the ricochet of the solid shot, and the more the damage, especially the other side of the hill. But this seems unlikely: time was the one commodity that Napoleon had always said was not his to dispose – 'Ask of me anything but time,' he told his marshals – and therefore not to be squandered. The truth is probably that his officers couldn't muster the army into its battle positions any more quickly (they'd been dog-tired), and that Napoleon and his gunners made the best of this with the consolation that 'at least the ground is drying out with every minute'.

The common narrative of the battle is divided into five phases. It began just before midday with a colossal bombardment by Napoleon's massed batteries directed at the centre-left of the allied line, together with a diversionary attack on Hougoumont to tempt Wellington to reinforce that flank at the expense of his centre and reserve. The French ploy was a shade too obvious, however, especially since the attack on Hougoumont was practically unsupported by artillery (which any serious attempt to turn a flank would have needed), and so Wellington simply stood his ground. Indeed, the attack soon began to serve him, for the Guards held out so resolutely that they drew in and tied down more and more French – all day, in fact, in a sort of mini Spanish ulcer. There would be many heroes of that day-long action, but none more praiseworthy than the admirable Corporal Joseph Brewer of the royal waggon train who, when powder was running low, volunteered to gallop his ammunition tumbrel from the ridge, under fire, and into the chateau – which he did, to the cheers of the defenders.

Just before launching his main attack on the allied centre (at about 1.30 p.m.) – the second phase – Napoleon learned that the Prussians had withdrawn not east and out of supporting range, but north towards Wavre. He therefore hurriedly formed a defensive right flank, and this would draw increasing numbers of troops from his reserve for the rest of the day – just as Hougoumont drew in more and more of Ney's left wing. Meanwhile, the great juggernaut that was the assaulting corps – 16,000 men, a quarter of Napoleon's whole force, under the Count of Erlon – began its march in column towards the ridge and to the east of La Haye Sainte. They had 1,300 yards to march, over wet, loamy earth, through corn 6 feet high, and in full view of the allied guns now being rapidly run forward along the chemin d'Ohain.* The preliminary bombardment by the massed battery had done some damage to Wellington's troops, but not nearly as much as Napoleon hoped or supposed (for he could not see the defenders behind the crest of the ridge), and the allied infantry now came forward in line two deep and began volleying into the densely packed columns which were already under a galling fire from the skirmishers – especially from the 95th Rifles in the sand-pits. Unsupported by artillery, and with the cavalry on their flanks unable to influence the fighting to their front, the French columns began to waver and then turn tail – but not before the French cavalry had cut up a battalion of Hanoverians sent to support La Haye Sainte, forcing the nearby battalions on the ridge to form square (a salutary reminder that it didn't do to make a mistake in front of French cav-alry) and allowing the assaulting columns almost to gain the crest. Seeing this, Uxbridge, without waiting for orders, launched his two heavy cavalry brigades – the Household and the Union (so-called because it consisted of English, Scots and Irish dragoon regiments) – at the French right flank, driving them off and turning the repulse into rout. But the Scots Greys (Royal North British Dra-goons) especially galloped on too far, cutting up some of the grand battery, and were in turn cut up by French lancers. They were saved from complete disaster only by a counter-charge from the light drag-oon brigade on the far left of the allied line, their brigadier, Sir John Vandeleur, disobeying Wellington's instructions not to move with-out his express order. For some minutes he'd tussled with himself over it; but the essence of cavalry was the *coup d'œil* – the ability to

---

* 'Corn 6 feet high' is sometimes disputed, but selective cultivation has reduced the height of wheat by almost a half since Waterloo.

take in a situation quickly, to judge it in relation to the whole, and then to act.

Despite their casualties, the heavies had delivered a huge blow. In the space of twenty minutes they'd destroyed five infantry brigades, inflicting perhaps some 5,000 casualties and taking 2,000 prisoners – herded to the rear by the same British infantry who before the charge must have thought their time was up.

Some who saw it all – including, by several accounts, Wellington, though that seems unlikely – thought it signalled the imminent collapse of the French, but skirmishing continued throughout the afternoon along the whole length of the ridge and in front of the three anchor points of Hougoumont, La Haye Sainte and the villages on the left of the allied line. The next real challenge came from the massed French cavalry. In this third phase of the battle, some 7,000 assorted horsemen – cuirassiers, dragoons, hussars and lancers – but with little horse artillery and no supporting infantry, came on in a great host towards the allied centre-right between La Haye Sainte and Hougoumont. The allied infantry formed squares to meet them. In fact the squares were largely oblong-shaped, with the defenders forming the sides in two ranks, the front kneeling – a bristling hedge of bayonets and a fair length of musketry. Outside the squares, the gunners fired until the last safe moment and then ran for the cover of the nearest square, racing back out to their guns again as soon as the French had swept past.

A sort of stalemate thus developed: the French horsemen galloped – and trotted, and even walked – about the ridge with impunity, but in turn could do no harm. The infantry, secure in their squares save for the occasional plaguing artillery (though some did suffer badly from the French guns), could do nothing to send them back. Uxbridge's heavies were in no state to mount much of a counter-attack, and Wellington's orders to his cavalry brigadiers were now holding them to their places (Wellington himself, with his staff, had to keep taking refuge in the nearest square as he rode about the field). The attacks continued for an hour and more, but they could make no impression on the unity of the line. At about half-past four it seems that Wellington thought the scales of the battle were beginning to tilt his way, for he was heard to say, 'The battle is mine, and if the Prussians arrive soon there will be an end to the war.'* This, if true, was optimistic, and perhaps deliberately so; but soon afterwards cannon fire to the east signalled that the Prussians were indeed making progress.

It was as well they were, for despite Wellington's confidence things were looking distinctly shaky for the allies on the ridge, where casualties were mounting terribly. Indeed, Wellington had to do a deal of realigning and reinforcing. Recollections refer to his intense concentration, his pale look as he rode about the field giving orders – sometimes unnecessarily and to the irritation of the more experienced commanders. Then, at about six-thirty, disaster threatened as La Haye Sainte fell to a coordinated attack by French infantry, cavalry and artillery (the defenders had simply run out of ammunition). This was the fourth phase, and the only decent piece of French coordination in the entire battle, making the allied centre look distinctly vulnerable just as the duke was managing to stabilize the battered inner flank above Hougoumont. The infantry casualties in the centre, just behind the crossroads, had also been rising alarmingly, for the ground here wasn't so favourable to the defenders, offering less shelter. The 27th (Inniskilling) Regiment alone had lost 400 men to the grand battery before firing a single musket, and their brigadier now sent a note to Wellington asking if his brigade, by this time down to a third of its starting strength, could be relieved for a while. He received one of the 'backs to the wall' orders that in

---

* Rees Howell Gronow, *Reminiscences of Captain Gronow: Formerly of the Grenadier Guards, and M.P. for Stafford: being Anecdotes of the camp, the court, and the clubs, at the close of the last war with France. Related by himself* (London, 1862).

desperate moments have often screwed the British army's courage to the sticking place: 'Tell him', said Wellington to an aide-de-camp, 'that what he asks is impossible: he and I, and every Englishman [*sic*] on the field, must die on the spot we now occupy.'

And for many on the ridge that day, it looked as if that indeed would be the outcome: a battle in which all were killed. Yet Wellington himself, riding to wherever the action was most intense, remained not only alive but untouched, even as others of his staff were maimed or killed at his side. His senior ADC Lieutenant-Colonel Sir Alexander Gordon and his inestimable chief of staff Sir William de Lancey were mortally wounded; another of his ADCs, Lord FitzRoy Somerset, lost an arm; and Lord Uxbridge famously a leg. 'By God, sir, I think I have lost my leg,' he said quietly to Wellington as grapeshot smashed his knee. The duke's reply, more solicitous than it perhaps sounds, was simply, 'By God, sir, I believe you have!'

Imperturbable throughout, Wellington now moved what few unengaged troops he had to the centre. A little later, on learning that Prussian cavalry had reached the furthest end of the allied line, he also ordered Sir Hussey Vivian's hussar brigade to the centre from the left flank, where it had stood inactive for most of the day with the light dragoon brigade. Coming up, Vivian was shocked by what he found: 'the ground actually covered with dead and dying, cannon shots and shells flying thicker than ever I heard musketry before, and our troops – some of them – giving way'. Wellington himself had to gallop to where some Brunswickers were recoiling. If ever there was a general with a perfect grasp of how in war the tactical was sometimes short-wired to the strategic it was he, which is one of the reasons he was everywhere that day. By about seven o'clock that evening he'd at last managed to stabilize the allied line.

The Prussians now began arriving on the left flank in large numbers, and with them, as Wellington had supposedly foreseen two hours or so before, came the prospect not just of winning the battle but of strategic victory.

Napoleon knew this perfectly well too. He had two options, therefore. The first was to form a covering force and retire: the British were exhausted, after all, and the Prussians, though scarcely engaged that day, had force-marched a fair distance; it might have been possible under cover of darkness to get away to see to the defence of Paris. Or else he could throw the dice once more – one last time – in an attempt to break through the allied line and get into the Forest of Soignes before nightfall and thence towards Brussels, perhaps driving in the wedge finally between the two armies. What good that might bring ultimately, when the Austrians and the Russians came to the borders of France, and with a Prussian army bruised but intact, could only be conjectured. His whole campaign, however, soon to be known as 'The Hundred Days', was always more visceral than cerebral. And what good would come of defending Paris? Without *La Gloire* Napoleon was nothing.

So he threw the dice one more time: indeed, he threw in the Garde – the Garde Impériale, which had never been defeated. In fairness, perhaps he genuinely believed the allied line to have been so weakened that the moral superiority of an attack by the Garde would be irresistible. But it's unlikely. Either way, he was wrong. The Garde – five battalions of the 'Middle Guard' backed by three of the 'Old', in all some 5,000 men – marched for the ridge between La Haye Sainte, which was now in French hands, and Hougoumont, dividing into two distinct masses as they came up the slope.* And by one of those

---

* The numbers taking part in the attack, and their precise formation, have never been firmly established. By this time the smoke on the battlefield was thick and widespread, and there is even some doubt as to whether all the attacking troops were from the Garde. Some of the battalions advanced in column, and some appear to have done so in square.

quirks of war, the force advancing on the left marched directly for the place where the British Guards lay prone – as ordered – behind the crest of the ridge.

Again, Wellington was at the perilous – decisive – place: 'Now, Maitland! Now's your time!' he called to the brigade commander as the French broached the ridge. And knowing, almost certainly, that this wasn't just the decisive place but, as Clausewitz would have it, the culminating point, he couldn't resist giving the order direct to the brigade: 'Stand up, Guards! Make ready! Fire!'

At 50 yards the effect was devastating. And as two allied brigades from the right flank moved to join the musketry, Colonel Sir John Colborne commanding the 52nd Oxfordshire Light Infantry took his men forward to open an enfilading fire from the Garde's right flank.

It was enough. 'La Garde recule!' – the most astonished cry the Grande Armée had ever heard. But even as they fell back, their supporting artillery checked the ardour of the allied troops following up.

'Go on, Colborne! Go on! They won't stand! Don't give them time to rally!' called the duke. And then, making sure they wouldn't, he took off his hat and began waving the whole line forward.

It was all over but the pursuit – and that he would leave to the Prussians.

Had Blücher saved the day? Would Wellington have been beaten if the Prussians hadn't come? The questions are facile: Wellington simply wouldn't have given battle at Waterloo if the Prussians hadn't been able to support him. It was exactly as he and Blücher had planned. Though when the two of them met as the French were streaming from the field – at the inn so aptly named La Belle Alliance – Blücher could only splutter: 'Mein lieber Kamerad: Quelle affaire!' And he wasn't exaggerating.

POSTSCRIPT

Napoleon surrendered for a second time, and was taken into the custody of the British crown on the allies' behalf. And this time there'd be no short measures when it came to exile: no pleasant and accessible island in the Mediterranean, but a remote volcanic vestige in the South Atlantic – St Helena.

The Congress of Vienna resumed its work, concluding a peace that would ultimately prove as illusory as that hammered out at Versailles in 1919. But for the time being, France would pose no threat; unlike in 1814, the restored Louis XVIII disbanded the entire army to remake it in a thoroughly non-Revolutionary image.

And Victor Hugo's claim, that Waterloo had been won by a general of the second rank – with its implication that he'd won against the superior man? 'My true glory is not to have won forty battles,' said Napoleon on St Helena; 'Waterloo will erase the memory of so many victories . . . But . . . what will live forever, is my Civil Code.'

That may be so; but the material point is the outcome of the final battle – the 'forty-first', as it were. In his celebrated staff college lectures, the great Victorian military historian Colonel Charles Chesney summed up the import of the battle, and with more objectivity than many a later attempt:

Yet not in this battle – as I hope presently to show – however heroically fought or dexterously won, should the glory of the allied generals rest;

but on the noble devotion of each to the common object in view, and the perfection of mutual confidence which enabled each so to act separately as to produce with their united armies at the right moment the greatest possible result. Never in the whole of military history was the tactical value of the troops more entirely subordinated to the strategic operations . . . Waterloo was, in fact, viewed in its proper aspect, but the crown and finish of a splendid piece of strategy . . . Had it been any other general [than Napoleon] that acted thus on that eventful day, it would long ago have been said that his tactics in the battle were as defective as the strategy which placed him in it at such fearful odds.*

Wellington's great legacy in campaigning was his 'harness of ropes' approach, in which he likened the art of military organization and planning to the practical business of horse furniture: 'The French plans are like a splendid leather harness which is perfect when it works, but if it breaks it cannot be mended. I make my harness of ropes, it is never as good looking as the French, but if it breaks I can tie a knot and carry on.' To do this required personal reconnaissance in the widest sense, an eye for ground, the supervision of the execution of detail, and sheer hard work ('My rule always was to do the business of the day in the day'). And also a pragmatic yet robust political sense: Wellington was careful to secure his political as well as his tactical flanks. In this he shared Marlborough's genius for logistics and ability to work in coalitions, which obliged them both to fuse the military with the political. Both were as much strategists as tacticians, a combination that's proved remarkably elusive in the British army – and most others – ever since.

And yet these very qualities had their downside. When, after Waterloo, Wellington said, 'By God, I don't think it would have

---

* Charles Cornwallis Chesney, *Waterloo Lectures* (London, 1868).

served had I not been there!' he was almost certainly right. He had some capable and experienced generals in the field with him that day, but none who – on past form – was equal to his own task. It is curious, therefore, that he took no great efforts to make sure that if he did become a casualty all would not be lost. He was criticized both at the time and later for his tight-gripped 'top-down' tendency. In his commentary on the diaries of Sir John Moore, for example, Major-General Sir Frederick Maurice, the official historian of the late Victorian army, observes sharply of Wellington's one criticism of the Corunna campaign (that Moore ought in anticipation of the retreat 'to have sent officers to the rear to mark and prepare the halting-places for every brigade') that

> if it really was the practice in Wellington's own army towards the end of the Peninsular War for headquarters to interfere in such a matter, then all that can be said is that it is an extraordinary illustration of the extent to which Wellington, in his utter contempt for his subordinate generals, had reduced the whole army to the condition of a mechanical instrument in his own hand.*

In the duke's hands, of course, the instrument worked. In the hands of others it didn't work nearly so well. As the years went by after Waterloo, the instrument, like a well-sprung clock, lost time (and in the Crimea it eventually stopped for a while) because it was never wound or serviced properly. Nevertheless, for a century and more, British officers, when faced with a tricky problem, were inclined to ask themselves 'What would the duke do?'

---

* *Diary of Sir John Moore*, ed. J. F. Maurice (London, 1904).

PART FOUR

SWORD BEACH

The Battle for the Bridgehead

6 JUNE 1944

One cannot but acknowledge that the history of the war knows no other similar undertaking as regards breadth of design, vastness of scale and high skill of execution.

Joseph Stalin on the D-Day landings, 13 June 1944

The Allied landings in Normandy in June 1944 were the longest-planned battle in history, and the most complex. And despite the gravest misgivings at every level, they were spectacularly successful. They were in themselves a separate battle in the great Allied offensive in the West – the 'Second Front'. Had they failed, the consequences would have been almost incalculable. The shaping of the Normandy landings, unprecedented in their conception, scale and scope, as Stalin said, was an exercise in strategic and tactical thinking that can sometimes be lost in the sheer human drama of 'the longest day' itself. As a study in the relationship between grand strategy, military strategy, campaign planning and tactical execution, it is hard to beat. Especially is it a fine example of why and how there can be no area of warfare that is exempt from 'policy'. And nowhere is all this – as well as the human drama – more vivid and instructive than in events at Sword Beach, where the British would place their main effort that day in order to secure the vulnerable left flank of the entire Allied operation, and to seize Caen, which by historical coincidence had been the seat of William the Conqueror, but which in 1944 had become the key crossroads on the path to Paris and thence to the heart of Germany.

1

PLANS

Plans are worthless, but planning is everything.

General Dwight D. Eisenhower

The Allied landings in Normandy in June 1944 were planned in the most remarkable detail – they had to be – and few battles have gone so remarkably well to plan.*

Planning began in 1940, after the fall of France and the evacuation of the British Expeditionary Force from the Continent.† The return was first just a vision, seen as if through a glass darkly, in the mind of Winston Churchill, a dim, flickering light at the end of a tunnel of

---

* Operational concepts such as the Schlieffen Plan were developed over many years, but these weren't battles. Operation Neptune, the amphibious invasion and establishment of a secure foothold on the continent – 'D-Day' – was a battle in itself.

† Some 338,000 Allied troops (a third of them French) were got away, and more were to follow from ports on the Atlantic coast. Nearly 50,000 British troops were taken prisoner before France eventually fell.

unresolved direction and incalculable length, whose roof might at any stage collapse. 'Plans', said the man who would be Supreme Allied Commander during the Normandy landings, General Dwight D. Eisenhower, 'are worthless, but planning is everything.' His subordinate, the commander of the landing forces, General Sir Bernard Montgomery, would probably have taken issue with this. He was an advocate of 'the master plan', and preferred always to say that a battle had gone exactly to plan, even when instead it had quite evidently been more a masterpiece of improvisation (his own, indeed). But Eisenhower's apparent paradox simply states what the Elder Moltke had famously implied in his dictum that 'no plan survives first contact with the enemy'.* Moltke's system of devolved decision-making, if sometimes misunderstood and over-stated, in fact required subordinates to proceed with initiative and discretion in line with the general intention. For on the day, the details of a plan might no longer be apt, while the planning process – a thorough exploration of options and contingencies – would indicate the appropriate action as events unfolded. (It was no dishonour to Montgomery's 'master plan' for El Alamein that the details had to be urgently revised during the battle.) Further, Moltke recognized that strategy was not an exclusively top-down process. While 'strategy affords tactics the means for fighting and the probability of winning by the direction of armies and their meeting at the place of combat . . . strategy [also] appropriates the success of every engagement and builds upon it'. It is this observation that led him to conclude that 'strategy is a system of expedients'.

In essence, then, a plan is a vision, an outline, of how the objective is to be achieved. It can't be a prediction of how the battle will go, as the enemy has a vote. And so does nature; for although it can be said

---

* 'Therefore no plan of operations goes with any degree of certainty beyond the first contact with the hostile main force': Helmuth von Moltke, *Military Works*, vol. IV, *Operative Preparations for Battle* (Newport, RI, 1935).

that, for instance, 'the jungle is neutral',* it won't always feel like that. All this amounts to what Clausewitz called 'friction'.†

The planning for D-Day in general – and for the landings on Sword Beach in particular, from the dim and flickering light of 'ends' in the mind of Churchill to the 'means', the first footing of infantrymen on that easternmost of the Allied beaches, nearest to Caen – is an object lesson in strategy and its implementation. Churchill later reduced the reams of writing on strategy (before and since) to a simple observation that its art lay 'in foreseeing the outlines of the future and being prepared to deal with it'. Or as modern strategians prefer – ends, ways, means. Though some would say that as a secret, black and midnight process, strategy was never better 'explained' than by Henry Reed in 'Movement of Bodies':‡

> Tactics is merely
> The mechanical movement of bodies, and that
> is what we mean by it.

---

* The title of the wartime memoirs of Colonel Freddie Spencer Chapman (London, 1949), who organized the ill-fated 'stay behind' parties in the Malayan jungle in 1942, and who attributed his survival to the basic rule that 'the jungle is neutral', that one should view the surroundings as neither good nor bad.

† Clausewitzian 'friction' derives from the unpredictability of battle, during which combatants are subject to the physical and mental exertions and the life-threatening dangers of war; and from uncertainty, or the 'fog of war', arising from the imperfection of intelligence: 'Everything in war is simple, but the simplest thing is difficult. The difficulties accumulate and end by producing a kind of friction that is inconceivable unless one has experienced war ... Countless minor incidents – the kind you can never really foresee – combine to lower the general level of performance, so that one always falls short of the intended goal' (On War).

‡ Henry Reed, born 1914, was drafted into the Royal Army Ordnance Corps in 1941, but because of his language skills served later at the Government Code and Cypher School at Bletchley Park. Though a prolific poet and writer, he is now known mainly for his work 'Naming of Parts', which, along with 'Movement of Bodies', made up two parts of the poem Lessons of the War.

> Or perhaps I should say: by them.
> Strategy, to be quite frank, you will have no hand in.
> It is done by those up above, and it merely refers to
> The larger movements over which we have no control.

Reed's plangent wit would prove unerringly apt on that day in June 1944 when the planning was over and the action began:

> But tactics are also important, together or single.
> You must never forget that, suddenly, in an engagement,
> You may find yourself alone.

For although not alone – indeed, far from it – those infantrymen, tank crews, sappers and all the rest who struggled to gain a foothold on D-Day for what Eisenhower called the 'Crusade in Europe',* found themselves making many an individual choice, even if just a breathless 'Do I take cover *here*, or do I go on to *there*?'

But by what process, exactly, did evacuation from one beach in France lead to the storming of another four years later?

On 18 June 1940, a fortnight after the last troops had been taken off from Dunkirk, and France had to all intents and purposes capitulated, Churchill addressed the House of Commons and exposed, if only implicitly, the flickering strategic light:

> What General Weygand called the 'The Battle of France' is over. I expect that the Battle of Britain is about to begin. Upon this battle depends the survival of Christian civilization. Upon it depends our own British life and the long continuity of our institutions and our Empire. The whole fury and might of the enemy must very soon be

---

* The title of his wartime memoirs, published in New York in 1948.

turned on us. Hitler knows that he will have to break us in this island or lose the war. *If we can stand up to him all Europe may be free* [emphasis added], and the life of the world may move forward into broad, sunlit uplands; but if we fail then the whole world, including the United States, and all that we have known and cared for, will sink into the abyss of a new dark age made more sinister, and perhaps more prolonged, by the lights of a perverted science. Let us therefore brace ourselves to our duty and so bear ourselves that if the British Commonwealth and Empire lasts for a thousand years, men will still say: 'This was their finest hour.'

If, however, D-Day's seeds were first planted on Dunkirk's beaches, they lay dormant for eighteen months, until in December 1941 the United States was rudely blasted into the war by the Japanese at Pearl Harbor.* But then came the germination. Even as the fire hoses were still playing on the burning ships of the US Pacific Fleet, Churchill telephoned the President, Franklin D. Roosevelt: 'Mr President, what's this about Japan?' 'It's quite true,' replied FDR . . . We are all in the same boat now.' Indeed, four days later, Germany would add to the boat's troubles – or rather, from Churchill's point of view, ease them – by declaring war on the United States. If ever there were a case of Clausewitz's 'War has its own grammar but not its own logic', it was

---

* Although it was not until the Japanese attack that the US declared war on Germany, during 1940 and 1941 Britain and the US had developed extraordinarily close ties, notably through 'Lend-Lease' – the loan of military equipment in exchange for US leases on a number of military bases adjoining the Atlantic (payment, according to the Lend-Lease Act of March 1941, being made 'in kind or property, or any other direct or indirect benefit which the President deems satisfactory'). By the time of Pearl Harbor the two countries' joint military and logistical planning was quite advanced. And Churchill and Roosevelt had met, in Newfoundland in August 1941, and agreed in outline their war aims (that is, their post-war political objectives), which would become known as the Atlantic Charter.

this, for Hitler's decision is ultimately inexplicable. Almost as inexplicable as his decision to attack Russia six months earlier.

Churchill now proposed travelling to Washington so that 'we [he and Roosevelt] could review the whole war plan in the light of reality'. FDR was reluctant, given the tumult of Pearl Harbor, but then agreed, and on 13 December Churchill left for America aboard the newly commissioned battleship HMS *Duke of York* accompanied by his political advisers and military chiefs. What followed was the 'Arcadia' conference, the key policy decision of which was 'Germany First' – or rather, 'Europe First', i.e. that the defeat of Germany was to take precedence over the defeat of Japan, to the considerable relief of Churchill. (Both FDR and General George C. Marshall, chief of staff of the US army and FDR's de facto principal strategic adviser, acknowledged that Germany's warmaking capacity was far the greater, and that Japan's defeat would soon follow that of the Third Reich.) It was agreed that a Combined Chiefs of Staff committee would be established – Marshall's newly appointed assistant chief of the War Plans Division, the recently promoted 51-year-old Brigadier-General Eisenhower, had lobbied hard for a unified command system – with a permanent British representative, Field Marshal Sir John Dill, in Washington, to agree military strategy. The principle of unity of command in each theatre under a supreme commander was also agreed – a lesson from the First World War, as indeed was the Combined Chiefs of Staff.*

---

* The term 'combined' can be misleading. In the Second World War the British used it to mean activities that involved air, land or naval forces acting together. However, the Americans used the term 'joint' for that purpose, and so 'combined' was appropriated for operations conducted by forces of two or more allied nations acting together for the accomplishment of a common goal. The same usage continues today in NATO terminology, though 'multinational' is increasingly preferred. However, the British army still uses the term 'combined arms' when two or more arms – infantry, armour, artillery etc. – act together in a common task.

The 'ends' having thus been settled, the question now was – crudely – the ways and means. This task was much simplified by the prior agreement on the principle of unity in both effort and command. That said, 'simple' isn't the same as 'easy'. Military strategy would prove contentious, to say the least. Indeed, without the considerable personal 'special relationship' which FDR and Churchill enjoyed – not entirely cosy, but unquestionably special in the sense of being more than just united in a common cause – and the largely unsung military diplomacy of Dill, it's possible that things could have gone badly awry, even given the obvious necessity of defeating two potentially existential threats.

How best, then, to defeat Germany? From day one, US military leaders (the air force was then a branch of the army) were determined on direct confrontation in north-west Europe as soon as possible – 1943 or even 1942. This, the direct approach, was – is – very much 'the American way of war'.* The reasons are, of course, many, but in *Meet the US Army*, a pamphlet commissioned by the Ministry of Information in 1943 for schools and other institutions that might otherwise be 'puzzled' by these strangers who spoke the same language (more or less) but seemed so different, Louis MacNeice recounts what one American officer told him: ' "We don't want to hang about on the outskirts of this war, we want to get into action." Why? "Because," he went on, "our way home lies through Berlin and Tokio [*sic*]." War, that is, for an American, is only a means to an end.'† The

---

* It was certainly the case in 1917–18, and led to considerable friction on the Western Front, as I describe in *Too Important for the Generals* (London, 2016).

† Frederick Louis MacNeice, poet and playwright, born in Belfast in 1907 and a member of the 'Auden Group' (which included W. H. Auden, Stephen Spender and Cecil Day-Lewis), had lately taught at Cornell University, New York State. He returned to England in late 1940 and, barred from active service by bad eyesight, joined the features department of the BBC.

British, on the other hand, although – unlike the totalitarian powers – they saw war largely in the same way (both countries in peacetime had small armies relative to their populations), had experience of fighting German troops in Norway, France, Greece and North Africa that made both Churchill and the chiefs of staff much more cautious. (And they'd yet to meet the most feared Nazi troops, the SS, as Churchill was acutely aware.) Memories of the Somme and Third Ypres ('Passchendaele') haunted most of them to one degree or another. Churchill recalled that

> While I was always willing to join with the United States in a direct assault across the Channel on the German sea-front in France, I was not convinced that this was the only way of winning the war, and I knew that it would be a very heavy and hazardous adventure. The fearful price we had to pay in human life and blood for the great offensives of the First World War was graven in my mind.*

Among these graven memories was, no doubt, that of Gallipoli, for he had very personally advocated the Dardanelles offensive, only to see a strong strategic card played very badly tactically.

Senior British officers also had grave doubts about the battle readiness of US troops and the capability of US generals. In 1939 the US army ranked seventh in the world in terms of numbers, just behind Romania. It had no armoured corps, its few tanks being incorporated in the infantry for fire support. Only in July 1940, after seeing the success of the German *Blitzkrieg* in Poland, Belgium and France, did the War Department hastily form a separate corps. By December 1941, the British had had two years' up-to-date experience of fighting, largely through rude shocks; and they knew well enough that they still weren't up to the

---

* Winston S. Churchill, *The Second World War*, vol. V, *Closing the Ring* (London, 1951).

mark. Their concern for their new ally's capability was hardly surprising, therefore. What of course they couldn't have known was the speed at which the US army would acquire that capability. Even so, a cross-Channel offensive in 1943, let alone 1942, against battle-hardened German troops was inconceivable. Besides its sheer complexity, the Chief of the Imperial General Staff, Sir Alan Brooke, was sure that the Germans wouldn't be sufficiently weakened (by attrition on the Eastern Front and in the Mediterranean, and by strategic bombing) until 1944. The Dieppe raid in August 1942 (of which more below) would supply ample and bloody evidence that British misgivings were well founded, as the fifty US Rangers who accompanied the British commandos – those who weren't killed or captured – could testify.

Churchill's preference (and Brooke's) was undoubtedly for an indirect approach through the Mediterranean (Italy probably, or the Balkans), which he referred to as the soft belly of the crocodile. This phrase has caused endless trouble: Italy – both the terrain and the Germans fighting there – was to prove anything but soft. It was, though, undoubtedly softer than the snout.* Determined to get to grips with the German army somewhere in 1942, however, FDR and Marshall

---

* The term isn't found in any of Churchill's writing or speeches, but he used it widely none the less – perhaps for the first time when trying to persuade Stalin that a 'second front' (i.e. additional to the Russian front) couldn't reasonably be opened in north-western Europe in 1943. General Mark Clark, who commanded the US 5th Army, later the 15th Army Group, in the Italian campaign, heard him use 'soft underbelly' when he and Eisenhower took up the question of where British and American forces should strike first. In autumn 1942, the two generals explained to Marshall: 'A cross-channel operation was [then] utterly impossible. We could not even get across without the British showing us the way and taking us by the hand. We did not have the means. And so it was decided that we would take this matter up with Mr Churchill, which we did. And that is where his persuasive eloquence first impressed me. He got up before a map with his pointer and he kept pointing to Gibraltar, North Africa, the Mediterranean, Sicily and Italy. Finally he said, "We should slit the soft belly of the Mediterranean"' (General Mark Clark, address of 1 June 1970 to the Rt Hon. Sir Winston Spencer Churchill Society, Edmonton, Alberta, quoted in *The Heroic Memory* (Edmonton, 2004).

accepted Brooke's proposal for an invasion of North Africa, which would unify the Anglo-American war effort and finally secure the Mediterranean theatre as a whole. It also had the merit of being softer than soft, for the invasion beaches would be in Morocco and Algeria, which were Vichy French territory, and thereby offered the strong possibility of just token resistance. The Germans at this stage were still fighting in Libya; and in October, at El Alamein, they'd be dealt a blow from which they weren't able to recover, and would withdraw in some disorder to Tunisia. In supreme command of the combined operation, codenamed 'Torch', would be Eisenhower, who was promoted major-general in March and in July lieutenant-general.

The Torch landings in November 1942 went well – there was indeed little fighting – but demonstrated the naval and logistic challenges of a major seaborne operation. At the Casablanca conference in January 1943, codenamed 'Symbol' (aptly, for it was on ground captured by the US army), Churchill again persuaded FDR to postpone a cross-Channel attack and instead mount Operation Husky, the invasion of Sicily, once more under Eisenhower. But Churchill also proposed appointing a US commander for the eventual invasion of north-west Europe, codenamed 'Overlord' (the first appearance of the name), with a British deputy and/or a British chief of staff. Marshall, having reluctantly agreed to Husky, seized on the idea as a token of earnest intent – indeed, more than a token – to breathe life into the planning of the invasion. Consequently, Lieutenant-General Frederick Morgan would be appointed 'Chief of Staff to the Supreme Allied Commander (Designate)' – COSSAC – and the American Brigadier-General Ray Barker his deputy. The organization came formally into being on 13 April at Norfolk House in St James's Square, London, where Torch had been planned (and where Morgan first met Eisenhower during that planning). Its remit was to produce an outline plan for a Channel crossing by 1 August.

Overlord was under way.

Left: The death of Edward the Confessor, 5 January 1066: the struggle for the succession begins. (Detail from Bayeux Tapestry.)

Right: The Witan makes its choice: Harold Godwineson is crowned the day of Edward's funeral, 6 January. (Engraving by W. Ridgeway after a drawing by Daniel Maclise RA.)

Above: Harald Hardrada defeats the northern earls at Gate Fulford, York, 20 September. (Detail from Matthew Paris's *La Estoire de Seint Aedward le Rei*, mid-13th century.)

Right: A late nineteenth-century artist's more detailed, and more accurate, impressions of housecarls, or perhaps select fyrdsmen.

William of Normandy's knights attack King Harold's shield wall at Hastings, 14 October. Stylized and imagined, but the earliest near-contemporary image. (Detail from Bayeux Tapestry.)

The last stand of King Harold, as imagined by the late nineteenth-/ early twentieth-century artist Richard Caton Woodville. If some of the detail is fanciful, the savagery of the closing stage of the battle could hardly be exaggerated.

Left: At the butts: archery practice (Luttrell Psalter, 14th century). The 'Assize of Arms' of 1242 required all males between the ages of 15 and 60 who were able (*'qui possunt'*) to keep bows – except those living within royal forests.

Right: 'Chaplain, away! Thy priesthood saves thy life. As for the brat of this accursed duke, Whose father slew my father, he shall die.' The killing of Edmund of Rutland after the Battle of Sandal (Wakefield), probably in violation of sanctuary, fanned the flames of revenge among the Yorkists before Towton. (As imagined by a nineteenth-century German artist.)

Below: Margaret of Anjou, *c.*1445. Nine years her husband King Henry VI's senior, and infinitely his superior in willpower. (Detail from the Talbot Shrewsbury Book.)

Above: The son of York who made glorious summer: Edward, Earl of March (Edward IV), whose determination to lead from the front ultimately gave his army the edge despite the Lancastrians' continuing superiority in numbers.

Above: The old bridge at Ferrybridge, from the Lancastrian side (1805). It had been slightly widened in the preceding century. The church tower doubtless proved a vantage point in the battle. (The church was dismantled and rebuilt further south in the twentieth century.)

Right: Late 18th-century historical painter Henry Tresham's vision of *The Earl of Warwick at Ferrybridge*: 'Then let the earth be drunken with our blood: I'll kill my horse, because I will not fly.' (*Henry VI, Part 3.*)

Left: 'The lord Fauconberg, which led the forward of Edward's battle, being a man of great policy and having much experience of martial fields. . .' (Edward Hall, Tudor chronicler). The third and most decisive of Fauconberg's gambits: seizing the advantage of the wind to outrange the Lancastrian archers.

Right: 'Here on this molehill will I sit me down.
To whom God will, there be the victory!
For Margaret my queen, and Clifford too,
Have chid me from the battle;
  swearing both
They prosper best of all when I am
  thence.'

In fact, Henry remained in York throughout the battle at Towton. But Shakespeare is correct as to the reason, and his doleful image of the King is probably just as accurate.

Above: 'O piteous spectacle! O bloody times!' (*Henry VI, Part 3*). The slaughter in the Cock Beck — 'No Quarter!' — as imagined by Caton Woodville.

Above: Sahagun, 21 December 1808: the high-water mark of Sir John Moore's campaign. His death the following month at Corunna brought Sir Arthur Wellesley (the Duke of Wellington) to command, his first step on the road to Waterloo. (Painting by James Prinsep Beadle.)

Right: The Earl of Uxbridge, Moore's cavalry commander, who brilliantly covered the retreat to Corunna. As the Marquess of Anglesey, reconciled with Wellington (with whose sister-in-law he'd eloped), he would command the cavalry at Waterloo, disregarding orders and leading the charge that broke the main French attack.

Below: Talavera, 28 July 1809, one of the bloodiest battles of the Peninsular War, in which Wellington gained much experience in how to deal with French attacks. (Pen and wash by E. Walker.)

Left: 'Napoleon has humbugged me, by God! He has gained twenty-four hours' march on me.' British officers leaving the Duchess of Richmond's ball in the early hours of 16 June 1815 for the Battles of Quatre Bras and Waterloo, as imagined by the Victorian artist Robert Hillingford.

Right: Wellington and Blücher meeting before the Battle of Waterloo (Robert Hillingford). Blücher's refusal to abandon Wellington after the Prussians' mauling at Ligny, against the urging of his chief of staff, Gneisenau, would be the critical decision in the defeat of Napoleon Bonaparte on 18 June: 'I have given him my word.'

Left: Ligny by Ernest Crofts (1875). Napoleon and his staff at his command post, the windmill on the heights of Naveau. At the end of the day's fighting he was certain the Prussians were done for, and that he could now turn and defeat the British in detail.

The fruits of perseverance. 'What is truly admirable in the battle of Waterloo is England, English firmness, English resolution, English blood. The superb thing which England had there – may it not displease her – is herself; it is not her captain, it is her army.' Victor Hugo's encomium in *Les Misérables* misses the point, however, that the duke of Wellington was the epitome of firmness and resolution.

2

PLANNERS

It won't work, but you must bloody well make it!

General Sir Alan Brooke to
Lieutenant-General Frederick Morgan

At first Morgan hardly had a staff worth the name. Later he'd write that COSSAC was 'not highly regarded by the War Office' at all.* Brooke had told him it – the planning for Overlord – wouldn't work, but that he'd have to make it work, and Morgan was determined to. His directive from the Combined Chiefs of Staff was broad to say the least: in his words, 'to plan nothing less than the reconquest of Europe'.

Morgan was a shrewd but something of a chance choice. He'd been commissioned just before the outbreak of war in 1914 and served throughout on the Western Front, principally in artillery

---

* Sir Frederick Morgan, *Overture to Overlord* (London, 1950).

staff appointments. He was, as a result, and by temperament, nothing if not methodical. In 1940, as a brigadier, he'd commanded the
1st Armoured Division's support group in the battle of France. Two
years later he was a lieutenant-general in command of I Corps,
which during the planning for Torch was earmarked for the defence
of Gibraltar if the Germans made a riposte through Spain. Torch had
gone off without a riposte, however, and so his corps was stood down
and Morgan had been without a job. 'Pug' Ismay (Lieutenant-
General Sir Hastings Ismay, deputy secretary of the war cabinet and
Churchill's military go-between with the chiefs of staff) had known
Morgan in India, and Brooke (though eleven years his senior) had
known him as a fellow artillery officer, so they asked him for a
memorandum on planning for a cross-Channel invasion. Morgan
had admired Eisenhower's integrated approach to Torch, and
strongly urged 'complete British–American amalgamation of staff,
effort, troops, and everything else from the very beginning', with all
branches of both nations' services 'buying in'. When the time came
to appoint the supreme commander, he wrote, the general must
inherit a fully developed force structure, with effective command
and control, a reliable supply system, and a solid yet adaptable plan.
Morgan likened the role of chief of staff in this setting to that of
John the Baptist – a true believer working on behalf of the celestial
figure yet to arrive. Later he'd write that he hadn't actually seen himself in the part of the 'Baptist' he'd described: 'I had in my mind's
eye one who had borne much more of the heat and burden than had
I.' But Brooke disagreed, and so Churchill had invited him to dine,
afterwards telling the CIGS that his dinner guest 'would do'. And
thus it was that Morgan had been selected as chief of staff to the
celestial figure yet to arrive.

Morgan and his staff, which would only later in the year reach its
authorized size (320 officers and 600 other ranks in five departments –
land, air, maritime, intelligence, administration – each headed by a

two-star officer*), worked more than the proverbial long hours and without official leave in the twelve months of their planning, he himself frequently sleeping overnight in his office. At times, it seems, they worked more in faith than with assurance. After the war Morgan reckoned that COSSAC (the acronym was applied not only to his position but to the planning staff as a whole) was 'not highly regarded by the War Office, save as a high-grade training exploit', which was undoubtedly a reflection of the prevailing view – in other words, Brooke's – that a cross-Channel invasion of France was not coming soon, if at all.

Nevertheless, when his staff began to assemble in April 1943, Morgan gathered them together – half British, half American – and resolutely announced:

The term 'planning staff' has come to have a most sinister meaning; it implies the production of nothing but paper. What we must contrive to do somehow is to produce not only paper, but ACTION. In spite of the fact that it is quite clear that neither I nor you have by definition any executive authority, my idea is that we shall regard ourselves in the first instance as primarily a co-ordinating body. We plan mainly by the co-ordination of effort already being exerted in a hundred and one directions. We differ from the ordinary planning staff in that we are, as you perceive, in effect the embryo of the future Supreme Headquarters Staff. I do not think I can put the matter any better to you than by quoting to you the last words of the CIGS, who said: 'Well, there it is; it won't work, but you must bloody well make it.'†

---

* The star system in the armies works thus: five – field marshal (US general of the army); four – general; three – lieutenant-general; two – major-general; one – brigadier (US brigadier-general).

† This and following quotations from Morgan are all from *Overture to Overlord*.

His directive from the Combined Chiefs was crystal clear on the objective, at least: 'to defeat the GERMAN fighting forces in North-West EUROPE'. And to this end the Combined Chiefs would

> endeavour to assemble the strongest possible forces (subject to prior commitments in other theatres) in constant readiness to re-enter the Continent if GERMAN resistance is weakened to the required extent in 1943. In the meantime the Combined Chiefs of Staff must be prepared to order such limited operations as may be practicable with the forces and material available.

Specifically, COSSAC were to prepare plans for:

> (a) An elaborate camouflage and deception scheme extending over the whole summer with a view to pinning the enemy in the WEST and keeping alive the expectation of large scale cross-Channel operations in 1943. This would include at least one amphibious feint with the object of bringing on an air battle employing the Metropolitan Royal Air Force and the US Eighth Air Force.
> (b) A return to the Continent in the event of GERMAN disintegration at any time from now onwards with whatever forces may be available at the time.
> (c) A full scale assault against the Continent in 1944 as early as possible.

A month later, following the 'Trident' conference of May 1943 in Washington, Morgan received a supplementary directive from the Combined Chiefs. The initial landings of the full-scale assault were to be made by the Anglo-Canadian armies based in south-east England together with the advance elements of the US armies already assembling in the south-west. Then the main bodies of the US armies would sail direct from the United States to the bridgehead. No fewer than 100 divisions would thereby be assembled on the Continent to complete the destruction of German power. The directive said that a total of twenty-nine divisions could be available for the assault and immediate build-up. Of these, five infantry divisions were to be simultaneously loaded in the landing craft, with two more to follow as soon as the landing craft could return for them, and two airborne (parachute and glider-borne) divisions were to be inserted, making a total of nine assault divisions – possibly with the addition of a French division. The remaining twenty divisions would be available for movement to the lodgement area as quickly as it could be secured and the logistic buildup achieved. Plans were therefore to be drawn up to seize and develop continental ports in order that the initial assault and buildup of forces might be augmented at the rate of three to five divisions per month. (In the earlier phases of the assault, however, supply would have to take place over the beaches until the ports could be captured and put into working order, the assumption being that the Germans would have carried out extensive demolitions.) The target date for the operation was 1 May 1944, and the outline plans were to be in the hands of the Combined Chiefs of Staff by 1 August 1943.

COSSAC's key task, of course, was to determine where (c), the invasion, should take place. This really had to be addressed in three parts: getting to the beaches, getting across the beaches, and then getting beyond them. Morgan had stressed in his April staff briefing that

> our ultimate object is to wage successful war on land in the heart of EUROPE against the main body of the GERMAN strategic reserve. It is true that we have to cross the enemy's beaches, *but that to us must be merely an episode* [emphasis added]. True, it is a vital episode and, if it is not successful, the whole expedition will fail. We must plan for the crossing of the beaches, but let us make sure that we get that part of the plan in its right perspective – as a passing phase.

It was a passing phase that others, too, had been considering, to varying degrees, for some time. Not least among them was General Sir Bernard Paget, Commander-in-Chief, Home Forces, who in late 1942 (once the immediate threat of invasion was past), quite unbidden, had produced an appreciation – a feasibility study – for the invasion of France.* In March 1943 he'd passed this to the War Office, who in turn passed it to Morgan. Paget had concluded that there were but two options: the Pas de Calais and Normandy (specifically the Calvados Coast, the Bay of the Seine). Geographically, the Pas de Calais made the most sense. The Strait of Dover is but two dozen miles at its narrowest: Allied landing craft could therefore reach the invasion beaches quickly, and might even make more than one round-trip per day. On the face of it, therefore, surprise would be easier to achieve using this route; but in fact, taking into account the problem of concealing the buildup, Morgan would conclude that surprise would actually be harder to achieve here. Besides, Dover and Folkestone harbours were too small to assemble the major part of the force, so a lot of water would have to be crossed anyway from the more westerly Channel ports. Air cover would unquestionably be easier to provide, and if there'd been any doubt before the Dieppe raid that air supremacy was a prerequisite, there certainly wasn't afterwards. There was further temptation in the much greater proximity of the Pas de Calais to the invasion's ultimate objective – Berlin. However, the object of Overlord was to gain a lodgement area from which further offensive operations could be developed, and in that sense the distance to Berlin was immaterial.

The Germans had made their own appreciation, too, and had

---

* A military appreciation was an assessment of all options for an operation, stopping short of an actual plan, but in such detail that a third party could, after the decision on the course to be adopted, draw up a plan.

evidently also come to the conclusion that – surprise notwithstanding – the Pas de Calais offered the invader the most advantages. Or, at least, that it was the greater threat, and perhaps the greater danger. For, as Morgan observed bleakly, 'The Pas de Calais is the most strongly defended area on the whole French coast.' Perhaps they'd done as thorough an appreciation as Morgan, and concluded that without a port, an invasion would not be sustainable – and that if it were routed through Normandy, taking Cherbourg quickly and intact would be essential and also impossible. The Normandy coast, then, was a place for raiding – raiding on a large scale, even; but not for invasion. This conclusion, of course, would present the Allies with a significant opportunity for deception and thus surprise, which, after overwhelming strength, is the greatest advantage a general can hope for.

Nevertheless, to minimize pre-conceived bias, Morgan got his staff to prepare arguments for *both* invasion sites. And to reduce bias even more, instead of having all the staff examine both options, he divided them: the Americans would argue for Normandy (between Dieppe and Cherbourg), the British for the Calais area.

In the end, when the staff had chewed over every conceivable consideration, Morgan concluded that Normandy must be the target, remarking that '[the] Germans consider a landing there unlikely to be successful'.* Its two greatest drawbacks were, first, that there was no decent harbour; and second, that, unlike the Pas de Calais, the

---

* On 25 October 1943 the German C-in-C in the West, Generalfeldmarschall Gerd von Rundstedt, submitted an assessment of German defences for Hitler's consideration. In it he was certain the attack would come in the Calais area. How Morgan reached this conclusion isn't wholly clear. It is possible that 'Ultra' played a part – secret intelligence obtained through Bletchley Park's cracking of German Enigma encoding machine cyphers.

country beyond the beaches was bosky, *le bocage* – thick hedgerows, sunken lanes, orchards. And the roads led south and east, not north and east. These, however, were drawbacks in the third part of the operation; and although the third part was what Overlord was all about – waging war in the heart of Europe against the main body of the German strategic reserve – first getting to the beaches and then getting across them were the harder, the most complex and the most perilous parts.

Supply across the beaches was a prerequisite of the Normandy plan, and the difficulties could not be over-estimated. Fortunately, others had been thinking about this too. In July 1940, again at Churchill's urging, Combined Operations Headquarters (COH) had been set up to harass the Germans in raids carried out by combined naval and army forces, and in October 1941 Commodore Lord Louis Mountbatten was appointed its chief. In August 1942 COH mounted a large-scale raid on the German-occupied port of Dieppe, midway between Calais and the Calvados Coast, with the ostensible aim of destroying coastal defences and port structures in use by the Germans, but in addition – or even primarily – of testing the feasibility of such a landing and gathering relevant intelligence. It was, however, little short of a complete disaster. Aerial and naval support proved insufficient, the tanks couldn't get off the beach and the infantry couldn't take the town. Of the 6,000 or so men who landed, mostly Canadian, within ten hours 3,623 had been killed, wounded or taken prisoner. The RAF lost 106 aircraft, double the Luftwaffe's toll, and the Royal Navy thirty-three landing craft and a destroyer. It would have been difficult not to learn lessons from this fiasco – if only negative ones. As the Duke of Wellington said after a similarly ill-fated expedition, to Flanders in 1793–4: 'At least I learned what not to do, and that is always a valuable lesson.' There are, and were, of course, other ways to learn; but that's by the by.

When, where and how the solution to supplying the landing

forces across the beaches came about, and whose idea it was, is the stuff of legend, and difficult to pin down. But one key moment came at a conference held to discuss the lessons of the Dieppe raid soon afterwards, when a member of Morgan's staff, Captain John Hughes-Hallett RN, who'd been the naval commander at Dieppe, made an almost throwaway remark: 'If we can't capture ports, we must build them.' Now, at Norfolk House as head of the naval staff, he was able to press his case. Fortunately there'd been preliminary studies. As early as May 1942, COH had been thinking about 'piers for use on beaches', as Mountbatten put it in a memorandum to Churchill.

At the end of June 1943, a conference codenamed 'Rattle' was held at Largs in Ayrshire – at HMS *Warren*, No. 4 Combined Training Centre. Chaired by Mountbatten and attended by Morgan and forty other generals, admirals and air marshals, plus twenty senior US and Canadian officers, it resolved many of the technical questions, including supply across the beaches – concepts and proposals that would develop into what became known as the 'Mulberry' harbours. Innovative schemes abounded. When Morgan had addressed his staff in April he'd told them that they'd be planning 'mainly by the co-ordination of effort already being exerted in a hundred and one directions'. That figure was no exaggeration, in its order of magnitude at least: ideas and initiatives were burgeoning at all levels as a result of the enormous expansion of the British armed forces and the harnessing of civilian expertise. The challenge facing COSSAC and COH was to identify, evaluate and keep track of them, and the Largs conference did a lot in that regard.

One of the best-known of these initiatives was the 79th Armoured Division, an experimental force of armoured vehicles adapted for specialist tasks, especially in the assault across the beaches, and known colloquially as 'Hobart's funnies'. Major-General Percy Hobart, late of the Royal Engineers and Royal Tank Regiment, was nearing sixty when in October 1942 Brooke put him in command of the division.

His 'back story' is interesting in that it explains much of his single-mindedness in the job. Hobart – 'Hobo' to his (not many) friends – whose sister had been married to Montgomery (she died in 1937), was commissioned into the Royal Engineers just after the Boer War, and transferred to the Royal Tank Corps after the Great War. In 1934 he commanded the first permanent armoured brigade in Britain and was made Inspector Royal Tank Corps. Three years later he was appointed Deputy Director of Staff Duties (Armoured Fighting Vehicles) and soon afterwards Director of Military Training as a major-general. But in 1940 he was sent home from the Middle East, where he'd formed the 'Mobile Force (Egypt)', from which chrysalis 7th Armoured Division had emerged. His views on the employment of armour had clashed with almost everyone else's. In high dudgeon, he resigned his commission, joined the Home Guard and in Dad's Army fashion took the rank of lance-corporal and charge of the defences of his home village, Chipping Camden. But when the German *Blitzkrieg* of 1940 had seemed to justify his unconventional ideas, at Churchill's instigation he was reinstated to the active list and assigned to training the 11th Armoured Division, before Brooke put him to the task of raising and leading the 79th.

Driven by the lessons of Dieppe, Hobart's technical solutions were not only 'funny' in the 'peculiar' sense, but also sometimes comical in appearance. Nevertheless, although one or two ideas exceeded themselves, the majority answered well. No matter what the problem identified by the planners, Hobo's staff always had a solution. The sand was too soft for wheeled vehicles: 'bobbin tanks' unrolled flexible trackway like a carpet salesman. The promenade-wall was too high for tanks to climb: 'Ark' (armoured ramp carrier) tanks drove against the wall to allow other tanks to drive over them in a slow-motion game of leapfrog. Mines were sown everywhere: 'flail tanks' with heavy chains attached to a spinning drum that projected from the glacis would thrash the ground to detonate them prematurely. Whatever the problem, there was one of Hobo's 'funnies' to deal with it. Not only was D-Day the longest-planned battle in the history of warfare; never was so much technical energy applied to a single day's fighting. For the stakes, of course, could not have been higher.

The most ambitious, most extraordinary of the 'funnies' began its work well before anyone reached the shore, however. The infantry needed intimate fire support as soon as they hit the beach – indeed, just before they got to it – but getting tanks in with them was always going to be difficult because their landing craft, much bigger than those of the infantry, were even more vulnerable both to fire from the gun emplacements and to the explosive obstacles with which the Germans had studded the low-water line.* What they needed was a tank that could be launched out of range of fire from the shore to swim to the beach and arrive a few minutes before the assaulting infantry.

The concept had been in development since 1940. Indeed, the idea could be traced back to 1918, when the War Office was toying with inflatable buoyancy aids for the Mark IX tank. These had to be so large, however, that the design – mercifully – was quickly deemed impractical. In 1940, the Hungarian-born engineer Nicholas Straussler solved the problem by devising a flotation screen of waterproofed canvas which when erected encompassed the top half of the tank, creating in effect an upper canvas hull. This gave sufficient buoyancy, and with a freeboard of some 3–4 feet, the appearance of an innocuous small boat; on beaching, the screen

---

* The 'Atlantic Wall' stretched from the north of Norway to the Spanish border, and was at its most formidable on the old south Saxon shore, from the Scheldt to Brittany. The rows of steel stakes on the beaches, many with landmines attached, were likened to a petrified forest.

could be quickly collapsed to allow the tank its full mobility and firepower. Straussler demonstrated the buoyancy principle to Churchill by placing a brick in a canvas bucket and floating it in a paddling pool.*

The first trials took place in June 1941 in Brent Reservoir with a Tetrarch tank, which weighed 7.5 tons, followed by successful sea trials at Portsmouth. The mechanism's feasibility having been established, a heavier Valentine tank was adapted, with propellers driven directly from the gearbox – hence the term 'Duplex-Drive' (DD) – and trialled in May 1942. It performed well, although it subsequently sank during a trial in which it was subjected to machine-gun fire. The canvas screens were never going to be able to withstand bullets or shrapnel, but so low in the water the risk of both was reckoned acceptable, and the following month some 450 Valentine DDs were ordered. However, when in 1943 the first American Sherman tanks began to appear, it was soon clear that despite their extra weight – some 35 tons laden, twice that of the Valentine, necessitating a taller flotation screen of some 8 feet to give a freeboard of 3–4 feet – they were far more suitable, not only as battle tanks but for the seaborne assault. Because the Sherman's 75 mm barrel was considerably shorter than the Valentine's, it could be launched with its gun forward and therefore instantly ready to fire on 'touch-down' when the screen was collapsed. Nevertheless, the majority of the US, British and Canadian DD crews would do their preliminary training with the Valentine before conversion training – some of it very last-minute – on the Sherman. For the British and

---

* A vehicle's *displacement* (the occupation by a submerged body or part of a body of a volume which would otherwise be occupied by a fluid) being usually greater than its weight, it will therefore float. Heavily armoured vehicles, however, will usually have a density greater than water (their weight in kilograms exceeding their volume in litres) and therefore need additional buoyancy aids. These can take the form of inflatable flotation devices, much like the sides of a rubber dinghy, or a waterproof fabric skirt raised from the top perimeter of the vehicle to increase its displacement.

Canadian crews, that training began as early as April 1943, even before the Largs conference. The regiment that would eventually lead the assault on Sword Beach was the 13th/18th Royal Hussars. Their crews were simply told that they were 'to be put ashore in an entirely novel manner', and then made to sign the Official Secrets Act. Only on arriving in Suffolk later that month and parading on the edge of Fritton Lake did they learn they were to be a 'water assault regiment' – and what exactly that meant.

COSSAC's tight deadline to submit an outline plan to the Combined Chiefs by the end of July had driven a punishing schedule. As Morgan remarked to one of his staff, with a dry reference to Churchill's tribute to the Battle of Britain pilots, 'Never were so few asked to do so much in so short a time.' Nevertheless, they'd done it, and the Largs conference confirmed in Morgan's mind the choice of Normandy. On 15 July he submitted his 'Operation Overlord: Report and Appreciation' to the (British) war cabinet via the Chiefs of Staff Committee through whom his directive required him to work – 143 pages and thirteen maps. In the covering letter, Morgan wrote: 'I have come to the conclusion that, in view of the limitations imposed by my directives, we may be assured of a reasonable chance of success on May 1, 1944, only if we concentrate our efforts on an assault across the Norman beaches about Bayeux.' And he gave three conditions necessary for success: a 'substantial reduction' in German fighter strength in north-west Europe; no more than twelve German mobile divisions in France, of which no more than three would oppose the landings on D-Day itself; and a buildup of no more than fifteen German divisions in the theatre in the two months following the landings. And, of course, that at least two 'synthetic harbours' would be operating quickly.

Churchill wasn't convinced by the conclusions. Four days later he minuted the chiefs of staff: 'I do not believe that twenty-seven Anglo-American divisions are sufficient for Overlord,' citing 'the extraordinary fighting efficiency of the German army and the much larger forces they could so readily bring to bear against our troops, even if the landings were successfully accomplished'. He didn't specify, though he undoubtedly had in mind, that for the first time Allied troops would be up against SS units, whose fanaticism and ruthlessness would be a considerable force multiplier. Yet Morgan had had to build with the bricks given him, and this Churchill recognized perfectly well. To COSSAC's three conditions for success (four – including the Mulberries – in the case of Normandy), he added another: that Stalin must initiate an attack on the Eastern Front that would tie down German reserves. Whether he'd much confidence that Stalin would ever do so is open to question, but either way Churchill's wholehearted commitment to Overlord was still some way off.*

The US chiefs of staff, having been kept in the picture informally throughout, considered the appreciation and plan formally on 5 August, prior to discussions among Churchill, FDR and the Combined Chiefs in the middle of that month at the 'Quadrant' conference in Quebec. Whatever Churchill's misgivings and his hopes that the 'Mediterranean strategy' would obviate the need for Overlord (the invasion of Italy had begun in July with landings in Sicily – Operation Husky – and Italian capitulation looked increasingly likely), decisions had to be taken.† The upshot was that the target date for Overlord to begin – D-Day – was set for 1 May 1944,

---

* In the event, Stalin did agree and did deliver: Operation Bagration (named after the great tsarist general of the Napoleonic Wars) was launched with spectacular success on 22 June 1944, the third anniversary of Operation Barbarossa, the German invasion of Russia.

† On 19 July Churchill had minuted the chiefs of staff that he'd 'no doubt that the right strategy for 1944 is a) Maximum post-"Husky" ' – by which he meant that in the event of the expected Italian collapse (and the perceived subsequent German difficulties in holding on in Italy), the Allies should develop thrusts into southern France or north-east towards Vienna, while simultaneously clearing the Balkans and Greece.

though the supreme commander was still not named. Although earlier in the year Churchill and FDR had agreed he should be British – because the Americans were commanding in North Africa, the numbers of British (including Canadian) and American troops in the Overlord landings would be roughly equal, and the invasion would be mounted from Britain – and Churchill had told Brooke that the command would be his, by the time of Quadrant he'd realized that the huge buildup of American divisions after the landings made this wholly unrealistic.* He and FDR therefore agreed that Overlord's supreme commander would be American, while the British would take charge in the Mediterranean. Brooke, according to Churchill, 'bore the great disappointment with soldierly dignity'. And doubtless Churchill bore it with relief, for he knew he'd not find another to fill Brooke's boots.

With COSSAC's plan approved in principle, Morgan was now told to proceed with detailed planning and preparations. And once back from Quadrant, Churchill, despite his persistent hope that Overlord wouldn't in the end be necessary, continued to harry his staff on every detail as if it were now a certainty.

In his covering letter, Morgan had said that it was

> necessary, if my plan be approved, to adopt the outlook that Operation 'Overlord' is even now in progress, and to take all possible steps to see that all agencies that can be brought to bear are, from now on, co-ordinated in their action as herein below described, so as to bring about the state of affairs that we would have exist on the chosen day of assault.

The (b) of his minute was Operation Jupiter, the invasion of north Norway, which he argued could be prepared under cover of Overlord.

* A great deal more than Overlord was discussed at Quadrant, of course – the Mediterranean, the Far East, the strategic bombing campaign over Germany – but these are topics not directly relevant to this narrative.

This was certainly the sort of language Churchill liked, and one area of activity in particular attracted his personal attention – the 'synthetic harbours', or Mulberries. The story goes that one of Mountbatten's scientific advisers, Professor John Bernal, had floated paper boats in the bath in the prime minister's suite aboard *Queen Mary* during the first crossing to Washington, agitating the water to simulate waves, then used a loofah to demonstrate the pacifying effect of breakwaters, and that Churchill had at once dashed off a memo demanding action. The story doesn't perhaps bear too close an examination, but throughout the summer and autumn of 1943 various floating breakwater devices were trialled and then abandoned, including the 'Lilo', which had flexible rubber air-filled chambers on the outer edges to counter the heavy stresses set up by the waves on a rigid body, and the 'bubble' breakwater, in which air bubbles were used to create a surface current to counteract the waves. Instead, floating steel and concrete cruciform 'Bombardons' 200 yards long and 25 wide were chosen. Trials were also carried out with concrete caissons ('Phoenix') and surplus ships ('Gooseberries') towed to a given point and sunk, block-ships being an old device whose breakwater effects had long been observed. Slowly a plan emerged for Bombardon units to provide outer anchorages inside which the Phoenix caissons would form harbours to allow ships to unload whatever the weather. Gooseberries would be used to give shelter for the landing craft in the follow-up, to be in position on D+1 (the first day after the initial landing).

Next, connections from the Phoenix caissons to the shore ('Whales') had to be devised: no easy proposition where there was such a great tidal range. Fortunately, fuel resupply by tanker vehicles or jerry-cans via Mulberry would be only a temporary expedient. Experiments were already under way with submarine pipelines that would be laid from shore to shore – from the Isle of Wight to the Cherbourg peninsula (over 70 miles), and later across the Dover Strait – dubbed Operation

'PLUTO' (Pipe-Line Underwater Transport of Oil; or, as some had it, 'Pipeline under the Ocean').* But for Mulberry as a whole, 'difficulties abounded', says COSSAC's official history, with the understatement perhaps that only ultimate success permits: 'Time was short, labour was scarce, constructional facilities were lacking, the weather interfered with practical trials, and the spheres of responsibility were uncertain.'

Morgan remained concerned that he'd still no 'big name' supreme commander to lever extra resources and bang heads together. This difficulty was in part eased by the Combined Chiefs' issuing an addition to their original directive after Quadrant, to the effect that, pending the appointment of the supreme commander or his deputy, Morgan himself was to be responsible for 'taking the necessary executive action to implement those plans approved by the Combined Chiefs of Staff'.† Only in December, however, did the various actors really begin pulling together – COSSAC, the Admiralty, the

---

* In the event, PLUTO wasn't the success hoped for, or as legend has it (if an understandable legend for its sheer ambition). The first line to France was laid on 12 August, but failed when it was caught by the anchor of an escorting destroyer. A further three would be laid, but it wasn't until 22 September, nearly three months late, that a pipeline finally became operational. As the fighting moved closer to Germany, seventeen lines were laid from Kent to Calais (Ambleteuse, to be precise) but PLUTO's overall success was limited: only some 8% of the fuel delivered between D-Day and VE-Day came 'under the Ocean'. As Sir Donald Banks, Director-General of the War Office's Petroleum Warfare Department, wrote: 'The technique of cable laying had been mastered but we were not yet sufficiently versed in the practice of connecting the shore ends, nor in effecting repairs to the undersea leaks which were caused fairly close inshore through these faulty concluding operations': *Flame over Britain: A Personal Narrative of Petroleum Warfare* (London, 1946).

† Montgomery too recognized the unfairness of Morgan's situation: '[Morgan] had to work on information supplied by the Combined Chiefs of Staff as to the forces which would be available; he had no alternative': *Memoirs of Field-Marshal Montgomery* (London, 1958). A *commander* would have been, and in the event was, in a position to insist upon greater resources.

War Office, the Ministry of Supply (and the respective US agencies).
Men were now released from the army to provide the urgently
needed skilled labour, while increasingly the unskilled work was
done by Irish labour (an often overlooked Irish contribution to the
war effort). This was due in part to the efforts of Major-General Harold Wernher, an engineer and pre-war territorial who in August had
been appointed 'Co-ordinator of Ministry and Science Facilities' to
get a grip on Mulberry. In January he was able to report that they
would indeed be ready by the target date of 1 May.

And only in December, too, was the question of the supremo
resolved. At the Teheran conference ('Eureka') – the first meeting of
the 'Big Three', running from 28 November to 1 December – Stalin
demanded to know who was to command Overlord. It wasn't, of
course, something he needed to know, and he couldn't have taken
objection to a particular general, even if he'd knowledge of him. The
point was that without a named commander, the invasion – the
Second Front for which he'd been pressing for more than a year – was
hardly a reality, certainly not a credible one. And so FDR, whose privilege it was, at last named the man. It was not Marshall, as he himself
had hoped; it was Eisenhower, just (the month before) fifty-three,
who'd not heard a shot fired in anger until the year before, and even
then only distantly. For just as Churchill would conclude that he
couldn't do without Brooke, his 'master of strategy', so FDR decided
that he needed Marshall in Washington to see the war to a close –
which, of course, meant the subsequent defeat of Japan.

The question was now who would command the ground forces –
21st Army Group, consisting of 2nd (British) Army and 1st (Canadian)
Army, and the US 1st Army until the buildup of troops permitted the
formation of 12th (US) Army Group – during the initial landings.*

---

* An army group is a four-star (full general's) command of two or more discrete armies,
and is usually, but not always – one exception being the later part of the Normandy

There were three contenders: Montgomery, whose stock stood high after Alamein and Sicily; General Sir Harold Alexander, commanding 15th Army Group in Italy; and General Sir Bernard Paget, who already had some title to it, being in charge of Headquarters 21st Army Group, established in July to direct the armies' training and administration. Eisenhower suggested to Brooke that General Sir Henry ('Jumbo') Maitland Wilson, Commander-in-Chief Middle East, replace him as supreme commander in the Mediterranean, and 'Monty' replace 'Alex', who would then come home to command the land forces for Overlord. Brooke agreed that Wilson should take over from Eisenhower, but was adamant that Montgomery – three years older than 'Ike', but with experience of command at every level, a good deal of it in battle – should command on Overlord. For while Brooke had the highest regard for Paget, he hadn't commanded a large formation in action; nor did he believe that Alex was up to it. For a week or so in mid-December the decision hung in the balance, before Churchill (and the Combined Chiefs) agreed that Montgomery would command. On New Year's Eve, having handed over 8th Army in Italy, 'Monty' arrived in

---

campaign, when Eisenhower took charge of the two army groups – associated with a particular 'front' (indeed, the Russians called their army groups 'fronts'). An army is a wholly self-contained command, capable of planning and executing the land element of a campaign, and is usually led by a three-star but sometimes a four-star officer. An army consists of two or more army corps (three-star commands), which are themselves capable of sustained operations but are dependent for overall operational direction and logistics on the army level of command. A corps in 1944 would typically comprise three or four divisions, with additional corps assets such as intelligence and heavy artillery. A division, numbering about 18,000 men, consisted usually of three brigades (infantry, armoured, or mixed) and additional assets such reconnaissance, signals, heavy artillery and specialist engineers for tasks such as bridging. In 1944 the division was the real focus of tactical fighting power, with the corps commander allocating and reallocating assets such as heavy artillery as the battle developed.

Marrakesh, where Churchill, having flown to Tunis from Cairo after Teheran, was recovering from pneumonia.*

The plans for the D-Day landings were now about to start taking real shape.

---

* In the entry for 11 December 1943 in Brooke's diaries, there's a startling aside after Eisenhower's suggested substitutions: 'This almost fits in with my idea, except I would invert Alex and Monty, *but I don't much mind* [emphasis added].' But then, in a post-war addendum, Brooke writes: 'I am surprised . . . that I wrote . . . "I don't mind much"! I certainly minded a great deal and would have had little confidence in Alex running that show': *War Diaries 1939–1945: Field Marshal Lord Alanbrooke*, ed. Alex Danchev and Dan Todman (London, 2001). What is the explanation? Perhaps because the diary that day was written after a flight from Cairo to Tunis on which he'd been unable to sleep and a day in conference with Eisenhower and Air Chief Marshal Tedder, commander of the Allied air forces in the Mediterranean and Eisenhower's deputy (designate) for Overlord. He'd certainly expressed his concerns about what he perceived to be Alexander's limitations in earlier entries, in unequivocal terms, and likewise his confidence in Montgomery.

3

UNITY OF COMMAND

For I have served him, and the man commands
Like a full soldier.

Shakespeare, *Othello*

In the end, the intelligence, character and experience of the commander is probably the greatest factor in shaping the battle. Unless his force is caught entirely on the hop, it's his decision where exactly, when and how to give battle. Eisenhower had his doubts about the commander of the land forces for D-Day. In March 1943 he'd confided to Marshall that Montgomery was

of different calibre from some of the outstanding British commanders you have met. He is unquestionably able, but very conceited. For your most secret and confidential information, I will give you my opinion, which is that he is so proud of his successes to date that he will never willingly make a single move until he is absolutely certain of success – in

other words, until he had concentrated enough resources so that any-
body could practically guarantee the outcome.*

These remarks were made when US forces had lately begun fighting in Tunisia, alongside the British for the first time. The following
month, Montgomery wrote to Brooke in similarly 'cautious' terms:
'[Eisenhower] is a very nice chap, I should say quite good on the political side. But I can also say, quite definitely, that he knows nothing
whatever about how to make war or to fight battles; he should be
kept away from all that business if we want to win this war.'

It didn't look promising.

What are we to make of their opinions? Perhaps it's best, in the
words of a song written at the time, to eliminate the negative and
accentuate the positive: Monty would leave nothing to chance if he
could help it, and Ike had the necessary qualities to be an *Allied*
supreme commander. The important thing was for both to recognize
this when exasperated with the other's defects.

It is fair to say that Eisenhower got this better than Montgomery did.

Also, although Eisenhower may only have been a lieutenant-
colonel with no operational experience in 1940, when Montgomery,
a major-general, was commanding a division in Belgium during the
German *Blitzkrieg*, Eisenhower understood more of war and battles
than Montgomery gave him credit for. Or, at least, he did by October
1943, after nine months' experience of war with the Germans.
Indeed, the most astute British officers conceded that the Americans
at all levels were quick learners; and the US army boldly promoted
the quickest, while unsentimentally removing the slowest. In October 1943, when Marshall was still earmarked for supreme commander
(at least in his own mind), Eisenhower was shown the COSSAC plans

---

* Quoted (along with much other unfraternal opinion) in Omar Bradley (and Clay
Blair), *A General's Life: An Autobiography* (New York, 1983).

and asked his opinion. Morgan, working only with the bricks he'd been given, had proposed a (sea) landing by three divisions, with two in reserve. Eisenhower thought it too weak; he suggested an increase to five, with two in reserve. Montgomery would insist on even more, but Eisenhower's misgivings – and his readiness to express them – suggest more than just an affable figurehead in the Alex mould.

When Montgomery flew to Tunis to meet Churchill at the end of December 1943, he'd called on Eisenhower in Algiers en route. Here they'd discussed the COSSAC plan and Montgomery agreed the troops were too few and the frontage too narrow. When he met Churchill, however, he apparently pretended he'd not seen the plan before. 'Apparently' because it's not entirely clear from the record whether he'd actually *seen* the plan at Algiers or been given a résumé by Walter Bedell Smith, Eisenhower's chief of staff; still, either way it was more than a shade disingenuous – and perilous – to omit any mention of discussions with Eisenhower. That said, a commander has an image to maintain with a political master, particularly a commander who's about to take charge of a great national make-or-break operation, and who must answer throughout to both a military superior (Eisenhower) and a political one (Churchill). That night he took the COSSAC plan to bed, and the next morning gave the PM a handwritten memo telling him it wouldn't work unless expanded to a five-division sea-landing (with all the considerable increase in naval capacity that demanded), augmented by three airborne divisions – i.e. landed by parachute and glider.

Eisenhower reached his new headquarters – SHAEF, Supreme Headquarters Allied Expeditionary Force (in essence, COSSAC 'weaponized') – at Bushy Park in south-west London on 17 January 1944. Montgomery arrived at his headquarters, which by astonishing coincidence were at his old school, St Paul's, in not-too-distant Hammersmith, soon afterwards. Authoritative directives and instructions – orders – could now at last be issued, first of which was

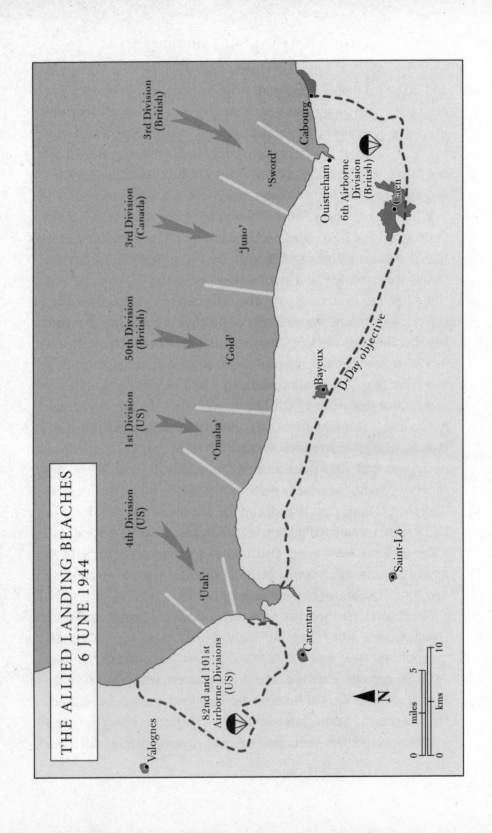

the Combined Chiefs of Staff directive on 12 February formally instructing Eisenhower to plan and execute a cross-Channel invasion of German-occupied western Europe. The target date was pushed on by a month, however, to the end of May, to allow more time for the buildup of the extra forces and logistical support. A month later, SHAEF issued a detailed directive to the naval, land and air subordinate commanders: Admiral Sir Bertram Ramsay, the Allied Naval Commander, Expeditionary Force; Montgomery, Commander-in-Chief, 21st Army Group; and Air Chief Marshal Sir Trafford Leigh-Mallory, Air Commander-in-Chief, Allied Expeditionary Air Force. It confirmed Overlord's objective – to secure a lodgement area from which further offensive operations could be developed – and that the operation was to be carried out in two phases. Phase I would be an assault landing on the Normandy beaches between Quinéville in the west and Cabourg-les-Bains in the east, followed by the early capture and development of airfield sites and the port of Cherbourg. Then, in Phase II, the area would be enlarged to secure the whole of the Cherbourg, Loire and Brittany group of ports. The supreme commander would 'control and co-ordinate the planning and execution of the operation as a whole', while C-in-C 21st Army Group would be 'responsible for the command of all ground forces engaged in the operation until such time as the Supreme Commander allocates an area of responsibility to the Commanding General, First (US) Army Group'.

One of COSSAC's stipulations had been that the initial assault must include as many men as possible with recent battle experience. Morgan had told his principal staff officers as early as May 1943 that most of the US troops as well as many of the British forces taking part would be new to the realities of war, and that even the most intensive training and 'battle-inoculation' – with live ammunition under simulated battle conditions – couldn't achieve the same results as actual fighting. 'As those of us know who have taken part in battle,' he said, 'it is one thing to manoeuvre freely when secure in the knowledge that the man behind the gun is doing his best to miss us, but it is quite another thing when that same man is doing his utmost to liquidate you.' Complete battle-tried formations (brigades and even divisions) from North Africa were needed, he said; men who understood battle and who'd inculcate the offensive spirit into the novices – 'high grade stock from which we must breed with the utmost rapidity'. And the same applied to the staffs and logistic and administrative troops, and indeed the air-force ground crews.

The Combined Chiefs agreed, and at Quebec in August they directed that three British and four US divisions should be returned to Britain, beginning in November – not necessarily for the assault landings, but for the subsequent offensive operations. This made sound sense, of course. But it would create problems, too, for some of these troops thought they'd done enough fighting – North Africa, Sicily, Italy – and that it was now the others' turn, those who'd been training all that time in England. And, indeed, some experienced units, and even some commanders, would prove distinctly wary in battle once in Normandy. Besides the feeling of having done their bit, it was a maxim that while moral courage increased with the exercise of it, physical courage decreased. Field Marshal Sir William Slim, who commanded 14th Army in Burma, likened it to a bank account: being morally courageous – 'doing the right thing' when it was easier not to – deposited money in the account, while acts of physical courage *drew* on the account, which could eventually be overdrawn.*

---

* 'All men have some degree of physical courage, it is surprising how much. Courage you know is having money in the bank. We start with a certain capital of courage, some large, some small, and we proceed to draw on our balance, for, don't forget, courage is an expendable quality. We can use it up. If there are heavy, and, what is more serious, if there are continuous calls on our courage we begin to overdraw. If we go on overdrawing, we go bankrupt – we break down': Field Marshal Sir William Slim, *Courage and Other Broadcasts* (London, 1957).

One division brought home from Italy and earmarked for the landings, the 50th (Northumbrian), known colloquially as the 'Tyne-Tees', a Territorial Army formation – that is, consisting in large part of pre-war volunteer part-timers – had already seen a show of dissension. In September 1943, 200 or so troops from this division and the 51st (Highland), veterans of the North African campaign, some just recovered from wounds or sickness, refused to follow orders to join other units. They were part of a reinforcement of 1,500, including fresh recruits, that had sailed from Tripoli to – as the veterans thought – rejoin their old battalions in Sicily and then return home to prepare for the invasion. Instead, at sea they were told they were being taken to Salerno, just south of Naples, to join the 46th and 56th Divisions, which had suffered heavy losses in the recent landings there. Many of them felt they'd been deliberately misled; and then at Salerno things were made worse by poor administrative arrangements. They were angry and frustrated, and they had a legitimate gripe, although picking and choosing where and with whom you were prepared to fight was hardly a privilege that could be guaranteed in war. A thousand or so, including the fresh recruits, were persuaded without too much trouble to give up their remonstrations and join their new units, and after a while some 200 of the veterans followed suit, but 300 more set up camp in a nearby field and simply refused to budge. The corps commander, the highly regarded Lieutenant-General Dick McCreery, came and addressed them. He admitted a mistake had been made, explained the situation at Salerno and promised that they'd rejoin their old units once the bridgehead there was secure – the immediate concern. And, of course, he also warned them of the consequences of mutiny in wartime. A hundred of them then buckled to, but the rest continued to refuse to be posted to unfamiliar units. The mutineers, as now they were, having failed to obey a lawful command, were shipped to Algeria and court-martialled. Three sergeants were sentenced to death, subsequently

commuted to twelve years' penal servitude (forced labour), with pro-
portionate punishments for the others.

It was an unedifying affair, but it serves – and served – as a reminder
that morale in war isn't a given.

It was also – *may* also have been – significant that the mutineers
were territorials. The Territorial Army (TA) originated in the volunteer movement of the mid-nineteenth century, in which groups
arose spontaneously and locally for home defence and with little
connection to the regular army, most of which was serving overseas.
It was more egalitarian than the regulars, the officers coming largely
from the middle class rather than the gentry, and the other ranks
from the artisan rather than the unskilled working class. It was less
deferential, less 'feudal'. Its members tended to believe they had
rights akin to those of workers in their civilian occupations, including the right to withdraw their labour – or, at least, to negotiate. This
had been a concern in the First World War. Many TA divisions performed admirably on the Western Front, but they were generally
regarded as 'unpredictable', more so even than the 'New Army' divisions which had been raised in 1914 and 1915 in tearing haste at
the bidding of the war minister, Field Marshal Lord Kitchener, and
incorporated in the regular army.

Morgan couldn't perhaps say it – or at least, couldn't put it in
writing – but the British 2nd Army, which was to see Overlord
through and serve beyond it, would have to include divisions that
were not just battle-experienced but regular. Indeed, they'd be
needed to bear the brunt of the fighting on D-Day. There were, however, only two available: the 3rd Infantry, which in the First World
War had gained the nickname the 'Iron Division', and had fought
skilfully in France and Belgium in 1940; and the Guards Armoured.
The others were fighting in Italy and the Far East. As early as December 1942, 3rd Division had been reassigned from home defence to be
the lead formation of any invasion of Europe – or occupation in the

unlikely case of a sudden German collapse – and training had begun accordingly. At several points in 1943 it looked as if the division would be sent to Italy, but as the probability of a cross-Channel invasion rose, Brooke confirmed its lead status (and that of Guards Armoured), and in December at Montgomery's recommendation he brought back Brigadier Tom Rennie from Italy to command.

Rennie was just forty-three. Commissioned in 1919, he'd been taken prisoner in 1940 as a major with the Black Watch (infantry) at Saint-Valéry-en-Caux on the Channel coast, but escaped a week later and made his way home by foot and bicycle through France, Spain and Portugal. He'd then taken command of the 5th Black Watch (TA) in North Africa, leading them at the battle of El Alamein, and afterwards of the 154th Infantry Brigade in the invasion of Sicily. Still a major after twenty years, then rising to major-general in three and a half years, and catapulted into command of the leading regular formation for Overlord – such are the fortunes of war.

The men of the 3rd Division themselves – of Guards Armoured too, as well as of the regular divisions in Italy and Burma – weren't by any means all pre-war regulars or even volunteers, for conscription had been introduced in 1939. In fact, the proportion of regulars in the 3rd Division was probably only 30–40 per cent. But the majority of the field officers (i.e. major to colonel) and senior NCOs were pre-war regulars, and the conscripts had been formed like regulars within the disciplinary regime of a regular battalion or regiment, and to a large extent therefore had absorbed its *esprit de corps*. Rather as HMS *Victory*, though most of her original timber has been replaced over the years, remains the *Victory*, so the '1st Loamshires', though many men had been posted out since Dunkirk and as many new ones had joined, were still the '1st Loamshires'.

The Guards Armoured Division, as the name implies, was predominantly a tank formation. Their role, clearly, would be in Phase II of Overlord and beyond – waging war in the heart of Europe against the main body of the German strategic reserve. The assault phase, which was now given the codename 'Neptune' (aptly, the Roman god of the sea), was quite evidently a job for infantry, albeit with armoured support. It followed, therefore, that the most vital sector of the British assault, the most decisive place of landing in the bay of Normandy (although they were all critical to gaining and securing a lodgement area) would fall to the 3rd Division. This would have given Montgomery a certain satisfaction, just as setting up headquarters in his old school had (indeed, taking the headmaster's office for his own), for he'd commanded the division during the battle of France.

Monty and his staff now began the detailed work on the landings, in particular the selection and allocation of beaches. There were to be five sectors (loosely called 'beaches'), one for each of the assault divisions – two British divisions and one Canadian in 2nd (British) Army, and two American in 1st (US) Army. Each beach sector was given a codename. The American sectors, the furthest west, were initially designated 'X-ray' and 'Yoke' – X and Y, according to the phonetic alphabet at that time – but these were later changed to 'Omaha' and 'Utah'. Why Omaha and Utah isn't entirely clear, but one story goes that they were selected at random, when General Omar Bradley, commanding 1st (US) Army, asked two NCOs where they were from. Their brevity seems fortuitous, but he may of course have rejected answers by NCOs from Mississippi and Massachusetts.

The three British sectors were labelled more methodically, but not at first entirely felicitously. For some reason it was thought useful to name each after a type of fish – Swordfish, Goldfish and Jellyfish – and then to drop the suffix in the operational orders. When Churchill was told, supposedly, he objected with predictable irritation: 'Sword' and 'Gold' were fine, but he wasn't about to send Canadians to die on a beach called 'Jelly'. (Sometimes the military mind can indeed be obtuse.) So 'Jelly' became 'Juno' – the mother of Mars and Bellona, the Roman god and goddess of war.

In fact, during the initial planning there was a sixth beach to the east of Sword: 'Band' beach. There is indeed a 'bandfish', whose habit is to burrow in sandy or muddy seabed – not a characteristic one would wish to associate with a beach assault, although as it isn't a fish native to Britain, Churchill was probably unaware of this. But the River Orne, with its mouth at Ouistreham, would have separated Band from the others, leaving the troops there in a perilous position if the Germans counter-attacked from the east, and the idea was abandoned.

Each sector – Utah, Omaha, Gold, Juno and Sword – comprised two or more beaches, named sequentially from the west according to the Allied phonetic alphabet at the time, and stretching from the Cotentin Peninsula to the mouth of the Orne: from 'How' Beach at Port-en-Bessin to 'Roger' at Ouistreham. In turn, each of these was further divided, but not evenly, into 'Green' (west), 'White' (centre) and 'Red' (east) areas, allowing the planners to be highly specific in both intelligence-gathering and allocation of tasks.

In early March, Montgomery's concept for the assault and subsequent offensive operations was agreed, and the layout – the sea approach and landings – for Neptune finalized. In other words, the shape of the battle of D-Day was fixed. The British would land in eastern Normandy between the Orne and Arromanches and take Caen, the key communications centre a dozen miles inland. This would cover the Americans' left flank as they landed in western Normandy and the Cotentin peninsula to seize Cherbourg. Both would then move deep inland, the British threatening to break out towards Paris by the most direct route, with the Americans covering their right flank and rear. That breakout attempt would be a feint, however, drawing the bulk of the German reserves on to it in order to leave the way open for the Americans, having seized Cherbourg, to move on west and take the remaining Brittany ports, then turning east to link up with the British. Together, the Allies would then begin the push

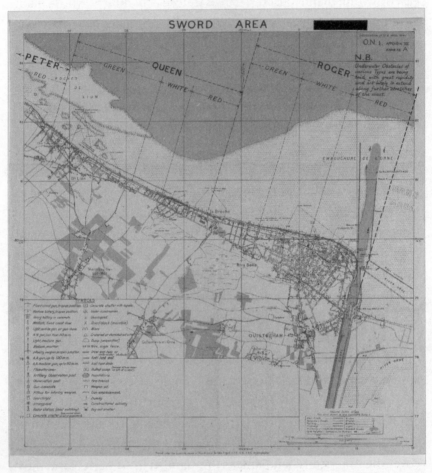

'No army in the history of war had such a wealth of intelligence on both the ground and the enemy' (p. 216). A section of one of the planning maps for Sword Beach. Similar and highly classified 'Bogus' maps with names of places disguised were issued for briefing and lower-level planning – for instance, Ouistreham became 'Oslo' and Caen 'Warsaw'. The topographical information and intelligence of enemy dispositions had come from multiple sources, principally aerial photo-reconnaissance and clandestine beach surveys, and also from the French Resistance and the Special Operations Executive.

towards the Seine on so broad a front that the Germans would have no opportunity to take them in either flank.

Although much has been written about the German belief in the superiority of American generalship – their praise of Patton, for example – and indeed much else, in fact at this stage of the war they believed quite the opposite, having seen the Americans' early mistakes in North Africa and to some extent in Italy. They, like the British, were slow to realize how quickly the Americans learned. So a British thrust for Caen would play to their expectations (once, that is, they were sure the Normandy landings weren't a diversion). Seizing Caen early was indeed central to Montgomery's plan – or, at least, the maximum effort to do so was. Clearly, therefore, the task would be assigned to the 3rd Division (in I Corps, which with VIII, XII and XXX Corps comprised 2nd Army), with its three regular infantry brigades (8th, 9th, 185th). The shortest route to Caen was across Sword Beach, and it followed that Sword would be the 3rd Division's landing place.

The topographical intelligence that the planners had gathered for the Allied landings was immense, from water depths, beach contours, gradients and tidal patterns to coastal obstructions such as reefs, soft sand patches or sandbars. Beyond the beaches the terrain had to be assessed for four purposes: defence (the lodgement); as a logistic base for subsequent operations; for 'advanced air landing grounds' (improvised airfields); and for routes inland for the breakout.

I (British) Corps' sector consisted of flat sandy beaches with rocky outcrops above the low-water mark except for short stretches at the mouth of the Rivers Seulles and Orne, with clay patches in the western half that might hamper vehicle movement. Generally, beyond the beaches lay sand dunes, but in places sea walls and low cliffs posed obstacles to getting off the beaches. Further inland the ground rose to 200 feet, through both rolling farmland and *bocage*. On the right (western) flank of the I Corps sector, the River Seulles and its tributaries created obstacles to wheeled movement, while on the left flank the Caen canal and the Orne, save for a very few bridges, would block all lateral movement – foot, wheeled or tracked. The water level in the canal was regulated by lock gates in Ouistreham defended by bunkers with armoured cupolas, and by a barrage in Caen. Beyond to the east, thickly wooded, dominating high ground divided the valley of the Orne from that of the Dives.

Within Sword sector, Ouistreham and the smaller holiday settlements of Hermanville and Lion-sur-Mer had many buildings that were suitable for the Germans to fortify, but would also serve as reference points for landing craft on the run-in. Beyond was a crescent of higher ground, a mile or so inland at its points and two at the centre, which gave a commanding view of the Channel and the far bank of the Orne; this the Germans had studded with strongpoints. Beyond this again was the Périers ridge, not very high, where the ground became more broken, interspersed with small villages connected by narrow roads. Just north of Caen, guarding its approaches, lay the thickly wooded Lébisey ridge, which then fell away to the city itself. The Germans had displaced civilians in large stretches of the Atlantic Wall to a depth of sometimes up to 15 miles, although in Normandy it was generally about 5 miles, with fishermen and farmers usually allowed to continue working. This undoubtedly gave them freer rein to fortify, but it also allowed the Allies to bombard the coastal strip with less regard to potential French casualties.

On the whole, however, the lodgement area wasn't promising for heavy military traffic. Troops advancing inland would be doing so through *bocage*, with hedges atop embankments separating the fields, and an overhanging tree canopy which cast deep shadows on the roads and tracks. It wasn't tank country; and it wasn't infantry country either – except for the defenders.

A detailed engineers' report for Sword sector, made in October 1943, had concluded that the eastern approach to Caen, via Roger Beach and Ouistreham, wasn't promising because of probable delays in clearing the town, and the paucity of good roads inland. The centre, from La Brèche d'Hermanville west for about half a mile, was also problematic because the Germans had flooded the area behind the beaches. The western part, fortunately, according to the engineer appreciation was however 'very favourable for the assault along the frontage of 1500 yds'. The 500 yards on the eastern edge of this stretch had sand dunes 20–30 yards deep, while the remaining beach front-age had a vertical sea wall 7–10 feet high and then cliffs of 20–30 feet. The engineers' comment was that 'the dunes and seawall constitute only minor obstacles'. There was a good seafront road, and another a further 700 yards back, with ten connecting roads. The report con-cluded that 'the possibilities for beach exits in the section are good', and said much the same for the routes running further inland. This section, of some 500 yards or so, which would be designated 'Queen White' Beach, was clearly key to rapid movement on Caen.

All this topographical information had come from a wonderful array of sources. Pre-war holiday postcards and family snapshots had been gathered from a willing British public – ten times and more than was needed, for the appeal couldn't be any more specific than 'the coast of France'. Special forces, and Combined Operations 'pilotage parties' made up of members of the navy, marines, Royal Engineers and the Special Boat Service, carried out close reconnaissance through-out the preparatory period – so close at times that they were able to hear the Germans exchanging banter. The secret army of local French Resistance, helped by the Special Operations Executive, the organiza-tion charged by Churchill in 1940 'to set Europe ablaze', provided sketches of German strongpoints in astonishing detail. The RAF flew countless photo-reconnaissance missions. Electronic surveillance intercepted radio emissions from throughout occupied Europe, and could narrow down their surveillance even to the level of individual radar sites and command posts. The most dramatic source of signal intelligence was the 'Ultra' intercepts – signals encoded by the 'Enigma' encryption machines, which the Germans thought indecipherable but which were famously proved otherwise by the codebreakers of Bletchley Park. However, they could only be decrypted, of course, if they were first intercepted, which meant if they were sent by radio telegraphy, Morse code. Messages in France were almost invariably sent by landline, except by the Luftwaffe, and so here Ultra played a relatively small part in tactical intelligence-gathering. Nevertheless, no army in the history of war had such a wealth of intelligence on both the ground and the enemy, even if intelligence on the latter was ultimately incomplete. In 1916, after disastrous assumptions about the ground and the enemy on the Somme, one staff officer had declared: 'It is a sin to assume anything that can be verified.' In 1944, no one was going to commit the sin of assumption again, especially not Montgomery.

However, the Germans had made the same detailed appreciations and taken measures to mine and obstruct both the beaches and the exits, and the potential glider landing grounds, and to cover them by both direct and indirect fire. This was, after all, the Atlantic Wall, the outer curtain of *Festung Europa*, 'Fortress Europe'. Field Marshal Erwin Rommel himself had been brought back from Italy and given responsibility for defending the French coast – but as Inspector General of the Western Defences, a staff position, not a command. Nevertheless, he was able to do a great deal to strengthen the wall in the next six months, although the Commander-in-Chief West, Gerd von Rundstedt, was convinced the attack wouldn't come in Normandy and insisted on the Calais region taking priority.

Rommel was certain, too, that any attack must be checked well forward – that it must not be allowed to develop from the initial landing zones – and that armour must therefore be stationed forward for immediate counter-attacks. 'The first twenty-four hours of the invasion will be decisive,' he'd said in April 1944, adding the prophetic and memorable conclusion: 'The fate of Germany depends on the outcome. For the Allies as well as Germany, it will be the longest day.'*

But Rundstedt disagreed. The experience of Salerno, he argued, suggested that the Allies would have massive naval firepower in support, and that it was better therefore to let them advance, even to draw them deeper into Normandy, beyond the range of that covering fire, and then destroy them with massed armour kept in reserve close to Paris. The dispute would rage all the way up to Hitler himself, who in due course took the easy option and divided the armour, like ancient Gaul, into three parts – one for Rommel, one for Rundstedt, and the other for his own personal control. A rare Ultra decrypt told the Allies what they'd face: in May a signal from the Japanese naval attaché in Berlin to Tokyo confirmed that Rommel intended to destroy any invasion 'near the coast, most of all on the beaches'.†

The 3rd Division Planning Intelligence Summary issued in February had concluded

> that the area SW of CAEN seems the most likely concentration area from which an attack could be launched against 3 British Division bridge-head. It seems possible that the panzer division might already be stationed in that area before D day, or if not, that elements of a panzer division might have moved into it from the SOUTH on reports of the approach of assault convoys. 3 British Division must therefore be prepared to beat off a tank attack, probably launched from the direction of

---

* '. . . the enemy most likely will try to land at night and by fog after a tremendous shelling by artillery and bombers. They will employ hundreds of boats and ships unloading amphibious vehicles, waterproofed and submergible tanks. We must stop them in the water, not only delaying him and destroying all enemy equipment while still afloat. Some units do not seem to realise the value of this type of defence': Rommel to unknown recipient, 22 April 1944, CAB146/329, National Archives.

† F. H. Hinsley, *British Intelligence in the Second World War*, vol. III (Cambridge, 1988).

CARPIQUET 9669, on p.m. D day. It does not follow that this will in fact be put in on that day, as the German Command may wait before committing armoured formations to counter attacks.

This necessity – being prepared to beat off a tank attack that afternoon or evening – became the dominating factor in the 3rd Division's planning, as indeed in that of the 3rd (Canadian) Division on the right, I Corps' other assault division. Whatever their progress inland, therefore, be it promisingly deep or frustratingly shallow, the division had to be able to hold on to its gains that evening. It simply couldn't risk being thrown back into the sea. The I Corps plan – its mission as given to it by 2nd Army – was 'to secure, *on D Day* [emphasis added], a covering position on the general line PUTOT EN BESSIN 9072 – CAEN 0068 – thence R ORNE to the sea, preparatory to a further advance in accordance with the Second Army plan'. And for this advance, 2nd Army needed to get its two remaining corps quickly ashore in the following days.

The 3rd Division's battlefield was now neatly shaped: a triangle tapering towards Caen, some 9 miles at its base (the coast) and 11 long, its left side the Orne (although the division would push its left boundary beyond the river for security), and its right the railway line from Langrune-sur-Mer to La Délivrande and thence to Caen.

The development of the several plans – at army, corps, division and brigade level – was unusually collaborative. 'Unusually' because there was time for commanders to discuss things, rather than simply the cascading of orders that active operations usually demand. And also because the dispositions in Britain were imaginative and favourable. The assault divisions of 2nd Army – 3rd British, 3rd Canadian and 50th Northumbrian (Tyne-Tees) – had each been allocated a primary training area. The 3rd British Division's was in the north of Scotland, with headquarters in Cameron Barracks, Inverness. They'd been there since the summer of 1943, and in late autumn and early winter were joined by other elements of 'Assault Force S', as those ear-marked for Sword Beach were known – in particular, specialist armour from 79th Division.

In summer there's no finer place than Nairnshire and Ross and Cromarty. The Moray Firth was ideal, too, for practising assault landings, not just for the landing craft but for Hobart's 'funnies', especially the DD tanks. The beaches, too, were similar to Norman-dy's. In winter, however, the north of Scotland is short of both daylight and good weather (though freer of fog than England), but is at least a long way from prying eyes. Rennie himself arrived at Inverness on Christmas Day.

From December to May, the 3rd Division took part in seven major exercises. To begin with, these practised assaulting with 'two up' – two brigades side by side, and the third in reserve; or rather, in depth, for they would have specific objectives beyond the beach. After Exercise 'Crown' in early February, however, with the actual beaches now earmarked, although known to only a very few in div-isional headquarters and the brigadiers, Rennie changed plan. On Exercise 'Anchor' at the end of the month he landed with the three infantry brigade groups in echelon – that is, following one another.* There'd be just one in the initial assault, then one for objectives inland, and one as a true reserve (that is, with no specific task but to avert failure or reinforce success). This decision was driven to an extent by the practicable beach frontage and availability of landing craft, but also by the need to maintain momentum inland. It was a bold one, but risky – just a third of the force committed to the fight on the beaches, and a slower buildup of troops ashore – but then the entire operation was risky, and the soldier's maxim is 'take one's risks early'. The gain on offer was that if the assault brigade could get

---

* A brigade group is an infantry (usually) brigade with additional arms attached, prin-cipally armour, artillery and engineers.

across the beaches and into the dunes quickly, the division would have two fresh brigades to launch inland. It also meant that the second DD armoured regiment could now land direct from the tank landing craft (LCTs) rather than swimming ashore, giving the division greater assurance of more tanks in the push on Caen.* Meanwhile, 2nd Army's other two assault divisions, the Canadians (I Corps) on Juno and the Tyne-Tees (XXX Corps) on Gold, would assault two up – side by side – establishing a broader bridgehead. Besides the practical considerations, it was also perhaps a compromise best suited to the temperament and experience of the divisional commanders. Major-General Douglas Graham, commanding the Tyne-Tees, was fifty-one, a veteran infantryman of the Western Front (he'd been with the 1st Cameronians in the retreat from Mons). He'd commanded divisions in North Africa and Italy, and would have prized the idea of 'balance' – that is, depth and reserves (or, in the case of the landings, width and reserves). Rod Keller, commanding the Canadians, had been promoted major-general at forty-one and had no operational experience of command. Caution on his part therefore was only to be expected.

To protect the left flank of 2nd Army, and in particular Sword Beach, the 6th (British) Airborne Division would land by night east of the Orne, and the 1st Special Service Brigade (later renamed 1st Commando Brigade), including French 'commandos', would come ashore at Sword Beach after 3rd Division had secured it to take Ouistreham and relieve the glider-borne troops on the Orne. For sound reasons of control, and for support, the brigade would be

---

* By the most optimistic estimates, it could hardly be supposed that even half the tanks launched 7,000 yards offshore to dodge the mines and caltrops on the beaches and then to slog it out with the Germans in their concrete defences would survive much beyond the high-water line.

under command of 3rd Division until reaching 6th Airborne. It was messy, but if Ouistreham had to be reduced, there was probably no other way.*

After Exercise Anchor the divisional and brigade planning staffs spent more than a week at Aberlour House – an even more isolated spot, on the Spey – studying all the available photographs of the assault area and working on their respective plans, which were then submitted to Rennie for his approval. When exactly, and why, Rennie chose which brigade would do what, isn't known. Battles turn on such decisions sometimes, as well he'd have known, although the overall design for Sword Beach and beyond was now pretty much set in concrete. Which brigade would lead – carry out the actual assault of the beach – was probably now his first decision. His mission was admirably clear: 'The 3rd British Infantry Division will land on QUEEN RED and WHITE beaches and capture CAEN, and a bridge-head south of the R ORNE at that place.'† But that mission was just one part of the greater Overlord design to secure a lodgement area from which further offensive operations could be developed, and the 2nd Army objective to seize enough ground by the end of the day to hold against German counter-attacks. Yes, the corps plan required him to push rapidly inland to Caen; but the whole operation rested on taking the beaches, and rapidly. Not just to forestall local counter-attacks, but because there was a timetable governing the landing of the forces following up.

On the face of it, there was little to choose between his three infantry brigades. Each was made up of regular battalions of English, Scots

---

* 4th (British) Special Service Brigade would likewise come ashore at Juno Beach to relieve or reinforce the airborne troops landing towards Bayeux.

† 3rd British Infantry Division Operation Order No. 1, 14 May 1944 (author's collection).

or Irish county regiments.* These had their own regimental pride, but none had seen action, as units, since 1940, and two – in 185th Brigade – hadn't seen any action at all. Instead they'd been keeping watch against invasion, and training continually. There hadn't been the same opportunity of 'winnowing' as in real fighting – the dramatic weeding out of commanders who proved they weren't up to it, and accelerated promotion of those who were – but conversely there'd been opportunity for even closer observation of performance by superior officers. The armoured brigade – the 27th – had two regiments which had fought in 1940, the 13th/18th Royal Hussars and the territorial 1st East Riding Yeomanry, although only a third of the Yeomanry had been able to get to Dunkirk and thence home, and therefore had been made up to strength since then by unseasoned men. The third regiment, the Staffordshire Yeomanry, had fought in North Africa, including El Alamein. They joined the brigade in February as part of Montgomery's bid to leaven the leading divisions with recent fighting experience, replacing the 4th/7th Dragoon Guards, who'd fought alongside the 13th/18th Hussars (13/18H) in 1940 and were now transferred to 8th Armoured Brigade supporting the Tyne-Tees.

The 27th Armoured Brigade's commander was the 41-year-old Erroll Prior-Palmer, who'd seen action with the 9th Lancers in France in 1940 and had lately been chief instructor at Sandhurst, which was then the officer cadet training unit for the Royal Armoured Corps. Armoured brigade commanders tended to be younger than their

---

* An infantry battalion was made up principally of four 'rifle' companies, each commanded by a major and comprising three platoons of thirty-six riflemen, each commanded by a subaltern (lieutenant or second lieutenant). The support company comprised four specialist platoons – 3-inch mortars, 6-pounder anti-tank guns, assault pioneers (in effect, sappers) and tracked carriers; and the headquarters company consisted of the battalion signallers and administrative staff.

infantry counterparts, sometimes spectacularly so: Brigadier (and ultimately Field Marshal) Michael Carver, for example, landed at Sword Beach on D+1 in command of 4th Armoured Brigade at the age of twenty-nine. But the infantry brigadiers in the 3rd Division were older even than the norm. Edward 'Copper' Cass (8th Brigade) was forty-six, as was Kenneth Pearce Smith of the 185th, while James Cunningham of the 9th Brigade was fifty-one. All had seen service in the Great War, Cunningham as early as 1914. Much ink could be used speculating on how and why they were older than usual, and what the consequences were. The divisional commander was younger than any of them. Even the corps commander, Lieutenant-General John Crocker, was only forty-eight, and the army commander, Miles Dempsey, almost a year younger than Crocker. Luck had played its part – the opportunity to shine, being in the right place at the right time – as, of course, had ability. But at this stage in the war, infantry brigadiers were at something of a premium. The outstanding ones – those who'd proved themselves in North Africa and Italy (and survived) – had been accelerated to divisional command and beyond, or to key staff appointments. Others had become 'stuck', as it were, in the appointments made after Dunkirk. Paradoxically perhaps, the need to pull the army together to be ready for invasion, and then to begin preparing for the return push, called for rather more stability in command than actual fighting on the battlefield. But in 1940, too, the army was expanding, and 'solid' battalion commanding officers in their early to mid-forties, peacetime promotion being slow, suddenly found themselves in brigade command. In turn, the need for more regimental commanding officers pulled able majors upwards and then often as not 'sideways' into new or territorial battalions, where the need for continuity in training kept them for the duration (or until wounded and invalided out). The brigadiers of the Tyne-Tees Division, veterans of North Africa and Italy, weren't markedly younger than Cass and Cunningham.

Rennie chose the 8th Brigade – Cass's – to lead the assault. It was hardly surprising, as Cass had commanded the 11th Brigade in the Sicily landings and had been transferred to command of the 8th in the 'leavening' process. Rennie would almost certainly have known him, or at least of him, as a fellow brigadier in 8th Army. 'Copper' Cass had been commissioned from Sandhurst into that most soldierly of regiments, the King's Own Yorkshire Light Infantry (KOYLI), in 1916, and the following year joined the 2nd Battalion in France, where he was badly wounded; rejoining in 1918, he won both the MC and DSO. Short and wiry, a crack rifle shot (a member of the Army VIII and in the King's Hundred at Bisley for ten years) and an army rugby player, in 1940, aged forty-two, he'd been second-in-command of 1st KOYLI in the 15th Brigade when it was withdrawn from France for the Norwegian campaign, and had unexpectedly succeeded to command when the incumbent was given command of the brigade. In the shambles of Norway, Cass won a bar to his DSO. There could be little doubt that here was the man to train and then lead ashore the brigade in the first wave.

Rennie formally issued the divisional orders for the Assault Brigade, as it was now called, on 14 May:

8 British Infantry Brigade Group with under command 13/18H, 5 Assault Regt RE (less two squadrons) and 4 and 41 Commandos will carry out the assault on QUEEN RED and WHITE beaches and secure the beach head to include [manuscript amendment] *high ground about* PERIERS-SUR-LE-DAN – ST AUBIN-D'ARQUENAY 0976.

Detailed tasks were given – not prioritized, surprisingly (unless the list itself was understood to be in order of priority): to clear the beaches of aimed fire to allow the engineers to clear obstacles and construct vehicle exits; to capture specified strongpoints and gun batteries inland (notably that nicknamed 'Hillman' just to the east of the centre line); to relieve 6th Airborne Division at the Bénouville and Ranville bridges some 3 miles inland (or, if the 6th hadn't done so, actually to take them); to 'establish a firm base quickly with one battalion on the PERIERS-SUR-LE-DAN feature so as to deny this ground to the enemy until the original assault battalions have completed their mopping up tasks and are available to reinforce that position'; and finally, on the orders of the divisional commander, to take over the bridgehead at Ranville and Bénouville with a battalion group.

There is really only one way to assault a beach: frontally, with unchecked momentum and huge fire support. The latter would principally be the job of naval gunfire and the Royal Air Force, with field artillery firing from the landing craft during the approach, and then intimately – that is, on the beach itself – from the tanks. The morale-boosting effect alone of having tanks to suppress enemy fire as the infantry stormed the beach was incalculable: hence the extraordinarily risky expedient of the DD.

Clearly, Brigadier Cass had no room for manoeuvre in the assault. The only thing he could practically do was land 'two up', with the third battalion following on close as a reserve, but with definite tasks if necessary, and the two commando battalions to mop up left and right. His battalion commanders were young: Charles Hutchinson (2nd East Yorkshire) and Richard Goodwin (1st Suffolk) were both thirty-six, and Richard Burbury (1st South Lancashire) thirty-eight; and there was little to choose between them. Cass decided to assault with 2 E Yorks left, 1 S Lan R right, and 1 Suffolk in reserve. Why exactly, there's no record to tell us. The Suffolks were the senior regiment by date of raising, and might have expected to lead. Then if the Suffolks weren't to lead, the E Yorks, as next senior, might have had the honour of taking the right (west) of the line – if such a thing meant anything at this stage of the war, which it almost certainly didn't. Perhaps Cass thought it was simply easier to remember that Yorkshire is east of the Pennines (with 'East' help-fully in their title), and Lancashire west. Who knows? (Cass left no record.) Stranger things determine choices sometimes when it largely makes no odds. Lieutenant-Colonel Dick Harrap (13/18H) was also thirty-eight. He'd been adjutant during the fighting with-drawal to Dunkirk, commanded a squadron on return, and later become second-in-command. In April he suddenly found himself promoted when the commanding officer was invalided out. The 8th Brigade would pay a high price during the assault. Of its four infantry and tank commanding officers, by D+10 only one would still be in command; two of the others would be dead and one badly wounded.

For the assault, each battalion was to be supported by a squadron of 13/18H tanks:* 'A' Squadron with 1 S Lan R (right), 'B' with 2 E Yorks (left), and 'C' with 1 Suffolk. A and B Squadrons had converted from the Valentine to the DD Sherman, while C was being re-equipped with the standard (non-DD) Sherman and the 'Firefly' variant – a Sherman with the long 17-pounder gun which could penetrate the frontal armour of the German Tiger tank. The intention was for A and B Squadrons to swim ashore to land seven and a half minutes before the infantry – 'H–7½', H-Hour being the time the assaulting infantry hit the beach. C Squadron would land dry-shod, or wade, from the LCTs at H+45, fifteen minutes ahead of the Suffolks.

When the rest of 8th Brigade had landed – between H+75 and H+150

---

* Each of the three 'sabre' squadrons, commanded by a major, consisted of four troops each of four tanks. Four more in squadron headquarters could, in extremis, act as a fifth troop. Regimental headquarters also had four tanks, allowing the commanding officer to command well forward during the battle. Headquarter Squadron had an anti-aircraft troop of six modified Crusader tanks mounting twin 20 mm cannon, a reconnaissance troop of eleven Stuart light tanks, an 'intercommunication' troop of nine Humber scout cars, a signal troop, administrative support and a large REME (Royal Electrical and Mechanical Engineers) light aid detachment.

(the leading elements of the Commando brigade at H+30) – the 185th Brigade – now referred to as the 'Intermediate Brigade' – would come ashore, complete with vehicles and supporting arms (primarily artillery and engineers) and the Staffordshire Yeomanry. Their task was to capture Caen and the bridgehead south of the Orne specified in the corps plan. 'This advance will be carried out with speed and boldness,' said the divisional operation order, 'so that the enemy's local reserves can be overcome quickly and the Brigade established on its objective ready to meet counter attacks by reserve formations which may develop towards the evening of D Day.' Further, having taken the city, the brigade was to push forward a covering force of a squadron of tanks and a company of infantry 'with the task of denying the enemy reconnaissance of the area SE of Caen'.

Rennie's operation order stressed that

armour will be used boldly in this advance but when defences are encountered which cannot be overcome by the advanced guard a co-ordinated quick attack *supported by all the available artillery* [emphasis added] will achieve the best results. It is very important in an advance of this nature that the commander should retain a reserve battalion in hand and keep control of his armour so that any weakening of the enemy can be immediately exploited.

A restricting factor in this, though, was artillery ammunition. Only a limited quantity could be got ashore the first day, and the operation order specified that 'expenditure will be strictly controlled . . . 50% of 1st line ammunition of Field Regiments will be held in reserve to meet enemy counter attacks which may be expected on D Day evening'. There again was the trade-off between progress inland and the need to defend what gains had been made by evening.

Curiously, too, the operation order gave no by-passing policy – what size of enemy 'pocket' could be left for follow-up troops to deal with – the implication being perhaps that clearing the beaches of aimed fire meant every strongpoint had to be reduced, including all those further inland covering the exit routes. But clearing every strongpoint en route to Caen would cost time as well as ammunition.*

Finally, at H+150, the reserve brigade, the 9th, with the East Riding Yeomanry under command, would begin landing. A reserve has no definite tasks – if you plan to use it, it's not a true reserve – but it will have a number of 'be prepared to . . .' contingency tasks. In principle, in defence a reserve is used to avert collapse, while in attack it's used to reinforce success. However, as the course of battle can't be foreseen – the very reason for having a reserve – even if the initial plan of attack fails, it may well be that another option presents itself. So one of the 'be prepared to' contingency tasks was, on the orders of the divisional commander: 'In the event of 185 Infantry Brigade failing to penetrate the Northern defences of CAEN, to attack CAEN from the WEST should that course appear to offer immediate prospects of success.'

It is fair to say, then, that the 8th Brigade, the Assault Brigade, had the most hazardous job; that the 185th, the Intermediate, had the most imperative (the capture of Caen); and that the 9th, the Reserve, had the most uncertain. Hence it was the most senior of the brigadiers, Pearce Smith, the divisional commander's designated replacement if incapacitated, who was charged with the most imperative task, with the Staffordshire Yeomanry, the most experienced of the armoured regiments, under his command.

The 27th Armoured Brigade, as an entity, had no initial tasks. The divisional operation order said only that it was 'the intention to concentrate the armour as soon as it becomes available from initial tasks with Brigades in the area CAZELLE 0276', and that 'under

---

* It's possible that the 185th Brigade decided its own by-passing policy, since it had the job of sprinting for Caen, but there's no record of it.

certain circumstances' it might be sent 'to anticipate the enemy on the high ground about CRAMESNIL 0857 [south and east of Caen]' – in which case it would be supplemented by a battalion from the Reserve Brigade, a field artillery regiment, an anti-tank battery and others. Clearly the 'certain circumstances' were the failure to take Caen and a counter-attack by German armour. This was only prudent, of course, but it did underline the fact that the divisional commander saw the battle for Caen as essentially an infantry battle with armoured support; he didn't envisage 27th Armoured having a role as an entity in taking the city.

It would surely have crossed his mind during planning, though. That said, Erroll Prior-Palmer, though a superb trainer, had relatively little experience of battle tanks. In 1940 the 9th Lancers had been equipped with light and 'cruiser' (medium-light) tanks, and although they'd been heavily engaged in the 1st Armoured Division's ill-fated counter-attack at Arras, Prior-Palmer had no first-hand knowledge of what a battle tank such as the Sherman – one which truly combined firepower, mobility and protection – could achieve in large numbers. Nor had he actually commanded a regiment. The 27th Armoured was seen essentially as a training organization and supplier of tanks for special tasks – the 'funnies' – for which the new brigadier, as a hands-on and demonstrative leader, was admirably equipped (as a cadet he'd won, uniquely, both the sword and the saddle of honour). Even if he'd conceived the idea of keeping the brigade as an entity to drive hard for Caen, it seems unlikely that he'd have had the credibility with Rennie to persuade him. At the back of the divisional commander's mind – the minds of all the divisional commanders, undoubtedly – was the imperative of clearing the beaches of aimed fire and having a defensible bridgehead by evening. And even then, this must have seemed a touch-and-go objective. It's telling, perhaps, that the corps commander, Crocker, a tank man, endorsed Rennie's plans. But then Crocker, whose nickname 'Honest John' speaks for itself, had had something of a cautionary bloody nose in Tunisia.*

But of course, Neptune – Overlord, indeed – rested to a high degree on surprise. Strategic surprise was impossible to achieve: both sides knew that there would be an invasion some time in 1944. To Berlin's certain judgement, the western Allies had no other option, given the Soviet offensives. At the substrategic, the theatre level, surprise was another matter: would it be Normandy or the Pas de Calais? Here were more possibilities for misleading the enemy. As for tactical surprise – the exact date and method – the possibilities were even greater. Huge effort would have to be put into security and deception operations to protect the truth.

Theatre-level deception would be the major prize. For the entire Overlord design might yet be defeated if the Germans deployed their theatre reserves against the landings in the initial stages, as Rommel wanted to do. But as a minimum, the battle of D-Day, as it ought rightly to be called, the battle to gain by evening a secure army group bridgehead, needed tactical surprise. Otherwise Eisenhower might indeed have to release the alternative communiqué that he'd write the evening before the assault, possibly the grimmest notice of failure in the history of war, so discomforting in its implications perhaps that he actually dated it wrongly ('5 July'):

Our landings in the Cherbourg–Havre area have failed to gain a satisfactory foothold and I have withdrawn the troops. My decision to attack at this time and place was based upon the best information

---

* In his first battle as GOC IX Corps in April 1943 during Operation Torch, he attempted to cut off the Italian 1st Army at Fondouk Pass, but underestimated the strength of the defences facing him, and the action went badly wrong, allowing most of the enemy to escape. Ten days later he was wounded during a training demonstration and evacuated home.

available. The troops, the air and the Navy did all that Bravery and devotion to duty could do. If any blame or fault attaches to the attempt it is mine alone.

The Dieppe raid was still imprinted on even the most optimistic minds.

Operation 'Bodyguard' is a story in itself.* Bodyguard was the overall plan to mislead the Germans as to the time and place of the invasion. Its major sub-operation was codenamed 'Fortitude', and consisted of two parts: 'Fortitude North', to convince them that the Allies would also launch an attack on Norway, and 'Fortitude South', to convince them that the main invasion would be in the Pas de Calais – both later in the year. Fortitude had everything: double agents, fake armies and fake radio traffic; raids on coastal targets in Norway and the Pas de Calais; dummy tanks and aircraft in Kent; even a 'dummy' Montgomery in Gibraltar – every conceivable technical and psychological trick.†

The other side of the coin was operational security – guarding the actual details of Overlord. 'Bigot', codename for the additional layer of security relating to particulars such as the landing beaches and the date of the invasion, was instituted by the war cabinet's joint intelligence subcommittee in early 1943, and in turn adopted by the United States. In addition to the clearance for graduated access to documents classified Secret, Top Secret (until 1943 'Most Secret') etc. was the 'need to know' principle. Only those needing to know details of Overlord

---

* 'In wartime, truth is so precious that she should always be attended by a bodyguard of lies': Churchill.

† In Operation Copperhead, Meyrick Clifton James, an actor serving in the Pay Corps and bearing a striking resemblance to Montgomery, made a well-publicized visit to Gibraltar and North Africa shortly before the landings. The idea was that Monty's presence there would suggest that the invasion wasn't imminent. Such evidence as there is suggests that the ruse didn't so much deceive the Germans as baffle them.

and its associated operations would be given access, even if otherwise cleared for the highest level of security classification. An officer could be cleared to 'Most Secret', for instance, but if his name wasn't on the 'Bigot List', he didn't get to see a paper classified as *Neptune Bigot Top Secret*. Obviously, the list would grow with time as more and more officers further down the chain of command came to have need of the details, but security was maintained to a remarkable degree. Indeed, the lengths to which the Allies went to contain the spread of information were extraordinary. Not only were troops physically sealed off in their concentration areas as the day approached, but specially printed 'bogus maps' were used to brief them, on which the gridlines were renumbered and place names disguised. In Sword sector, for example, Luc-sur-Mer was renamed 'Vienna', Hermanville was 'Mexico', Colville was 'Brazil', Ouistreham was 'Oslo' and the ultimate objective, Caen, was 'Poland'.

Overlord documents had additional handling instructions, such as 'not to be taken in aircraft' and 'not to be taken on shore [in France]'.* Nevertheless, huge efforts were made to make sure troops were well briefed on what they faced and what was expected of them. Units set up special briefing marquees with 'bogus' maps, models and aerial photographs, under tight supervision of the intelligence officer. In general, however, it wasn't until the first two weeks of May that commanding officers and their immediate staff were allowed to know the whole of the divisional plan and to study the real maps. Even then the actual date of the assault wasn't disclosed, although no one could have supposed they'd have to wait very long. Needless to say, once 'locked down', no leave was granted

---

* The author's copy of the 3rd Division's operation order is marked 'NEPTUNE/ BIGOT/ NOT TO BE TAKEN ON SHORE'. How it got onshore and subsequently to the author 75 years later is testament to the good judgement of one of the divisional intelligence officers.

except in the most exceptional circumstances, and letters out were strictly censored.

But if the ground, the enemy, and the Allies' will and capabilities would be the principal shapers of the battle once ashore, for Neptune itself – the sea transport and landing operation – *the* shaper was the weather. Air operations – the glider and parachute landings, and precision bombing – needed clear skies and a good moon; and, when daylight came, clear enough conditions for aerial spotting for naval gunfire. The naval operation needed low winds and calm seas, and the ground troops needed to land at low tide, when the beach obstacles were exposed and easier to deal with – though in places, particularly the British beaches, they needed high enough water for landing craft to get over the sand bars; they also needed rising water in order to beach without the landing craft getting stranded. For at its extreme, the tidal range was 19 feet, which with an ebb tide could mean the landing craft, needed for subsequent waves, might be left high and dry for as long as twelve hours.

The lunar and tidal window of opportunity was 5–7 June. The next opportunity wouldn't be for a fortnight, and the moon would then no longer be full. The 5th had therefore been chosen as D-Day so as to have two days in reserve.* The weather in early June 1944 proved more than usually complex to predict, however. Although Admiral Ramsay would record in his diary that Tuesday, 30 May was 'another boiling hot day', cyclonic disturbances as far west as the Rocky Mountains were even then generating turbulence in the eastern Atlantic.

---

* The position of the sun and moon relative to the Earth determines the strength of the tides and the times of high and low waters. The Allies needed a low tide near sunrise, and on the Normandy coast this conjunction occurred only near the times of either a new or a full moon. Even so, the demolition teams would only have some 30 minutes or so to accomplish their task (under enemy fire) before the rising tide became too deep. By 7 a.m. the water level would be rising 1 foot every ten minutes, and accelerating.

Two deep depressions in particular exercised the SHAEF forecasters. The chief meteorologist, Group Captain James Stagg, wrote later that 'each by itself was a mid-winter phenomenon', the conditions being more like April than the start of summer.* The point wasn't so much the depressions, though, as what was happening in between them. On Saturday, 3 June, with the assault troops embarking, and some from the more distant ports even under way, the weather looked fine from the windows of Southwick House near Portsmouth, where Eisenhower and his subordinate C-in-Cs were gathered. But Stagg told him that bad weather was imminent – too bad for the operation to proceed given the parameters, although by no means all his forecasters agreed.†

Ike said he'd reserve final judgement till their early morning meeting.

At dawn on Sunday the 4th, they assembled again. Stagg's view hadn't changed, and despite Montgomery's urging that the operation go ahead (to the dismay of Eisenhower's deputy, Air Chief Marshal Sir Arthur Tedder, and the Air C-in-C Sir Trafford Leigh-Mallory), the supreme commander postponed the operation for at least twenty-four hours.

Later that Sunday, however, even though wind and rain were now

---

* J. M. Stagg, *Forecast for Overlord* (London, 1971). Strictly speaking, Stagg was a geophysicist with little forecasting experience compared with the meteorologists in the sections he coordinated – the (Air Ministry's) Meteorological Office, and those of the Royal Navy and the USAAF's 8th Air Force. But he was an experienced administrator, and steadfast. He regularly rehearsed the meteorologists with trial forecasts which were then checked for accuracy.

† It is important to note that in 1944 forecasting techniques did not rely on satellites, real-time communications and computer programs, but on observations by weather ships in the Atlantic, reconnaissance flights and westerly lighthouses, made with anemometers, barometers and slide-rules – and, occasionally, the weather reports from German U-boats, whose signals Bletchley Park were routinely reading. Public weather forecasts were, of course, suspended for the duration of the war.

rattling the same windows, Stagg reported that there was a consensus in his section for 'a fair interlude' the following day, with a steady reduction of both the swell and the sea state: 'Swell – In Western approaches to English Channel, and south of 50 degrees N up Channel as far as the Cherbourg Peninsula: 6 to 7 feet Monday [5 June], decreasing to 4 to 5 feet Tuesday, 3 to 4 feet remainder of period, westerly direction throughout'; and for 6 June they forecast a 3-4-foot mixed sea and swell. This was good enough for landing craft, but the DD Shermans had a freeboard of just 4 feet. The margin would be very tight indeed. In addition, gusts of force 6–7 were measured in the English Channel, with winds blowing a steady force 4–5. Force 4 was enough to swamp the landing craft, but Admiral Ramsay said he was prepared to accept 4–5 as marginal with the possibility of the occasional 4–6.

Eisenhower said he didn't like it, but was quite sure they'd have to go; nevertheless, he'd take the final decision at their dawn meeting next day. Ramsay said he'd give the warning order to sail.*

At four o'clock next morning, the 5th, Eisenhower held his 'go/no-go meeting'. As he drove in the grey light to Southwick House from what he called his 'sharpener camp' a mile away – the tents and caravans from which he'd command in Normandy – there was, he wrote later, a 'wind of almost hurricane proportions shaking and shuddering', and he wondered why he was even bothering. There was a fire burning in the grate at Southwick as the commanders

---

* Ramsay, as C-in-C Dover, had planned and commanded the evacuation from Dunkirk, been Deputy (Allied) C-in-C for the Torch landings, and had commanded the Eastern Task Force in the Sicily (Operation Husky) landings. Neptune – his operation – was a never surpassed masterpiece of planning and execution, yet he remains one of the least known commanders of the war, perhaps because after D-Day the focus was on the land battle and Bomber Command, and also because he himself was killed in January 1945 when the aircraft taking him from SHAEF in Paris to a meeting with Montgomery in Brussels crashed on take-off.

assembled, and hot coffee, which gave a little comfort; but then, according to Ramsay, 'this time the prophets came in smiling'. Stagg said that the predicted high pressure was holding, and even building. Eisenhower asked his three subordinate C-in-Cs their opinion. All said 'go'. He paced up and down for a minute or so, drawing heavily on his cigarette, and then said: 'OK. We'll go on 6 June.'

Then he retired to his camp bed to chain-smoke and read cowboy fiction for several hours. It was undoubtedly the best therapy.

4

THE LONGEST DAY

Well, is it or isn't it the invasion?

Hitler to Field Marshal
Wilhelm Keitel,
afternoon, 6 June 1944

Shortly after midnight, 18,000 Allied paratroopers dropped into Normandy in order, as it were, to secure the perimeter of the invasion area. Most spectacularly of all, six Horsa gliders, each carrying a platoon of the Oxfordshire and Buckinghamshire Light Infantry and a detachment of sappers, swooped on the two bridges over the Orne and the Caen canal, the only eastward exits for the Sword landings (and German counter-attack routes westward). Intelligence reported that both were strongly defended and wired for demolition. Both were captured in minutes.

Meanwhile some 7,000 warships, transports and landing craft were making for the French coast, their task to put 150,000 men ashore by evening. 'You could have walked across from the Isle of

Wight to France without getting your feet wet, there were so many ships,' said more than one soldier who saw even just a part of the great armada as day broke. The English Channel had long been the moat that defended Britain. Now it was the bridge that would liberate Europe.

And overhead were the Allied air forces, with air superiority at last – indeed, with complete mastery of the air: *air supremacy*, the enemy incapable of effective interference. They would fly more than 14,000 sorties in support of the landings.

The man in command of the ground troops, Montgomery, exuded confidence – necessarily so, for there were many unknowables. Others didn't share his assurance – among them the CIGS, Alan Brooke. Confiding in his diary in London, Brooke expressed his great unease 'about the whole operation. At best, it will fail the expectation of the bulk of the people, namely all those who know nothing of its difficulties. At worst, it may well be the most ghastly disaster of the whole war.' But Monty had kept telling his men: 'We have a sufficiency of troops; we have all the necessary tackle; we have an excellent plan. This is a perfectly normal operation which is certain of success.'*

As for its being a normal operation, he was right in one sense: no one was being asked to do what had never been done before – either for real or in training, although for real it hadn't always been successful. What *wasn't* normal was the sheer size of the operation. But Montgomery knew the concept was sound, and so were the

---

* As an aside, Brooke's diary entry suggests that although a 'master of strategy' (as inscribed on his statue in Whitehall), he would not have been the man for Overlord. Does it suggest that he'd have said 'Go' the day before, as 'Ike', the 'lesser general', did? As for Monty, his appreciation of the situation in what he told his troops justifies the accolade 'master of the battlefield', the title of the second volume (1984) of Nigel Hamilton's three-part biography. (This, of course, will be an unfashionable opinion.)

individual parts – the commanders, the troops and the technical resources. Colonel Paul R. Goode, US Army, addressing the 175th Infantry Regiment (brigade in British terms), who were to land at Omaha Beach, took perhaps a more 'robust' view: 'You get your ass on the beach. I'll be there waiting for you and I'll tell you what to do. There ain't anything in this plan that is going to go right.' But even in his candour he was expressing a determination that they'd succeed somehow. And probably somewhere between this cussed resolve – rather than Brooke's pessimism – and Monty's breezy assurance lay the attitude of most of the assault forces.

Certainly the 13th/18th Hussars weren't too troubled, according to the adjutant:

As the invasion fleet sailed at about midday . . . the feeling uppermost in nearly every mind was that this was just another exercise. This was the result of the many rehearsals and exercises we had done both in Scotland and the South and our rather phlegmatic attitude had been somewhat intensified by a twenty-four hour postponement spent with little or nothing to do in overcrowded and uncomfortable LCTs. Even such dramatic moments as the hoisting of the Admiral's signal 'Good Luck and Press On' or the opening of the sealed packages of operation orders and maps which told us where we were going failed to ruffle any-one's outward calm.*

Each squadron had twenty tanks, five in each of four LCTs. The crews were confined to the well-decks and could only see the sky, so that tank exhaust fumes and the wallowing motion made for a great deal of nausea. They'd practised many times, and launching into the sea, perilous as it was, always came as something of a relief. This time,

---

* War diary of Julius Neave, privately published.

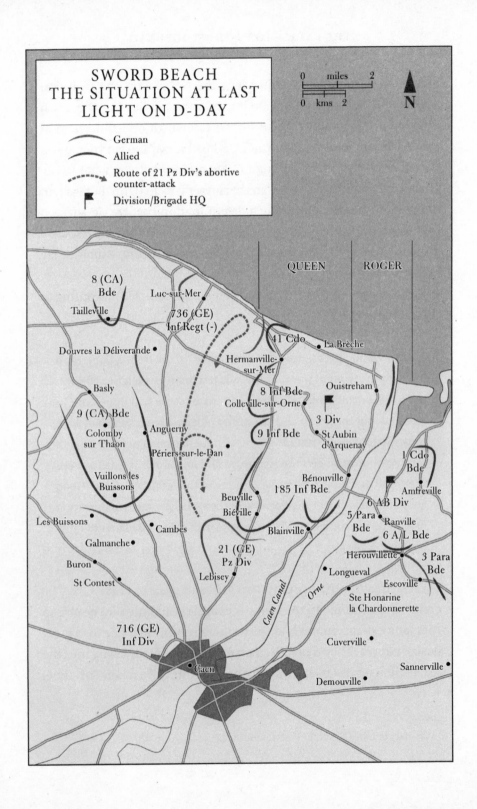

SWORD BEACH
THE SITUATION AT LAST
LIGHT ON D-DAY

0 — miles — 2
0 — kms — 2

N

‐‐‐ German

‐‐‐ Allied

‐‐‐▶ Route of 21 Pz Div's abortive
counter-attack

🏴 Division/Brigade HQ

QUEEN   ROGER

8 (CA) Bde
Luc-sur-Mer
Tailleville
736 (GE) Inf Regt (-)
41 Cdo
La Brèche
Douvres la Déliverande
Hermanville-sur-Mer
Basly
Ouistreham
8 Inf Bde
9 (CA) Bde
Colleville-sur-Orne
Colomby sur Thaon
Anguerny
3 Div
St Aubin d'Arquenay
Périers-sur-le-Dan
9 Inf Bde
1 Cdo Bde
Vuillons les Buissons
Amfreville
Bénouville
Beuville
185 Inf Bde
6 AB Div
Les Buissons
Biéville
5 Para Bde
Ranville
Cambes
Blainville
6 A/L Bde
Galmanche
Hérouvillette
3 Para Bde
Buron
21 (GE) Pz Div
Longueval
Escoville
St Contest
Lebisey
Ste Honarine la Chardonnerette
716 (GE) Inf Div
Cuverville
Caen
Sannerville
Demouville

though, the sea was heavier, and they'd never had so long a passage, or faced so long a run-in once launched.

The 'lowering position' – the point at which the LSIs (landing ships, infantry) lowered their LCAs (landing craft, assault) – was set for 10,000 yards from the beach. At that point too the LCTs would begin forming line, so that by the time they reached the DDs' launching position at 7,000 yards they'd all be in line abreast. Here they'd drop anchor, and after ten minutes for the crews to get the flotation screens up, the ramps would be lowered and out the tanks would plunge. Each squadron would then swim in columns of five tanks ('line ahead' in the naval parlance they'd adopted), led by an LC(N) – landing craft, navigation – making headway at an average of 1,000 yards in ten minutes. At about 1,000 yards from shore, the columns were to come into line abreast, and as soon as the tanks 'touched down' – the tracks made contact with the beach – they'd break struts to drop the screens, and go into action.

'A' Squadron Leader, Major Derrick Wormald (aged twenty-eight), who'd won the MC in France in 1940, recorded in the squadron war diary that

The night was uneventful except for the unpleasant weather and conditions on the Landing Craft. I think that all of us looked forward to being on dry land, wherever it might be. Before dawn I went to the bridge of my Landing Craft and asked Charles [Lieutenant-Commander Charles Creighton RN, commanding the flotilla, and with whom the squadron had trained since Scotland] how we were getting on. His reply was 'You and I, Derrick, seem to be the only people carrying out this invasion.' However, soon afterwards the other craft of his flotilla appeared astride us and the invasion fleet emerged astern. At 06.16 all tanks were launched, after closing to 5,000 yards [the wind, blowing force 5 from the west, and the swell were judged by Prior-Palmer – and Captain Eric Bush commanding 'S3', the leading edge of the naval assault force – to be too high to launch at the planned 7,000 yards]. The sea looked alarming from the craft but FLOATER [launch] proved to be the right decision. Only Corporal Sweetapple's tank failed to swim towards the shore. This was because he could not get his propellers to fall and to engage with the drive off the tracks. His tank sank but he and his crew were picked up from their inflatable dinghy [carried by each tank]. Naval and Air Bombardment was tremendous and occasional glimpses of the shore were possible, due to the offshore wind which carried the smoke of the bombardment towards us. The tanks were performing well beyond what we thought to be practicable for the apparatus. Four columns each of five tanks (less Cpl Sweetapple's) followed the lead of a Landing Craft Personnel (Navigational) the task of which was to lead us to the correct point of 'TOUCH DOWN' on the beach. Our tanks touched down at 07.23. Sixteen tanks got their tracks on the sea bed, moved into water sufficiently shallow to allow them to deflate their screens and to engage the beach defences. I still remember very clearly the 'brewing-up' of the leading AVRE [Assault Vehicle Royal Engineers] Churchill tank as it drove down the ramp of an LCT which was beached a few yards to my left front. The turret and the contents thereof spun into the air after a violent explosion, presumably caused by a penetrating direct hit by an anti-tank shell, which detonated the explosive charges which the AVRE was carrying for the purpose of destroying concrete emplacements. I immediately got my gunner to engage a bunker from which I thought that the shot had been fired. His first round hit the target and the gun became silent. We then continued to fire at suspected defensive positions until we could neither see nor hear any firing from the defences. The Assault Engineers crossed the beach and started to carry out their task of creating exits from the beach. The assault companies of the South Lancashires came ashore, crossed the beach with very few, if any, casualties and passed inland. We had, therefore, successfully completed our first task, which was to neutralise the beach defences. We could now only wait for the Engineers to open the exits so that we could escape from the beach to support the infantry in the capture of their inshore objective – the village of HERMANVILLE.

However, Wormald's account doesn't tell the whole story; the losses in both men and tanks are noted separately in his diary. Indeed, Wormald's own second-in-command, Captain Noel Denny (aged twenty-four), who'd also fought with the regiment in 1940, was almost lost during the run-in. One of 'A' Squadron's tank commanders, Corporal Pat Hennessy, tells the story:

> Each side of us other DD tanks were launching. To my right and behind me I saw Captain Denny's as it came down the ramp and into the sea. It straightened up and began to make way, but behind it I could see the large bulk of its LCT creeping forward. The distance between them closed, and in a very few minutes the inevitable happened. The bows of the LCT struck the DD tank and forced it under the water.*

Denny managed to surface and was picked up, but the rest of his crew, despite their escape apparatus and buoyancy aids, didn't. He'd been lucky. On the run-in, the crews, apart from the driver, stood on the engine decks, the drill being (perhaps counter-intuitively) to get inside once fire from the shore threatened, though the commander had to remain on the deck to give steering instructions to the driver – which was why Denny survived when the tank was pitched over on its beam, sinking in 25 feet of water, upside down.†

---

* Neave's and the squadron diaries are archived at Home Headquarters, The Light Dragoons, Newcastle. Hennessy's account, *Young Man in a Tank*, is privately published.

† In fact, it was Sweetapple's tank. Denny's was run down about half a mile from shore by an LCT carrying assault engineers. In the rougher water, the DDs couldn't make the planned 4½ knots, only about 3. The assault engineers were supposed to land behind the DDs and begin work under their covering fire, but the slow swimming speed of the DDs presented problems for the LCTs carrying the next wave. This had been foreseen

Hennessy's own experience of the fight on the beach wasn't untypical:

As we approached, we felt the tracks meet the shelving sand of the shore and, slowly, we began to rise out of the water. We took post to deflate the screen, one man standing to each strut. When the base of the screen was clear of the water, the struts were broken, the air released and the screen collapsed. We leapt into the tank and were ready for action.

He recalled very clearly the first shot: '75 HE, Action – Traverse right, steady, *On!* 300 – white-fronted house – first floor window, centre' – (Gunner's reply) 'On!' – 'Fire!'

With other tanks coming in on both sides, and now under fire from several positions, Hennessy's tank continued the action with both main armament and 'co-ax' (coaxial Browning machine gun). Then the South Lancashires' landing craft began beaching, ramps dropping fast and men forging through the surf. 'We gave covering fire wherever we could,' he recalled, 'and all the time the build up of men and vehicles continued.'

It was much the same on the left in the East Yorkshires' sector, with 'B' Squadron providing a heavy weight of intimate fire support, allowing the infantry to get across the beach to the cover of the sea

---

during training, and it had been decided to accept the risk of getting the sappers and their specialist equipment on to the beach ahead of the DDs even if it meant potentially ramming some, and not having their immediate covering fire. Bush, who as a 15-year-old midshipman had seen his first amphibious operation at Gallipoli, took the decision to proceed through the late-running tanks. Two tanks and all but one of their crews (Denny) were lost as a result – the price of clearing the way for the infantry and the follow-up armour and artillery. But thirty-one made it to the beaches.

wall and then beyond. The Hussars estimated that they silenced three or four 7.5 cm PAK 40 (anti-tank guns), four or five PAK 38s (5 cm guns), and 'numerous 20 mm' PAK. Direct fire at the beaches was steadily subdued, and other than the odd suicidal sniper had ceased by H+20 (minutes).

It's worth reflecting on Corporal Hennessy's 'We gave covering fire wherever we could, and all the time the build up of men and vehicles continued,' for this indeed was the first trial of Overlord, the culmination of a year and more's planning – how to maintain the momentum of the assault so that tactical checks wouldn't defeat the vital object of gaining a defensible bridgehead by evening. And how to do so with the absolute minimum of casualties, the determination not to – as in the last war – simply send men 'over the top' more in hope than in realistic expectation.*

Getting across the beaches was, of course, just the beginning, but it shaped – guaranteed the planned shape of – the battle of D-Day. Or rather, the five individual battles of D-Day – Sword, Juno, Gold, Omaha, Utah.

The base of the Sword 'triangle' – Ouistreham to Langrune-sur-Mer – was pretty much secured in the first hour, and so was the left side by the airborne operation, especially the *coup de main* glider actions. The right side also looked promising with the successful landings on

---

* The frontal attacks on the Western Front had certainly been in the minds of Morgan and others, and in Montgomery's *a fortiori*; as, indeed, had that first assault landing against machine guns – at Gallipoli, when without support a battalion of the South Lancashires' fellow-county-men threw themselves heroically at the Turkish defences. The 1st Lancashire Fusiliers started that day in 1915 with 27 officers and 1,002 other ranks; twenty-four hours later, just 16 officers and 304 men answered the roll-call. The assault, in broad daylight, on beaches meshed with barbed wire and covered by machine guns on the heights, had been the 'idea' of the divisional commander, and had all the tactical sophistication of a Highland charge in the Jacobite rebellion of 1745.

Juno by the Canadians, and to their right by the Tyne-Tees. The question now was how far the 3rd Division could get towards the point of the triangle – Caen – before the opposition hardened.

In fact, and perhaps contrary to expectations, this would prove harder than the beach assault. To begin with, the South Lancashires and the East Yorkshires found that they'd fewer tanks supporting them than they'd hoped for. Very few tanks had been put out of action by the enemy; rather more by the rising tide. The crews' orders had been to collapse flotation screens as soon as they grounded in order to give immediate covering fire and to minimize the chance of being picked off by anti-tank guns – in other words, to fire 'hull down' – but hull down in the water rather than the usual sense of being behind solid cover. They'd first practised this in the Dornoch Firth, and found that if they kept the rear of the screen inflated, it helped keep the water off the engine deck. They'd also been ordered to switch off the engine after grounding to save fuel, no resupply being expected till at least evening, and instead to use the auxiliary generator for turret power. However, the fast-rising tide was greater than anticipated, and many of the engines were flooded. Had they been diesels like those with the US regiments, requiring only compression to fire up, it wouldn't have mattered much, but petrol needed a spark – and that wasn't forthcoming in engines drenched by breakers.

Corporal Hennessy's tank was one that succumbed, although he'd decided to ignore the order to switch off the engine:

Harry Bone's voice came over the intercom: 'Let's move up the beach a bit – I'm getting bloody wet down here' . . . The sea was beginning to come in over the top of the driver's hatch and by now he was sitting in a pool of water. The problem was that the promised mine clearance had not yet taken place so we had to decide whether to press on through a known minefield or wait until the path had been cleared and marked. Suddenly, the problem was solved for us. One particularly large wave broke over the stern of the tank and swamped the engine, which sputtered to a halt. Now with the power gone, we could not move even if we wanted to. Harry Bone and Joe Gallagher [co-driver] emerged from the driving compartment, soaking wet and swearing.

They took out the Brownings and several cases of ammunition, inflated the dinghy, and using map boards as paddles began making way for the beach. A burst of machine-gun fire hit them, wounding Gallagher in the ankle, and the dinghy turned over.

Somehow, we managed to drag Gallagher and ourselves ashore. We got clear of the water and collapsed onto the sand, soaking wet and shivering. A DD tank drove up and stopped beside us with Sergeant Hepper grinning at us out of the turret. 'Can't stop!' he said, and threw us a tin can [of self-heating soup] . . . As we lay there on the sand, in the middle of a battle taking turns to swig down the hot soup, we were approached by an irate captain of Royal Engineers who said to me 'Get up, Corporal – that is no way to win the Second Front!*

---

* Hennessy continues his account with wry humour. In their unarmed state, they weren't much use to the infantry, 'so I found the Royal Navy beach master and reported our presence to him. He was a very busy man at the time, and advised me to "Get off my bloody beach!" We made our way to the road which ran parallel to the sea, some four or five hundred yards inland, and then we met up with some other un-horsed tank crews. I could not help feeling a bit unwanted at that stage. There was plenty of action taking place, but there was not a lot that we could do to influence the course of the battle and nobody seemed keen to invite us to join in. Of course, we had already played a part, and we could look back with some satisfaction. We had done what most people thought was impossible, we had swum a 32-ton tank through 5,000 yards of savagely rough sea and had given that vital support to the infantry to enable them now to have the chance to do their job of clearing the beach . . . Eventually, we were found by Major Wormald, who directed us to make our way to the village of Hermanville . . . As he drove off in his tank, we felt a return of confidence as we started the 3 mile trek to Hermanville . . . [Here] what was left of a squadron came together.' After the war, Hennessy gained a commission in the RAF, rising to the rank of group captain.

In fact, having immediately 'lost' a troop to the commandos making for the bridges on the Orne, 'A' Squadron was down to single figures. However, at H+45 (8.10), as planned, the LCTs carrying 'C' Squadron and regimental headquarters beached, so at least the Suffolks would have a full hand of tanks to support their assault on 'Hillman' and 'Morris'. The Suffolks landed at 8.25, only five minutes behind schedule – remarkable in itself – wading 50 yards in water chest-deep. One of the company commanders recorded a terse description in his diary: 'a background of shattered, smoking seaside houses with naked slats on the roofs. The narrow stretch of sand covered with tanks and men. Pungent, burning and explosive sort of stink.'* Remarkably, for the beach was still under sporadic *indirect* fire, the Suffolks lost only one man killed during the landing.

Their first objective, 2 miles inland, would also prove a walkover. Morris, with its four howitzers, surrendered before the Suffolks could fire a shot. Many of the defenders were Poles, and evidently they'd been thoroughly shaken by the naval bombardment, though their heart probably wasn't entirely in the fight to begin with. Certainly not as much as the defenders at Hillman, the next and much larger objective, which would prove unexpectedly hard to crack. It was only subdued as night fell, with many casualties, and not until the following morning did its commander formally surrender.†

Back on the beach, the Intermediate Brigade – the 185th – began landing at just after ten o'clock. The divisional operation order

---

* Major Charles Boycott, cited in Colonel W. N. Nicholson, *The Suffolk Regiment 1928–1946* (Ipswich, 1948).

† Hillman was headquarters of the 736th Grenadier (infantry) Regiment, with 150 all ranks in eighteen underground bunkers (with armoured observation cupolas) linked by tunnels, and surrounded by machine-gun pits, barbed wire and mines. It was the control centre for the entire defences of Sword Beach, although it had no artillery of its own.

stressed speed and boldness in the advance to take the high ground before Caen, and then the city itself. Speed and boldness were as much attitudes of mind as material capabilities, but both were meant to be characteristic of armour. The operation order also stated that the brigade commander should retain a battalion in hand so that any weakening of the enemy could be immediately exploited. Brigadier Pearce Smith's plan was therefore for the Staffordshire Yeomanry, landing on the most easterly sub-beach, to marry up with the 2nd King's Shropshire Light Infantry (2 KSLI) as soon as possible at Hermanville and then to advance, carrying the infantrymen on the tanks until either artillery or small-arms fire forced them to dismount. If fire checked the tanks' advance, as instructed he intended to use concentrated artillery and quick mopping-up by the infantry to maintain momentum. The two other battalions of the brigade, the 1st Royal Norfolks and 2nd Royal Warwicks, were to follow in reserve, and were equipped with folding bicycles to increase their mobility. Unfortunately, a good many of the bikes were lost – ditched – during the deep-wading ashore.

Maintenance of momentum – the key point: without it, the brigade would be sorely pressed to achieve its first objective, let alone take Caen. Yet almost immediately the action began to stall. Congestion on the narrowing strip of sand between the rising tide and the sea wall – which was now nowhere deeper than 25 yards, and in places only 10 – and the failure to open additional exit lanes, despite heroic efforts by the sappers and flail tanks of the 22nd Dragoons, meant that few of the Yeomanry could get off the beaches for over an hour. The Yeomanry's war diary records how there was 'a terrible jam on the beach when no organization appeared to be operating and no marked exits were to be seen'. The 185th's two artillery regiments were similarly stuck, and had to deploy into gun lines at the water's edge to answer increasingly urgent calls for fire from 8th Brigade. Even the brigade commander – on foot – found himself cut off for more than an hour trying to reach the rendezvous for his command post. As one of the KSLI remarked later, 'the operation became rather an impromptu affair'.

By noon the Yeomanry had managed to get just a squadron and a half to the rallying point at Hermanville, only then to discover a minefield astride their axis of advance. Here they began taking losses from 88 mm fire – five tanks to a single gun in not many minutes – and the plan to advance with infantrymen aboard was rapidly abandoned. Instead, the KSLI would advance independently by the main road towards Périers-sur-le-Dan, and the Yeomanry would catch up as soon as they could. Meanwhile the Norfolks and the Warwicks too would advance by another route from that they'd planned.

Such is war, and what so often happens when plans come into first contact with the enemy; but even so, the stillbirth of a plan can undermine confidence. There'd been concerns throughout planning about congestion on the beaches, with the assault forces landing according to a strict timetable while their egress depended on the enemy (the mines, the obstacles, the fire) – yet no alternatives appear to have been practised by 185th Brigade. Further, while 8th Brigade needed tanks to get them ashore – mentally as much as physically – did they really need them for the immediate objectives inland? Might the squadron assigned to the Suffolks, for example, have been better employed in the dash for Caen – especially with its Fireflies? Its support of the Suffolks' attack on Hillman was severely hampered by mines. And, indeed, was an infantry brigade, even with a regiment of tanks leading, best suited for a 10-mile dash? The brigade commander really needed to be well forward in such an advance, but that was only advisable if he were in a tank, or some sort of armoured vehicle. In fact, for at least half the day he was on foot or a bicycle. And while it was – and is – the usual practice to keep a third of the force in reserve, was it best for the division to keep a third of its armour (the East Riding Yeomanry) out of the battle at the outset, and also the armoured brigade headquarters? Brigadier Pearce Smith of the 185th had seen no real action during the war, having commanded a brigade under siege in Malta. Now he was entrusted with the day's great objective – 'The 3rd British Infantry Division will land . . . and capture CAEN' – which by the divisional commander's own reckoning could only be achieved with thrusting single-mindedness.

Adding to the congestion and confusion now was the arrival of the Reserve Brigade, the 9th. Their leading elements had begun landing at ten o'clock, a little further west, but soon the beachmasters were signalling the LCTs to hold offshore. Indeed, some of the brigade wouldn't land until three hours after schedule. By a perverse stroke of fortune, too, their brigadier was badly wounded early on, before the brigade could even begin rallying, and his deputy, Colonel Dennis Orr, wasn't immediately at hand to take over, having been sent to liaise with the airborne troops at the Orne bridges. The commanding officer of the lead battalion, the 2nd Royal Ulster Rifles, had to assume command in his absence, which inevitably prolonged the sense of drift.

The failure to take Hillman was also adding to 185th Brigade's problems. Mid-afternoon, Pearce Smith told the Norfolks to forget their intended line of advance along the road and to give Hillman a wide berth. In doing so, however, cross-country, they ran into trouble with machine guns. At the same time, a potentially dangerous armoured counter-attack was developing from the direction of Caen – doubly dangerous because 8th Brigade had been unable to secure the high ground between Périers-sur-le-Dan and St Aubin-d'Arquenay. Fortunately, the Staffordshire Yeomanry's commanding officer, Lieutenant-Colonel James Eadie, had already decided this was vital ground – it overlooked the beaches, and commanded the approaches to and from Caen – and as soon as his tanks were able to deal with the distant '88' opposition and shake off the minefield, he made a dash for it.

Pressure on the left flank beyond the Orne was already building, with a series of counter-attacks, though fortunately without much armour. These failed to dislodge the airborne troops, but checked progress towards the River Dives and slowed their consolidation. It certainly wasn't going to be an alternative route to Caen.

When the Staffordshire Yeomanry reached the Périers–St Aubin ridge they opened fire on some distant guns and transport, which probably also served to deflect the developing counter-attack by the 21st Panzer Division from its line heading directly for Ouistreham and Sword, sending it further to the north and west – which in turn exposed them to enfilading fire from the ridge. The division was under-strength but had re-formed around a cadre of 2,000 Wehrmacht veterans of the battles in North Africa, and was equipped with the formidable Panzer IV tank (with its long 75 mm gun). However, they'd suffered from air attacks all morning as they tried to get up to and through Caen (most of the divisional staff were killed in one attack), and they now began losing panzers to the Yeomanry and a 17-pounder anti-tank battery at the extreme range of 2,000 yards. Although a few actually reached the sea between Sword and Juno in mid-afternoon, there was nothing they could do, and they were only just able to withdraw from what was nearly a closing trap.*

By late afternoon, then, the Sword 'triangle' was pretty secure on all three sides; but the apex – Caen – remained elusive. Indeed, 185th Brigade were nowhere near capturing the city. The Staffordshire Yeomen were firmly in command of the Périers–St Aubin ridge, where

---

* They'd first been put on alert at 3 a.m. by the airborne landings, and then again by the landings at Omaha and Utah beaches, which because of the need for a rising tide had begun an hour before those at Sword. How definitively they'd identified the gap between the 3rd Division and the Canadians it isn't possible to say. They were probably, in the old manner, 'marching to the sound of the guns', and then adjusting their lines of advance to the air threat and anti-tank fire. Theirs was not an enviable situation.

they'd been joined by the KSLI and the Norfolks, and the Warwicks were just outside the village of Blainville-sur-Orne astride the main road from Ouistreham, 3 miles short of Caen. With German resistance stiffening, however, not least with the expected arrival of the 12th SS Division, the trappy going made for diminishing progress. The Reserve – 9th Brigade – couldn't help either, for they'd had to turn west just a mile inland to face the Panzer Division's flanking threat (which in the end petered out). As night approached, and with it both exhaustion and the casualty reckoning, all the division could now do was dig in and await the expected counter-attacks.*

It wasn't neat, it wasn't joined up, and they hadn't gone as deep as they'd hoped; but the landings – sea and air – hadn't been repulsed. The left flank of Sword – the Orne – hadn't been pushed out as far as they wanted, but it was solid. The right was open, with a gap of some 3 miles, but any counter-attack here risked being caught in a pincer by troops from Sword and Juno. The beaches were no longer under direct fire, nor could they be engaged by artillery with less than 12,000 yards' range – except from the left flank.† The I Corps plan had been 'to secure, on D Day, a covering position on the general line PUTOT EN BESSIN 9072 – CAEN 0068 – thence R ORNE to the sea'. By evening, although the line didn't conform exactly with those points, 3rd Division (and the Canadians and Tyne-Tees at Juno and Gold)

---

* For example, come evening the 2nd East Yorkshires had lost five officers and sixty other ranks killed, and four officers and 137 ORs wounded – some 25% of the battalion's assault strength, which called for considerable reorganization. Theirs were the highest casualties suffered by any battalion in 2nd Army on D-Day. (But far lower than those of Gallipoli or the Somme.)

† The feared 'Nebelwerfer' multiple rocket-launcher, for example, had a maximum range of 7,000 yards, and the standard 75 mm howitzer had also been pushed out of effective range, except from the eastern flank. Even so, fire from the left flank increased dangerously throughout June, until on the 30th the easternmost beaches, including Roger (Green), were closed – no longer used for landing.

had secured a practicable covering position, and in all, perhaps some half to two-thirds of the hoped-for ground.

Caen wasn't in the bag, however. Why not?

The first part of the answer, of course, was the enemy. Much was known about him, his dispositions, defences and probable intentions. He was quickly neutralized at the high-water mark, but inland he hadn't been bombed and shelled into complete submission. The 21st Panzer Division's counter-move seems also to have alarmed Rennie, and also no doubt Crocker, the corps commander, although a German counter-attack was the most predictable aspect of any Second World War battle. Then there was Clausewitz's 'friction' – 'Everything in war is simple, but the simplest thing is difficult.' And the landings weren't even the simplest thing. They were, indeed, the most complex technical challenge the British army had ever faced. Add to this that other of Clausewitz's malevolent elements, the 'fog of war' arising from imperfect intelligence, and the job facing 3rd Division's brigade commanders was perhaps the toughest of the war.

There is a saying: the brigade commander fights the enemy, and the divisional commander fights the battle. The idea is that while the brigadier is personally directing the troops and resources under his command to fight the enemy with whom his brigade is in contact (or moving to contact), the divisional commander sits back, as it were, with his eyes casting about and his mind ranging left, right and forward, *anticipating*; and, like a chess player, he moves the uncommitted elements of his division in response to or in expectation of his brigadiers' triumphs or troubles. To an extent this is the same for every level of command: the commander – even the platoon commander – tries to keep out of the actual firefight so as to judge what best to do, and to have something spare to do it with. But even a brigade is best fought tightly, with its elements in close cooperation, and with a hands-on commander. The 8th Brigade did well, although their taking of Hillman was reckoned a bit slow; and, indeed, seven days later

'Copper' Cass would take over temporary command of the division when Rennie was wounded, returning to his brigade a fortnight later and remaining in command until October. In some quarters, inevitably, there was criticism of 3rd Division's performance. The thrust of it was that, not having seen action since 1940, and two-thirds of its men not having seen any at all, the division didn't really know its job. Some said the infantry companies were too reliant on their officers, becoming disordered and even despondent when these became casualties. There are grains of truth in these criticisms, no doubt, but as a generalization it hardly seems to hold. The 13th/18th Hussars' astonishing feat of seamanship, and then their support to the assault battalions – for which five Military Crosses and twelve Military Medals were awarded, the greatest number of gallantry decorations ever won by a regiment in a single day – is one example of why not. And even if the East Yorkshires' 25 per cent casualties suggest poor tactics – which they by no means do – they're certainly not evidence of shirking.*

Pearce Smith, however, was sacked a few days later. There seems no doubt that he'd failed to 'thrust' – 'This advance will be carried out with speed and boldness' – becoming instead too mentally tied down by Hillman and too wary of counter-attack. Caen was, after all, his entire *raison d'être* that day: '185 Infantry Brigade Group ... will capture CAEN ...' This the brigade failed to do. That failure is understandable, but arguably there was, ultimately, no unavoidable reason for it. It is tempting to speculate on what might have been if 27th Armoured Brigade had been kept at least partly intact and assigned the task. Or

---

* In his memoir *March Past* (London, 1978), for example, Lord Lovat, commanding the 1st Special Service (Commando) Brigade, is particularly scathing of 3rd Division's infantry. I am not, however, inclined to give his criticisms much credence. He saw almost nothing of 3rd Division's fighting that day, except the bodies on the beach on which he landed half an hour after the East Yorkshires had stormed it.

if more, at least, of the infantry had been in carriers, like those of the motor battalions.*

That said, was Rennie's plan as good as it might have been? His divisional operation order is immensely detailed, elaborate even, trying as it does to knit together so many sub-formations and separate units, as well as others such as the commandos temporarily under his command, and reinforcing or replacing airborne troops east of the Orne. It reads more like a set of coordinating instructions – and one preoccupied with the flanks – than an order to the division *as a whole* to capture Caen. There's almost a sense of 'if we can all get across the beaches by nightfall it will be an achievement – and then we'll go from there'. And clearly, in the minds of some – Brooke springs to mind – not just an achievement but a miracle. The operation order is clear that taking Caen on D-Day is I Corps' intention (mission), but it isn't expressed as categorically as it might have been. And Rennie's own movements on the day don't suggest that getting the 185th or the 9th Brigade to Caen was his overriding concern. It's curious, too, that he allocated no role to his divisional reconnaissance regiment other than as contact detachments with the brigades and beach traffic control groups – that is, there was no independent scouting. Indeed, the bulk of the regiment didn't land until D+11. It meant that he was wholly reliant on what his brigades could tell him.

There just seemed to be too much on 3rd Division's plate.

And then we should ask why, if Caen was so critical to the

---

* The motor battalion of 1944 provided the armoured brigades with immediately available infantry, as distinct from the armoured division's main infantry contingent, the infantry brigade, which was on foot or lorry-borne. An armoured brigade therefore had a strong infantry component that was almost a match with the tanks in terms of mobility. The problem of congestion on the beaches would have remained – in fact potentially increased with the carriers – but an armoured brigade commander would have been more likely to fix on the problem during planning than would the commander of an infantry brigade, whose mind will always be focused on his infantrymen.

subsequent development of 2nd Army's operations, was the 6th Airborne Division not dropped south and east of the city to mask it – to prevent or at least delay the movement of counter-attacking forces? This had in fact been part of COSSAC's original plan, but had been dropped in February and the emphasis switched to left-flank protection.

Perhaps the answer to this (a question for 2nd Army, perhaps even 21st Army Group) and the questions about 3rd Division's performance is best found in 2nd Army commander's own post-war assessment, in which he said that he'd not wanted 'to get involved on too broad a frontage, because that would have consumed two-thirds of their [the assaulting forces'] strength', and that he was 'worried about the Germans on their left and on their front'. He wanted, he said, 'to be able to push 3 [Infantry Division] as far south towards Caen as I could and still keep sufficient troops in reserve to be quite sure of holding this flank'. Indeed, he 'never expected 3 to get to Caen on the first day, and I always said that if we didn't get it the first day it would take a month to get it afterwards'.

Then, Dempsey made his view quite clear: 'The important task on this sector was not deep penetration but strength on the flank.'*

So there it is: the army commander's mind, which by degrees, no matter how imperceptibly, shapes that of successive subordinate commanders – and ultimately therefore the battle itself.

---

* Dempsey to Basil Liddell Hart, LH15/15/130/8, Liddell Hart Centre for Military Archives, King's College London.

POSTSCRIPT

The Allies had succeeded in establishing a bridgehead on D-Day. Although many of the immediate strategic objectives of the landings hadn't been achieved, and the Germans still controlled most of Normandy, it's impossible to overstate this achievement. D-Day was a battle in itself – the battle for the bridgehead. Without that bridgehead, nothing could avail. Overlord would have been dead, as dead as Eisenhower's alternative communiqué implied.

The failure to capture Caen was a major setback; but ironically, given the strength of German resistance, it may in the longer run have been less of a catastrophe than has been widely supposed since. Montgomery now switched his tactics to drawing the German reserves towards the British and Canadians in order to let the Americans take the port of Cherbourg, which would be critical to any sustained advance, and thereafter to break out for Paris while the bulk of the Germans were fixed in battle towards Caen.* It's never been truly established whether this had been Montgomery's

---

* It is sometimes argued that, the Germans having moved several formations undetected much closer to the coast, as per Rommel's intention – especially the reinforcements north of Caen, including half of the infantry and a battalion of the 21st Panzer Division – by 15 May, the day of Montgomery's briefing to the king and others, a dash to seize Caen was no longer possible. When Caen had been set as an objective in 1943, the planning assumption was that the Germans would have (best case) twenty divisions, and (worst case) fifty. In fact by 6 June they had sixty, even if some were

intention all along, or even a contingency plan; or whether it was just an agile adaptation, as at Alamein. The trouble is, Monty always liked to give the impression of things going to (master) plan.

The Allies had complete air superiority, more men and far greater resources. And although the Germans put up the most determined defence, they were never able to launch a decisive counter-attack anywhere along the entire Normandy front. The Allies held and maintained the initiative throughout.

The Americans captured Cherbourg at the end of June, and were then able to increase their pressure south. Meanwhile the British and Canadians made slow progress around Caen, but forced the Germans to commit their best troops and tanks to hold them back.

Caen was finally captured, and the dominating ground to the south-east taken, towards the end of July, which allowed the Americans to break out around Avranches at the southern end of the Cotentin Peninsula. Hitler personally refused all requests to retreat, instead ordering a counter-attack towards Mortain. Without adequate air support, it had no chance of success, and the Germans soon found themselves trapped in a shrinking pocket at Falaise, where they suffered heavy casualties from Allied artillery and air attacks. While many did manage to escape, 60,000 were killed or captured, and almost all their guns, tanks and vehicles abandoned.

Overlord had achieved its strategic object – to gain a lodgement area from which further offensive operations could be developed. On 25 August 1944, Paris was liberated. With the Germans in full retreat, the Allies now advanced rapidly on a broad front through north-east France and Belgium towards the borders of the Third Reich.

---

under-strength. I remain unconvinced, however, that taking Caen wasn't possible; the point is that the plan wasn't optimized to do so.

In March 1945, after crossing the Rhine, Major-General Tom Rennie, whose division had won the battle of the bridgehead at Sword Beach, was killed by mortar fire. Having recovered from his D-Day wounds he'd taken command of the 51st Highland Division. He was the most senior of Montgomery's commanders to be killed in action.

PART FIVE

IMJIN RIVER

The Battle for Honor

22–25 APRIL 1951

> A bit sticky, things are pretty sticky down there.
>
> Brigadier Tom Brodie to his (US)
> divisional commander

While Rorke's Drift is familiar to many, if only from the 1964 film *Zulu*, fewer know of Imjin River, or have even heard of it. Yet the two battles have much in common: British troops, though massively outnumbered, putting up an heroic fight against wave after wave of frontal attacks by suicidally brave infantry. Sustained by regimental discipline and steadfast junior leadership, they beat off the attacks time and again, although eventually at Imjin the defenders were overwhelmed and had to withdraw. The two leading actors in *Zulu*, Michael Caine and Stanley Baker, had even featured in an earlier film about the Korean War, Caine himself having served in Korea as a national serviceman. The difference between the two battles, however, was their scale. At Rorke's Drift, an infantry company some 120 strong faced 3,000–4,000 Zulus, and sustained fewer than twenty fatal casualties. At the Imjin river, a British brigade of some 4,000 faced three Chinese divisions, upwards of 50,000 men, and at the end of three days' continual fighting had lost nearly a quarter of their strength. Imjin remains the British army's bloodiest action since the Second World War, and underwrote much of its defensive tactics in the Cold War.

1

A TRANSITORY STATE

When whales fight, the shrimp's back is broken.

Old Korean proverb

Old sins cast long shadows in Korea. The peninsula, similar to Great Britain in length and area, has seen repeated invasions and civil war. There was indeed an earlier battle of Imjin river,* during the Japanese invasions of the late sixteenth century in what is sometimes called the First Great East Asian War. The seven-year conflict shaped the relationship between China and Korea in the centuries between the first and second Imjin battles, a relationship which, when war came again to the peninsula in 1951, brought the West and the communist bloc perilously close to major conflict, and the use of nuclear weapons.

In May of the Korean year *Imjin* – 'water-dragon' – 1592, a Japanese army invaded via Pusan in the south-east of the peninsula, the

---

* See Samuel Hawley, *The Imjin War: Japan's Sixteenth-Century Invasion of Korea and Attempt to Conquer China* (Berkeley, CA, 2005).

closest point to the island of Kyushu, headquarters of Toyotomi Hideyoshi, first minister and de facto dictator of Japan. It was meant to be a stepping stone to the conquest of Ming China, which had been much weakened by Mongol incursions across the Great Wall, by rebellions in the north-east (in what later became 'Manchuria'), by pirates raiding the long length of the coast, and by trouble with its supposed vassal Burma. In theory, Peking (modern Beijing) had 2 million men under arms; in practice, by the late sixteenth century they could barely muster six figures. Hideyoshi had more than twice that number mobilized for the war, of which 150,000 were now landing at Pusan after a short but fierce battle to overcome the Korean garrison – short because the Koreans were armed with bows and the Japanese with Portuguese matchlock muskets; fierce because the Japanese would give no quarter.

The army began its march towards the capital, Hanseong (modern Seoul), against little effective opposition, and in June the royal family fled north for Pyongyang (now the capital of North Korea) – 125 miles as the crow flies. Hanseong, which had lapsed into anarchy and much of which lay in ruins, fell to the Japanese three days later. After resting for a fortnight, on 27 June the army resumed its advance, closing quickly on the Imjin river.

The Imjin rises near Wonsan on the east coast and flows north to south, turning south-west about 30 miles north of Seoul, where it's joined by the Hantan, and then meanders to join the Han downstream of the capital before entering the Yellow Sea. Near its confluence with the Hantan, the Imjin isn't more than 100 yards wide, a channel in an otherwise dry riverbed of some 400 yards bordered by almost vertical rock cliffs standing 75 feet and more. During the dry season the Imjin is fordable; during the rainy season, July and August, it becomes a torrent.

Here, the Koreans finally managed to steel themselves to a determined stand. With 15,000 soldiers on the north bank, they were in a commanding position, able to force an indefinite delay on the Japanese, who'd have to cross in small numbers. The Koreans, however, were hampered by disunity of command, being made up of a number of independent forces, not least some 3,000 northern border cavalry, not dissimilar to the English northern light horse of Henry VIII's day whose other occupation, cattle rustling and general plundering, gave rise to the name 'border reivers'. Being veterans of many a clash with the frontier tribes of Manchuria and practised reivers themselves, the border cavalry were certain of their superiority, and impatient of more sedentary tactics. So when after a fortnight the Japanese tired of trying to establish a bridgehead and decided to withdraw their main forces to the comfort and safety of nearby Paju fortress in the hope of tempting the defenders to cross, the Koreans were quick to fall for the feigned retreat. Although the Japanese had developed a healthy respect for the border cavalry, they'd calculated that, impetuous and not having faced the concerted fire of the arquebus (musket) before, once across the river they could be destroyed en masse.

Some of the northern cavalry who'd seen the border tribes use the same *ruse de guerre* were reluctant, however, and several officers were summarily executed *pour encourager les autres*. The Koreans began crossing at dawn on 7 July (by the Gregorian calendar), 13,000 of them by some estimates, and pressed on confidently past the ostentatiously abandoned camp. The Japanese sprang their ambush, reinforced rapidly by the main body at Paju; the Koreans broke and were harried back to the river. Casualties were heavy, including most of the field commanders. A government official on the north bank fled, and those left holding the dominating ground, mistaking him for Kim Myong-won, the titular commander-in-chief, panicked and fled too.

By the end of July the Japanese had taken Pyongyang, while in the meantime a second contingent, having marched some 600 miles directly from Pusan into the far north-east of the peninsula, crossed into Manchuria to test the fighting strength of the Jurchen tribes.

This, however, was as far as the Japanese got. In August, the Korean king, who'd crossed the Yalu river and taken refuge in Manchuria, appealed to the Chinese emperor, his suzerain, for military assistance. The emperor at once sent a small force, which got a bloody nose. Now thoroughly alarmed, in January he sent a larger army – some 35,000 – across the Yalu. Pyongyang was quickly retaken, and the Japanese withdrew to Seoul and sued for peace.

But the war had dealt Korea a major blow. Besides the death of at least 125,000 Korean warriors and the removal of 60,000–70,000 prisoners of war – by no means all combatants – to Japan, agriculture suffered severely from neglect and the Japanese scorched-earth policy. Cities especially felt the consequences: starvation and disease. Seoul's population fell from about 100,000 to 40,000, and by 1600 that of the country as a whole had shrunk from 14 million to 12 million. In addition, much cultural and technological loot was taken back to Japan – and, as if to maintain a defiant claim on the country, to be renewed at some future date, a Japanese settlement and garrison remained at Pusan. The war of the Korean year *Imjin* did indeed cast long shadows.

The Sino-Japanese War of 1894–5 darkened them even further. As Japan emerged from its internal blood-letting in the 1870s – the shogunate against the emperor – it became increasingly assertive in Korea. China became equally assertive in resisting interference in its most important tributary state. In 1894 a peasant revolt alarmed the Korean king into asking for Chinese military assistance again. When the Chinese informed Tokyo under the terms of an earlier 'confidence and security' agreement, Japan at once sent troops to the peninsula to crush the rebellion, and then stayed put. War with China followed, in which Japan's forces, modernized with considerable British help, particularly naval, were spectacularly successful. Indeed, the imperial Japanese navy sank or captured most of the northern Chinese fleet. A peace treaty followed which made Korea independent, but in effect merely exchanged Chinese suzerainty for Japanese. Ten years later, Korea formally became a Japanese protectorate, and then in 1910, again by pseudo-treaty, Japan annexed the country outright.

For the next thirty-five years, from the annexation to Emperor Hirohito's surrender in 1945 after atomic bombs were dropped on Hiroshima and Nagasaki, the Korean peninsula was subject to particularly brutal Japanese rule. During the Second World War, over 5 million Koreans were pressed into forced labour, in which one in ten died, and many tens of thousands of Korean women were conscripted as 'comfort women' for the Japanese military. New sins were lengthening old shadows even further. 'Rehabilitation' of Korea after 1945 was never going to be easy.

The first problem was forming an administration. Unlike other liberated countries of East Asia, Korea had no former colonial power or exiled government to retake control. At the Allies' Moscow conference in October 1944, the Russians had finally agreed to declare war on Japan as soon as Germany was defeated, but it wasn't until after the United States dropped the first atomic bomb that Stalin revoked the Soviet–Japanese non-aggression pact and on 8 August 1945 moved to invade Manchuria, where the Japanese had been lodged since invading in 1931 (subsequently invading the rest of China in 1937). Alarmed at what was now an unnecessary intervention, President Truman, who'd succeeded to the presidency in April on the death of Franklin D. Roosevelt, proposed a joint occupation of Korea.

Japan surrendered on 15 August – which North Korea celebrates as its national liberation day – and the Soviet Union, as the victorious ally with troops nearest the peninsula, moved quickly into the vacuum. As an interim measure to disarm the Japanese occupation forces and repatriate the 700,000 or so Japanese civilians, Moscow and Washington agreed to divide the peninsula along the 38th parallel and administer their respective zones under United Nations trusteeship – Russia to the north, the United States to the south. The US Army's XXIV Corps landed at Inchon just west of Seoul on 8 September.

As for restoration of Korean sovereignty, the candidates for leadership fell into two categories: communists, who'd fought against the Japanese in Manchuria and China with Mao Zedong's People's Liberation Army (PLA), and nationalists in exile in the West, mainly the United States. Of the communists, the Russian-trained guerrilla leader Kim Il-Sung (Kim 'one star') soon emerged pre-eminent. Of the nationalists, Syngman Rhee, a political refugee in America since 1904, emerged the strongest. Paradoxically, while Kim Il-Sung had been born into a Presbyterian family in the north, later abandoning his faith, Syngman Rhee had had a traditional Confucian education in the south, converting to Christianity in his late teens through the influence of American medical missionaries.

By the end of the three-year UN trusteeship, some 3 million Koreans, a third of the North's population, had migrated to the South despite the North's advantage in industry and raw materials (the South was largely agrarian, much poorer, and generally considered backward). The North then boycotted what were intended to be nationwide parliamentary elections. Consequently, in August 1948 the South declared itself the Republic of Korea (ROK), with Syngman Rhee as president. The following month the North formed the Democratic People's Republic of Korea (DPRK), with Kim Il-Sung as 'Eternal Leader'. The Soviet Union at once declared Kim Il-Sung's government to be sovereign over both parts. The UN, on the other hand, declared Rhee's to be the only legal government in Korea.

In July the previous year, the British (Labour) government led by Clement Attlee, who'd been Churchill's deputy in the wartime coalition, and who'd won the 1945 general election with a landslide majority for welfare and much other reform, had taken the unprecedented step of passing an act of parliament providing for conscription in peacetime.* When the Second World War ended there'd been a general expectation that it would be 'business as before' for the army, just as it had been when the First World War ended, with a return to pre-war voluntary recruiting. But the peace of 1945 was quite unlike that of 1918. The imperial situation was far shakier, in part because of a surge in nationalism, in India especially, and in part because of the spread of communism in Asia – allied to the uncertainty of how difficult it would be to recolonize territory lost to the Japanese in 1941–2. And in Europe the enemy had been replaced by an even more powerful threat: the Red Army.

The act provided for a year's compulsory military service for all able-bodied males aged eighteen, soon afterwards extended to eighteen months, followed by six years' reservist liability. The legislation was called the National Service Act, and conscripts were therefore national servicemen. It probably sounded more in keeping with the new socialist order in Westminster.†

But war with communism would break out further away than anticipated. Encouraged by the DPRK, communists in (South) Korea began an insurgency which led to sporadic fighting along the porous border, between the newly formed ROK army and the DPRK's Korean People's Army (KPA). Atrocities on both sides were common. Nevertheless, in December 1948 the UN established a commission for the unification of Korea and the withdrawal of the occupation forces. While the commission oversaw the withdrawal of almost all US and Soviet forces in 1949, it made no progress towards unification.

On 25 June 1950, with the encouragement of Stalin and Mao

---

* Unprecedented, that is, excepting the Military Training Act of April 1939, which was passed in the expectation of war.

† The legislation in 1939 at the outbreak of war was also called the National Service Act, but the term 'national serviceman' wasn't much used then, probably in part because the entire country was mobilized.

Zedong, advised by Soviet generals and inspired by the success of Mao's PLA against Chiang Kai-shek's nationalist troops, the KPA launched a massive offensive across the 38th parallel – a full-blown invasion of the South. The UN Security Council (UNSC) promptly passed a resolution calling for immediate cessation of hostilities and withdrawal of North Korean forces. Two days later, with no response from the DPRK, the UNSC passed an additional resolution calling on UN members '[to] furnish such assistance to the Republic of Korea as may be necessary to repel the armed attack and restore international peace and security in the area'.*

Truman authorized air and naval operations north of the 38th parallel by US occupation forces in Japan. However it wasn't until 30 June, following a sobering report on the military situation by General Douglas MacArthur, hero of the war in the Pacific and now US commander-in-chief in Japan, that he authorized the use of ground forces.

This would take time. Meanwhile, with no tanks or heavy artillery to speak of, the ROK Army proved no match for the KPA, who were well equipped, especially with the T34 tank which had served the Red Army so well on the Eastern Front, and swelled by Korean guerrillas (and some ethnic Chinese in Korean guise) recently returned from the PLA's war with Chiang Kai-Shek's nationalists. Not surprisingly, Seoul, the capital, fell quickly.

US troops were rushed from Japan via Pusan, while other UN members, especially from the Commonwealth, began mustering theirs.†

---

* The UN was only able to pass these resolutions because the Soviet Union was boycotting the UNSC over the issue of which China should be a permanent member of the council – Mao's communists, victorious in the civil war that had followed the defeat of the Japanese, or Chiang Kai-Shek's nationalists, who'd withdrawn to the island of Formosa (now Taiwan).

† Eventually there would be troop contributions from fifteen member states, of which Britain's would be second only to the US.

But by early August the KPA had largely over-run the South, ROK army and US forces falling back south-east on Pusan, where a British infantry brigade, the 27th, had arrived from Hong Kong to help hold the bridgehead. By 18 August the KPA had outrun themselves and were finally brought to a halt at the Pusan perimeter, although fighting continued for several weeks.

MacArthur, appointed commander-in-chief of UN forces in Korea (UN Command – UNC), in addition to all US forces in the region, now made one of the boldest moves in all of military history: an amphibious landing by two divisions – one marines and one US army, together with ROK units, in total some 50,000 men – at Inchon. They quickly recaptured the capital; the KPA, badly shaken, began withdrawing north, taking with them many thousands of civilian hostages and forced labourers, and executing many others. Indeed, the summary execution of large numbers of political prisoners by both KPA and ROK troops made for scenes reminiscent of the Second World War in eastern Europe.

On 27 September, the US Joint Chiefs of Staff sent MacArthur a directive stating that the primary goal was the destruction of the KPA, with unification of the Korean peninsula under Rhee as a secondary objective 'if possible', depending on whether or not the Chinese and Soviets intervened. Within days, UNC had pushed the KPA north of the border, and ROK troops were crossing in pursuit. The UN then authorized MacArthur to follow and, now with the bit between their teeth, UN troops made rapid progress.*

Kim Il-Sung at once appealed directly for help to both the Russians and the Chinese. Stalin responded by sending more and better arms, including aircraft – and pilots – while in late October Mao

---

* MacArthur, as US tri-service C-in-C in the Far East and C-in-C UNC, exercised overall command from Tokyo. The land forces commander in Korea was Walton Walker, Commanding General 8th US Army.

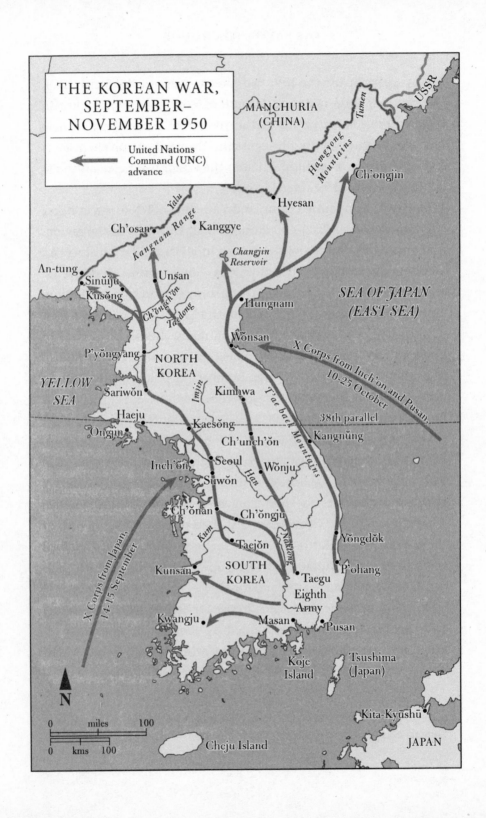

THE KOREAN WAR,
SEPTEMBER–
NOVEMBER 1950

United Nations
Command (UNC)
advance

MANCHURIA
(CHINA)

Tumen

USSR

Hamgyong Mountains

Ch'ongjin

Hyesan

Yalu

Ch'osan

Kanggye

Kangnam Range

An-tung

Changjin Reservoir

Sinŭiju

Unsan

Kusŏng

Ch'ŏngch'ŏn

Taedong

Hungnam

SEA OF JAPAN
(EAST SEA)

Wŏnsan

P'yŏngyang

NORTH
KOREA

X Corps from Inch'on and Pusan,
10–25 October

YELLOW
SEA

Sariwŏn

Imjin

Kimhwa

T'aebaek Mountains

38th parallel

Haeju

Kaesŏng

Kangnŭng

Ongjin

Ch'unch'ŏn

Inch'ŏn

Seoul

Wŏnju

Suwŏn

Han

Ch'ŏnan

Ch'ŏngju

Kum

Taejŏn

Naktong

Yŏngdŏk

X Corps from Japan,
14–15 September

SOUTH
KOREA

P'ohang

Kunsan

Taegu

Eighth
Army

Kwangju

Masan

Pusan

N

Koje
Island

Tsushima
(Japan)

Kita-Kyūshū

0   miles   100

0   kms   100

Cheju Island

JAPAN

redesignated the PLA's North East Frontier Force as the People's Volunteer Army (PVA) and sent them south to aid the KPA. MacArthur, given what he perceived to be the strengthening strategic momentum, now argued that hostilities should be extended into China itself to destroy depots supplying the war effort. Truman disagreed, ordering caution at the Sino-Korean border. So, having taken Pyongyang, UNC halted 25 miles from the border, formed largely by the Yalu and Tumen rivers on a line roughly south-west to north-east, although ROK troops pressed right up to it in the north-east.

In fact, with the intervention of Soviet air power and regular Chinese troops, the tide was already beginning to turn. After secretly crossing the Yalu, on 25 October the PVA 13th Army Group launched a counter-offensive. This took the ROK II Corps and the US 1st Cavalry Division by surprise, turning the US 8th Army's right flank and forcing UN troops to retreat to the Chongchon river, 30 miles north of Pyongyang. However, the PVA soon outran their logistics, and a fortnight later had to withdraw. This seemed to confirm the UNC's assessment that the Chinese had not intervened on any large scale, and MacArthur ordered the interdiction bombing of the bridges over the Yalu, telling Lieutenant-General Walton Walker, commanding the US 8th Army, to launch an all-out offensive: 'Home by Christmas'.

Hardly had Walker begun, though, when the Chinese struck again. The planners had underestimated the number of PVA troops already south of the Yalu – now some 180,000 – with reinforcements still managing to infiltrate despite the bombing. And although the Chinese leadership had originally intended to stand on the defensive till Soviet weapons arrived in the spring, their earlier success convinced them the PVA was ready to deliver a knockout blow.

After a week's fighting, in early December the US 8th Army was decisively beaten in an encircling battle astride the Chongchon river, precipitating a headlong retreat to the 38th parallel – the longest retreat of a US army in history. MacArthur loosed his Far East Air

Forces (FEAF) to stem the advance of the Chinese and the reinvigorated KPA, and to destroy any potential shelter for the coming winter. North Korean cities were devastated, including Pyongyang; images of the destruction even today play a major part in the DPRK's anti-American propaganda.

On 16 December, Truman declared a national state of emergency, effectively putting US forces on a war footing. The following day, Mao divested Kim Il-Sung of command of the KPA: from now on they'd operate under direct command of the PVA. He publicly justified China's open entry into the war as a response to 'American aggression in the guise of the UN', claiming that US aircraft had violated Chinese airspace and attacked Chinese targets.*

By Christmas, UN troops were back south of the Imjin again. At times their pursuers had only been held off by the US air force, and although here and there the retreat was skilfully conducted, particularly in the marines division, morale throughout 8th Army was low. Indeed, in some units, battlefield discipline was rapidly ebbing away. Then on 23 December, not long after his sixty-first birthday, Walton Walker himself was killed – in a traffic accident, just like his mentor General George S. Patton, in whose 3rd Army he'd served during the Second World War as a corps commander.†

---

* At the Washington conference earlier that month, Attlee had urged Truman not to allow the war to escalate – through being, as it were, drawn in by Soviet involvement – when the greater Soviet threat lay in Europe. British advice during UNC's advance to the Yalu had been to stop at the 39th parallel – the line on which Pyongyang sat, beyond which the peninsula widened significantly.

† Walker – nicknamed 'Bulldog' – was killed near Seoul when his northbound open-top command jeep collided in snow with a KPA weapons carrier coming south. His body was escorted back to the US by his son, a battalion commander with the 19th Infantry Regiment, also in Korea. On 2 January 1951 he was posthumously promoted to full general.

2

WHY ARE WE HERE?
WHAT ARE WE FIGHTING FOR?

The true soldier fights not because he hates what is in front of him,
but because he loves what is behind him.

G. K. Chesterton

The British – increasingly the Commonwealth – contribution to
UNC was now the best part of a division: two infantry brigades (the
27th and the 29th), a reinforced armoured regiment (with Centurion and Cromwell tanks), and supporting arms and services.* At this
stage, however, the brigades were still operating under command of

---

* In July 1951 the Commonwealth Division was formed, with Canadian, Australian
and New Zealand contingents, and an Indian field ambulance. At its peak, the British
contribution was just over 14,000 (some 60,000 in all took part over the two years of
fighting), compared with the US's 300,000, including naval and air forces, and the
ROK's 620,000 (out of a population of 20 million). The PVA peaked at 1.4 million (not
all south of the border), and the KPA at 267,000 (out of a population of 9 million).

US divisions. Most officers of the rank of captain and above, and most sergeants and above, had seen active service in the Second World War, but the junior ranks were largely national servicemen. Regiments were therefore made up, as in the Second World War, of a solid core of experienced professionals and conscripts of varying quality – most of them resignedly unenthusiastic, some of them positively recalcitrant, but some of them highly intelligent, capable men who'd never thought to find themselves in uniform and found it rather to their liking. In addition there were the reservists, men who'd previously served their time with the colours as either national servicemen or regulars and whose reserve liability hadn't expired. These latter, far from pleased to find themselves called up suddenly without warning and seemingly without compelling reason, were perhaps the most difficult to handle, although sometimes when the chips were down their previous service proved its worth.

Up to the direct intervention of the Chinese at the end of October, the British contingent had had things relatively easy, except for the weather, although there'd been sporadic bouts of intense fighting: the first post-war VC (posthumously awarded) had been won at the defence of the Pusan perimeter in September. The subsequent withdrawal to the Imjin and Han rivers, however, had seen some very desperate fighting indeed, not least by the 8th King's Royal Irish Hussars, who'd been in England as part of the strategic reserve when the KPA had crossed the 38th parallel in June. Initially there'd been no intention of sending tanks, but that changed as the KPA's T34s cut through the peninsula, and after hasty conversion to the Mark III version of the Centurion (with 20-pounder gun), the regiment were shipped east. Landing at Pusan in November, they were loaded at once on to railway flatbeds and sent north, only to find themselves after unloading in full retreat, covering the withdrawal of the two brigades back across the Imjin.

Here a tolerably defensible line was established, but in the depths of the coldest winter in a hundred years; and with the death of 'Bull-dog' Walker morale in American units sank even lower, while in most of the ROK divisions it was even worse.

It was at this point that the supreme shaper of battle came to the fore – the leadership. As soon as he learned of Walker's death, Mac-Arthur rang General Joe Lawton Collins, the US Army's chief of staff, asking for Lieutenant-General Matthew Ridgway to be sent to Korea at once.* Ridgway, aged fifty-five, had commanded the 101st (US) Air-borne Division in Normandy and then XVIII Airborne Corps on Operation Market Garden, and MacArthur had known him since Ridgway was a captain on his staff at West Point (when, so legend has it, MacArthur had been trying to get the military academy to stop thinking about refighting the war of 1812). Collins at once rang Ridg-way, who was at the home of a friend in Washington 'sipping an after-dinner highball'. After taking the call, Ridgway returned to his drink, saying nothing, but left soon afterwards with his wife and packed his bags. Next morning, Saturday (still the 23rd in Korea – a fourteen-hour time difference between Tokyo and Washington DC), he went to the Pentagon, and then in the evening took off by plane for Tokyo, landing shortly before midnight on Christmas Day. Next morning he had a briefing from MacArthur, the import of which was that 8th Army should continue to retire to successive defensive positions, to hold Seoul as long as they could, but not to risk encirclement.

After listening in silence to what must have been a deeply pessi-mistic summary of the situation, at length Ridgway asked: 'General, if I get over there and find the situation to my liking, do I have your permission to attack?'

---

* According to Ridgway's own account, he'd been selected – unbeknown to him – months before by Collins and MacArthur as the 'stand-by' commander: Matthew B. Ridgway, *The Korean War* (New York, 1967).

'The 8th Army is yours, Matt,' replied MacArthur. 'Do what you think best.'*

This was far greater latitude than MacArthur had given Walker. The reason may have been greater confidence in Ridgway, but given Walker's record in Germany, it's difficult to see why. However, it's been suggested that MacArthur was already trying to distance himself from what looked like a looming disaster. 'Bugout fever' was rife, with 8th Army looking all the time over its shoulder towards Pusan – not so much the Korean Normandy landings any longer as the Korean Dunkirk. It's also strangely unlike MacArthur. 'As soon as you can' would have been the more characteristic reply.

Certainly relations between MacArthur and Truman were increasingly fractious. The possibility of using nuclear weapons to halt the North Koreans had been discussed at a Joint Chiefs of Staff meeting as early as July, and MacArthur had rejected US air force proposals to fire-bomb North Korean cities, urging instead that atomic bombs be used to isolate North Korea by taking out bridges and tunnels. The army staff in Washington considered this to be impractical, but the Joint Chiefs decided nevertheless to send ten nuclear-capable B-29 bombers to Guam in the western Pacific as a deterrent to Chinese retaliatory action against Formosa. Truman, meanwhile, publicly denied that he was considering the use of nuclear weapons, but then authorized the transfer of 'disarmed' atomic bombs to Guam. With UNC forces now in full retreat, and the prospect of Seoul falling, MacArthur again advocated not only the use of nuclear weapons *per se*, but their use against targets beyond the Yalu – and that the decision should be *his*, not the president's.

By noon on the 26th Ridgway was in the air again, his plane

---

* This and following quotations from Ridgway are from *The Korean War*.

touching down four hours later at the 8th Army's main headquarters in Taegu, 60 miles north-west of Pusan. After calling on President Rhee and the US ambassador and reading himself in at his headquarters, a day or so later he set out to tour the front by helicopter and open jeep: 'I held to the old-fashioned idea that it helped the spirits of the men to see the Old Man up there in the snow and sleet . . . sharing the same cold miserable existence they had to endure,' he said later, but admitted that until a quartermaster dug up a pile-lined cap and warm gloves for him, he 'damn near froze'.*

He also, of course, wanted to judge for himself his command's morale: and what he found didn't please him. In forty-eight hours he saw all his corps and divisional commanders, most of whom he knew or had served with before, and all but one of the ROK divisional commanders, and he was not impressed, to say the least: 'The men I met along the road, those I stopped to talk to and to solicit gripes from – they too all conveyed to me a conviction that this was a bewildered army, not sure of its self or its leaders, not sure what they were doing there, wondering when they would hear the whistle of that home-bound transport.'†

He also saw Brigadier Tom Brodie, commanding the 29th Infantry Brigade. In his memoir of the war, Ridgway doesn't specifically exclude Brodie's headquarters from the observation that 'every command post I visited gave me the same sense of lost confidence and lack of spirit' – it's unlikely that he'd have spent time visiting a brigade headquarters – but judging by his remarks on the general 'alertness' of the British troops he saw, it's safe to conclude that he wouldn't have had any complaints:

---

* *Soldier: The Memoirs of Matthew B. Ridgway, As Told to Harold H. Martin* (New York, 1956).

† Ridgway, *The Korean War*.

I could not help contrasting their [US troops'] attitudes to that of a young British subaltern who had trotted down off a knoll to greet me when he spotted the insignia on my jeep. He saluted smartly and identified himself as to name, rank, and unit. Knowing that the British Brigade had hardly more than a handful of men to cover a wide sector of the front line, with a new Chinese offensive expected almost hourly, I asked how he found the situation. 'Quite all right, sir,' he replied quickly. Then he added with a pleasant smile: 'It *is* a bit drafty up here.' Drafty was the word for it, with gaps in the line wide enough to march an army through in company front.

By now Ridgway had abandoned hope for an immediate offensive, concluding that 8th Army 'were simply not mentally and spiritually ready for the sort of action I had been planning'. But he'd also told President Rhee there was no question of UNC pulling out of Korea. So first he'd have to restore the army's will to fight, and he'd come to the conclusion that a good many commanders would have to go: 'After I'd got the measure of these commanders in their own fields, up in their own terrain, I informed the Army Department that I needed top-flight regimental [brigade] and battalion commanders', he recalled, and sent the Pentagon a list of the men he wanted. This caused considerable consternation in Washington, not least given the prevailing Truman–MacArthur discord. Ridgway would eventually get rid of those in whom he'd no confidence, but not in one go. Instead he would send them home singly under the guise of a 'rotation policy'.

Nevertheless, in just one month he was somehow able to turn round morale, not least by tearing up plans for further wholesale retreat, much as Montgomery had done in the North African desert when he took over a weary British 8th Army in 1942. This evidently demanded shock action. When he visited I Corps and asked the 'G3' – chief operations staff officer – to brief him on their battle plans, the officer told him the plans to withdraw to 'successive positions'.

'What are your attack plans?' Ridgway growled.

The G3 hesitated. 'Sir, we are withdrawing.' There were no attack plans.

Ridgway ordered the corps commander to relieve him. It was brutal, but it doubled the effect by placing the onus on the man ultimately responsible for the dereliction (i.e. the corps commander) to carry out the execution. As intended, the story quickly got round every headquarters.

As for soldier comforts – the everyday elements of morale – Ridgway demanded urgent action from Washington to send warmer clothing, something which had also been exercising London. He sorted out, as only generals with a sore head can, the sluggish postal service and the dismal rations, adding steak and chicken to the menu, an obvious 'quick win', and with it a ferocious insistence that meals be served hot. If he'd not appreciated the importance of hot food in his early service, he'd certainly have learned to during the 'Battle of the Bulge', the German counter-offensive in the Ardennes in December 1944. Eisenhower had asked Montgomery to take charge of the hasty defences on the northern flank of the 'bulge', and the field marshal had been astonished to find American troops who'd not eaten hot food in days, and officers who thought it no great deprivation. Little wonder, Montgomery said, that their fighting spirit had gone. It would have been the same for British troops had they eaten cold for long. The issue is more than simply a culinary one of sustaining the troops; rather an indicator of poor overall administration and discipline.

Indeed, at the root of the deficit in morale was a deficit in infantry leadership. The American instinct for mechanization and overwhelming firepower diverted too many of the ablest men into the support, technical and administrative arms. By 1945, the experience of three years' battle had brought a little more balance into the quality mix, but five years' of peace had put the clock back – as, too, had the working of the Selective Service Act,* so that in the Korean winter of 1950–1 a disproportionately small percentage of the best the nation could offer were serving as infantry leaders. And yet it was the infantry, as always, who bore the greatest burden of battle and paid the highest price in casualties. If ever there was a place, too, where mechanization had its limits, it was Korea. Not surprisingly, the marines division under Ridgway's command was rather more steadfast. The US marines' historic purpose was assault from the sea, across the beaches, headlong – a job for the infantryman, for the well-led infantryman. And they'd known unfavourable terrain enough in the Pacific War.

In the British army, the 'infantry question' was different again. The Royal Engineers, especially, and Royal Artillery had always attracted capable men – not least because promotion had always been on merit, rather than, as in the infantry and cavalry before the reforms of the late nineteenth century, by purchase. But the infantry had a prestige based on the regimental system. Regimental names meant something, either locally in the county or nationally, and if, say, the regiment was good enough for princes, it was good enough for the rest. Public and grammar schools alike had a strong ethos of leadership, and there was a plentiful supply of subaltern officers. A number of national service platoon commanders in Korea wore different cap badges from those of the regiments to which they were attached, having volunteered for active service. This prestige attaching to infantry command was undoubtedly at least part of what

---

* The wartime Selective Training and Service Act had expired in March 1947, but, like Attlee, Truman worried that a peacetime army couldn't attract the numbers needed to meet its global commitments. The legislation was therefore re-enacted in June 1948, originally to expire in June 1950; but the outbreak of the Korean War prompted Congress to extend it for another year, and again in 1951. All males aged 18–26 were required to register for the draft. However, a series of deferments, based on family status or academic standing, soon crept in, the merits of deferment requests being weighed by local boards in a highly subjective process.

underlay the difference in the bearing of American and British troops that struck Ridgway with such force.

Another problem facing the US army that winter was that few commanders – only those, in fact, who'd faced the Japanese in the Philippines in 1942 – had any experience of defensive operations. Nor, by all accounts, was deliberate defence taught much, if at all, in the arms schools and staff colleges. Hasty defence against German counter-attacks in Tunisia, Italy and north-west Europe was different from methodical preparation to halt a major offensive. The American way of warfare was to go on the attack at the outset, taking the direct rather than the indirect approach. It had served them well in two world wars – with the occasional bloody nose – and on the surface there seemed no reason why this war, in which they'd have the overwhelming advantage in military technology, should be any different. The problem was, of course, that mass (Chinese infantry in huge numbers) now seemed to be trumping technological advantage.*

Here, too, Ridgway introduced a sense of purpose. Judging that another major Chinese assault was imminent, he told his corps commanders that he didn't just want to contain it, he wanted to inflict maximum punishment. He knew that for the time being he'd have to give some ground, but he wanted to exact a high price for it. In defence a commander needs 'balance', which is a product of depth and reserves, and Ridgway began preaching 'depth' to his subordinates. Although they lacked the manpower to halt the night attacks, he told them he wanted every unit to 'button up tight' and then in daylight to counter-attack strongly, with combined armour and infantry, superior firepower and air, to pinch out those who'd got

---

* Some British troops exhibited the same problem in reverse during the first Gulf War (1991). Having trained for years to face a massive Soviet Army offensive in Germany, in a strategy predominantly of fighting withdrawal, some found it hard at first to adjust to the idea of forward movement.

through the gaps. Their instrument would be the counter-attack, not just the firefight from 'foxholes'. No encircled unit was to be abandoned unless a 'major commander' after 'personal appraisal' at the front decided its relief would cost as many or more men. It was to be 'fought for' and rescued.

Further, Ridgway insisted that commanders pay more attention to the ground; in particular, that they make a rigorous assessment of 'vital ground' – that which if lost made a position untenable, or in the offensive made the objective unachievable. And especially that the army got off the roads:

> What I told the field commanders in essence was that their infantry ancestors would roll over in their graves could they see how roadbound this army was, how often it forgot to seize the high ground along its route . . . There was nothing but our own love of comfort that bound us to the road. We too could get off into the hills.

As well as improving ground–air cooperation (or perhaps the other way round: air–ground, for the USAF had been rather cherishing its newly independent status), he regrouped the artillery, especially the heavier, to make it decisive instead of just supportive. And to counter the shift in Chinese tactics to the night attack, whose moral effect was often greater than its material, he increased capacity to fire illuminating rounds.

But knowing also that for the time being he'd have to give some ground, he told his corps and divisional commanders to prepare 'switch' (reserve) positions, a normal tactic of defence in depth. And he had to prepare for the worst, however unlikely, unpalatable or inconsistent with his 'no withdrawal plans' message it was. His chief engineer, Brigadier-General Garrison Davidson, conscripted several thousand Korean labourers to construct a 'deep defensive zone' to guard Pusan, with a wired-in trench system and well-dug gun positions. It wasn't exactly the Lines of Torres Vedras, but the principle was the same. It would give Ridgway his army-level depth.

There remained the underlying moral element of fighting spirit to address. His American troops especially were, as Montgomery would have put it, 'bellyaching' – and, as Ridgway himself wrote, asking: 'What the hell are we doing here in this God-forgotten spot?' So, on returning to his tactical headquarters one evening in mid-January he tried to answer the question, which he reworked more elegantly as 'Why are we here? What are we fighting for?'

'Messages to the troops' are always perilous. Get the tone just a fraction wrong, and indifference, or worse, follows. Nor does it help when it's obvious to all that the cause is questionable – lacking, say, public support or unanimity on strategy at the top, so that to men on the ground the war doesn't seem worth the candle. But no message from the commander isn't an option. So Ridgway put pen to paper.

Professionals in the army would have responded to the question 'Why?' with the retort that they had orders to fight from the President of the United States, and that they were defending the freedom of South Korea. Conscripts needed something more. Ridgway wrote:

> Whether the power of Western civilization, as God has permitted it to flower in our own beloved lands, shall defy and defeat Communism; whether the rule of men who shoot their prisoners, enslave their citizens and deride the dignity of man, shall displace the rule of those to whom the individual and his individual rights are sacred . . . the sacrifices we have made, and those we shall yet support, are not offered vicariously for others but in our own direct defense.

High ideals, high-minded words; did they work?

There's no simple answer, of course, but on 7 January, PFC – Private (First Class) – James Cardinal of the 3/5th Cavalry, which was serving as infantry, had written home: 'The troops over here are mad, mad at

America, Americans and American leadership. We all feel we've been let down, by our incompetent blundering leadership, from the White House down. If we must fight Communism let's do it in Europe which is the cradle of western culture and our own civilisation.' On New Year's Eve, the Chinese and North Koreans had attacked, and the army had fallen back. Whole ROK divisions broke and ran, but Ridgway hadn't been surprised. He'd met their generals and knew that most of them had little more experience or expertise than a company commander, and moreover that they'd taken a terrible beating in the first six months of the war, more so perhaps than any of the armies of the Second World War. On 2 January, he ordered the withdrawal south of the Han River, abandoning Seoul, and then successively to defensive line 'D' close to the 37th parallel, anchored on dominating ground in the west around Chinch-on and running north-east to Wonpo-ri on the east coast. But this time, he observed, the army withdrew 'as a fighting army, not as a running mob', bringing with them all their equipment and, he said, their pride (although he was exasperated with two of his corps commanders for withdrawing too quickly rather than inflicting punishment and then breaking clean). The articulate and strategically informed PFC Cardinal had taken part in this withdrawal, and although sore at everyone 'from the White House down', he signed off his letter: 'I'm in the best of heath and spirits.'

Clearly something was beginning to work, even before Ridgway's exhortation 'to show ourselves and our people at their best – and thus to do honor to the profession of arms, and to those brave men who bred us'.

The Americans were by far the major fighting element in UNC, and they were Ridgway's primary audience. Nevertheless, some of the ROK units were quite evidently stiffened by his approach; and even if the British didn't need quite the same stiffening, they clearly appreciated the message. When they'd taken up their positions before Seoul at the end of December, Brigadier Tom Brodie had told his commanding officers:

> At last after weeks of frustration we have nothing between us and the Chinese. I have no intention that this Brigade Group will retire before the enemy unless ordered by higher authority to conform with general movement. If you meet him you are to knock hell out of him with everything that you've got. You are only to give ground on my orders.*

At about the time that Ridgway was composing his words to the troops, the Chinese and KPA, now well south of Seoul again and pressing on to the 37th parallel, were running into trouble. Their casualties, particularly the PVA's, were rising alarmingly, and the Korean winter was also taking its toll, PoWs reporting that as many as 50 per cent of front-line troops were suffering from frostbite. Chinese lines of communication were now sorely stretched, exactly as the UNC's had been as they neared the Yalu, although unlike the UNC they hadn't the benefit of plentiful mechanical transport and supply by air. MacArthur's headquarters estimated that on the Yalu the Chinese had been able to support a million men, that by the time they reached the 38th parallel the figure was 300,000, and that south of Seoul it fell to 200,000. Even if these estimates had been out by 100 per cent, which they certainly weren't, with nearly half a million Chinese and KPA troops now in the country it was clear they wouldn't be able to hold recent gains, let alone make further advances. Ridgway now had some 365,000 men in all, but this considerably lower figure distorts the true balance, for it doesn't reflect the huge UN superiority in materiel, above all in air power. Though it still

---

* Anthony Farrar-Hockley, *Official History: The British Part in the Korean War*, vol. I (London, 1990).

probably didn't look like it to many a GI and ROK soldier on the ground, the tide was on the turn. The advantage had undoubtedly swung back to the UNC. The question was how to take advantage of the advantage, both tactically and strategically.

In late January, Ridgway ordered a reconnaissance-in-force, which soon confirmed that the Chinese and KPA had dramatically thinned their lines. He followed up with a full-scale advance (Operation Thunderbolt) which quickly reached the Han river and the city of Wonju in the centre of the peninsula. In mid-February, the PVA counter-attacked at Wonju, but were seen off in short order by the US IX Corps (with a French battalion under command), despite at one stage being surrounded by five times their number.

To jaundiced observers in the press, 8th Army's performance in this and subsequent offensive operations was little short of miraculous. The BBC's René Cutforth wrote: 'Exactly how and why the new army was transformed . . . from a mob of dispirited boobs . . . to a tough resilient force is still a matter for speculation and debate,' while a correspondent of *Time* magazine probably best explained the miracle: 'The boys aren't up there fighting for democracy now. They're fighting because the platoon leader is leading them and the platoon leader is fighting because of the command, and so on right up to the top.'*

A week later, Ridgway launched Operation Killer (a name which caused some consternation in Washington), an offensive along the entire front to exploit UNC's reorganized firepower to destroy as many KPA and PVA as possible while they were at their greatest disadvantage. It was so successful that by the middle of March a follow-up operation ('Ripper') had levered them out of Seoul. This was the fourth time Seoul had changed hands in nine months, and the

---

* Thomas Fleming, *American Chronicles* (Rockford, IL, 2019).

capital was in ruins. The pre-war population of a million and a half had by now been reduced to barely 200,000.

Then, in the first ten days of April, UNC forces pushed north again to secure the 38th parallel, halting on the Imjin in the west and extending east roughly along the line held before the Chinese new year offensive. It was still short of the line judged best for strategic defence if ceasefire negotiations were to begin, as Truman certainly wanted them to; but it had been a remarkable turnaround none the less.

Meanwhile, however, there'd been two unexpected, if not unpredictable, developments. First, the Chinese setback had attracted closer Russian support. Stalin agreed to send two air force divisions, three anti-aircraft divisions and 6,000 lorries. The PVA's commander had told Mao that what his soldiers feared wasn't the enemy, but having no food, ammunition, or vehicles to evacuate them when they were wounded. From the end of January to the middle of April, they'd suffered 53,000 casualties. It wasn't a grievance that Mao could ignore. The second development came on 11 April, when Truman peremptorily relieved MacArthur of command. The disagreements over atomic weapons – MacArthur had again wanted to use them as the Chinese offensive gathered momentum – and the not always behind-the-scenes lobbying of Congress members to support his view of the conflict (that it was a fight with communism, that China was the existential communist threat to Asia, and that the United States should take the war to Chinese cities) had become too much for the president, the commander-in-chief. Truman had concluded – as had, indeed, the Washington political–military establishment – as early as December that reunification of the peninsula was no longer a worthwhile object. The aim now was simply a ceasefire restoring the *status quo ante*.*

---

* Many pages have been written about MacArthur's dismissal. Truman didn't handle it well, and there were undoubtedly domestic political factors in the decision. But the

Ridgway was appointed in his place.

The Chinese, though, certainly weren't finished, not in their own minds at least. With Stalin's promise of increased support, and now back on North Korean soil, the PVA were once more planning for an all-out spring counter-offensive.

---

fact was that MacArthur had forgotten who was ultimately the C-in-C. Now seventy-one – though fit and active – he'd simply been a very senior general for too long. Indeed, he'd been a proconsul for too long. As ruler of Japan and Korea from 1945, he had consciously or unconsciously (the majority view is that it was the former) modelled himself on a Roman aristocrat, initiating policies of his own that 'Rome' frequently found itself having to approve of retrospectively and with considerable misgivings. Tokyo had become his imperium to such an extent that when he met Truman for the first time, in October on Wake Island in the middle of the Pacific, he held out his hand – as would an equal – rather than salute. An astonishing discourtesy for a professional soldier.

3

A HILL IN KOREA*

For the first time I understood that the Regiment was more important than me, and my loyalty to my mates had become a matter of sovereign importance.

(Private) David Green†

---

* Title of a 1956 film based on the novel *Hell in Korea* by Max Catto (under the pseudonym Simon Kent), a fictional portrayal of the war at platoon level. The film title was changed at the last minute for 'distribution reasons', although not – perhaps predictably – for its release in the US. With a cast of (future) stars such as Stanley Baker, Robert Shaw and Michael Caine, who as a 19-year-old national serviceman had served in Korea with the Royal Fusiliers (in the 28th Commonwealth Brigade), it pulled no punches. Caine relates in his autobiography how he'd gone to Korea with sympathetic feelings towards communism, having been raised in an impoverished family, but that the 'human wave attacks' left him with the sense that the Chinese and North Korean governments had no care for their citizens.

† David Green, *Captured at the Imjin River – The Korean War: Memoirs of a Gloster 1950–1953* (Barnsley, 2011).

Exactly why the massive Chinese assault on the Lower Imjin took the defenders by surprise – at least, by tactical surprise – still isn't clear. It was certainly expected. And it was obvious enough that the Chinese would make their main effort here, on the historic route to Seoul. So much so that the commander of the 29th British Independent Brigade Group's engineer squadron, Major (later Major-General) Tony Younger, seeing speculation in the US army newspaper *Stars and Stripes* about a Chinese thrust towards the Imjin, flew back from leave in Tokyo to rejoin the brigade. On reaching them he was dismayed by the lack of field defences: 'We were not really in a defensive frame of mind. We had been crawling forward, probing forward for months. We didn't even really know exactly where on our front the Imjin was fordable.'*

Indeed, the commanders on the Lower Imjin, I (US) Corps' Lieutenant-General Frank Milburn, 3rd (US) Division's Major-General Robert Soule and the 29th Brigade's Tom Brodie – all three with considerable experience of war – were apparently in the frame of mind of the 'operational pause', the deliberate breather in offensive operations to rest, resupply, regroup and whatever. The term is modern, but the idea's as old as the hills. Troops in this position take precautions against counter-attack, but as they have the initiative, the precautions won't be the same as when on the forced defensive. This is reflected in such things as manning levels (the reason why Younger was on 'R&R') and the positioning and notice-to-move of reserves, while on the ground it affects such things as how extensively the field defences are constructed and what alert levels are maintained, especially patrolling. If men are to rest and get ready for the next phase of the advance, they can't put unlimited effort into constructing defence works which, almost by definition, are infinite: fire trenches, communicating

---

* Quoted in Max Hastings, *The Korean War* (London, 1987).

trenches, dug-outs with overhead cover and so on. Besides, defence stores – mines, barbed wire, steel pickets, sandbags and the like – are always in short supply. Defence measures during an operational pause are a fine balance, therefore, a matter of judgement. The Chinese had been on the back foot, giving ground, for two months, and the positions on the Imjin were supposed to be merely a springboard for I Corps' further advance.

This was also the reason why I Corps' frontages were so great. On the left was the 1st (ROK) Division, its left flank secure on the wide confluence of the Imjin and the Han, covering the major crossings at Munsan-ni towards its centre and extending in all some 16 miles as the crow flies. But as the Imjin here meanders, the linear distance was nearer 25 miles. On the corps' right, covering the main road and rail routes to Seoul from the north, was the 3rd (US) Division. They had a rather shorter frontage, but one which ran awkwardly north-north-east before its boundary with the 25th Division, whose line then ran almost due east. In the centre, and under command of the 3rd Division, was Brodie's 29th Brigade. Their straight-line frontage was 9 miles, but because of the ground and the course of the Imjin, in reality it was nearer 15. This was considerably more than a brigade would expect to hold, except during an operational pause. Even in similar country in Italy in the Second World War, 3 miles at most would have been the rule. However, the brigade was rather stronger than its equivalent in the US army, the regimental combat team, and had lately been reinforced by a Belgian battalion. Nor were there any permanent bridges in their sector, although there were two rough roads which headed in the direction of Seoul, and (south of the river) two connecting roads. If the Chinese could get across the river here they could outflank the rest of the 3rd Division, threaten the 1st (ROK) Division's right flank and the 3rd (US) Division's left rear, and have the shortest run to Seoul, less than 25 miles.

While some clearly felt, at least in retrospect, that the atmosphere on the Imjin was 'relaxed. Too relaxed',* the Chinese weren't actually giving anything away in terms of the usual tactical indications. There was simply no activity in front of the 29th Brigade's position. As late as 20 April, a strong armoured reconnaissance patrol of the 8th Hussars scouted nearly 20 miles north of the river but encountered only a small force of Chinese, who withdrew at once on contact. Nor did aerial reconnaissance discover anything. While 'strategic' intelligence was indicating a counter-offensive, tactical intelligence evidently suggested that the main effort would be elsewhere. The Lower Imjin was reckoned to be safe. It wouldn't of course be the first such mistake in history.

On the face of it, too, the 29th Brigade's position looked a strong one – or one, at least, that had capability. High ground south of the Imjin, in one place rising to 2,000 feet, overlooked almost every yard of river. However, at this time of year, for the most part, the river was fordable; there were, therefore, no channelled crossing points on which to concentrate the defence. So somehow the brigade would have to cover its entire length, at least by observation.

Brigadier Brodie, aged forty-seven, an infantryman who'd commanded one of the 'Chindit' brigades – officially, the Long Range Penetration Groups, in action against the Japanese in the Burma campaign – had three British battalions to dispose: the 1st Royal Northumberland Fusiliers, the 1st Gloucestershire Regiment ('Glosters') and the 1st Royal Ulster Rifles. Each was about 600 'bayonets' strong – the term for the actual fighting troops, those in the four 'rifle' companies and the support company (the 'heavy weapons': mortars, machine guns, and anti-tank guns towed by tracked carriers), as opposed to those in the command and administrative roles, headquarters company, numbering another 150–200. In addition, he had

---

* Major Guy Ward, a battery commander in 45 Field Regiment Royal Artillery, the 29th Brigade's close support regiment, quoted in Hastings, *The Korean War*.

the Belgian battalion, rather smaller, some 500 overall, but highly regarded by the British, all of them volunteers, including many veterans of the late war – Free Belgian commandos and former members of the French Foreign Legion or *maquis* (the Resistance). In support of the brigade were the three field batteries of 45 Field Regiment Royal Artillery, each of eight 25-pounder howitzers, and the eighteen heavy (4.2-inch) mortars of 170 Independent Mortar Battery RA, which were grouped in three troops of six. The 4.2-inch mortar fired a 20-pound projectile, not quite as lethal as that of the howitzers, and with only a third of their range (4,100 yards), but with three times the rate of fire and an extremely high trajectory which enabled it to deploy behind high cover. And in addition to Younger's sappers, 'C' Squadron of the 8th Hussars (sixteen Centurions) were under command.

In trying to make the best of a difficult hand, Brodie gambled on a compromise to achieve both coverage of his entire front and some degree of mutual support between the battalions. He sited the Belgians on the right, just north of the river, and two of the British battalions on the best of the high ground south of the river, the Fusiliers a mile to the Belgians' left, and the Glosters a mile and a half to the left of the Fusiliers. The Ulster Rifles occupied a blocking position in depth some 4 miles south of the Belgians astride 'Route 11', the dirt road south that served as the brigade's main line of communication (that is, supply). 'C' Squadron were concentrated in reserve, just to the rear of the Fusiliers.

The four rifle companies of the Fusiliers were sited four-square, and the Glosters' three-up, but not as tight as the commanding officers would have liked. As was the practice at that time, defensive positions were 'sited two down': the brigade commander selected the position the companies would occupy, the battalion's commanding officer selected the platoon positions, and the company commanders sited the sections. General Ridgway had said he wanted each unit

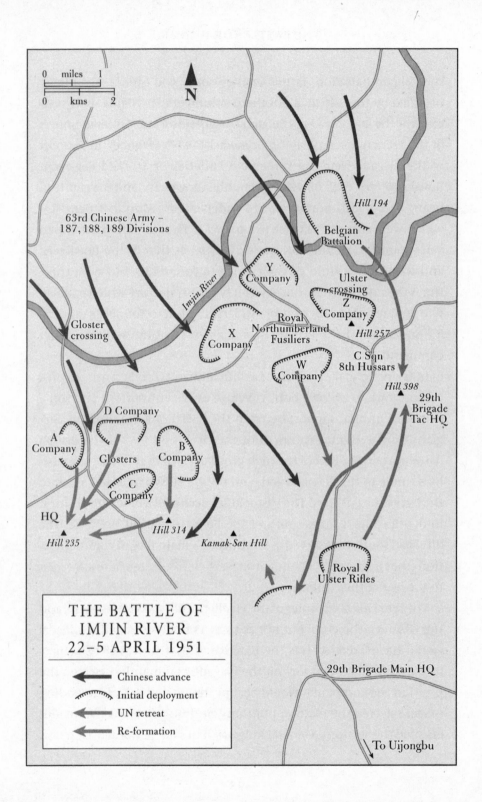

miles 0 — 1
kms 0 — 2

N

63rd Chinese Army –
187, 188, 189 Divisions

Hill 194

Belgian
Battalion

Y
Company

Ulster
crossing

Z
Company

Imjin River

Gloster
crossing

X
Company

Royal
Northumberland
Fusiliers

Hill 257

W
Company

C Sqn
8th Hussars

Hill 398

29th
Brigade
Tac HQ

D Company

A
Company

Glosters

B
Company

C
Company

HQ

Hill 235

Hill 314

Kamak-San Hill

Royal
Ulster Rifles

THE BATTLE OF
IMJIN RIVER
22–5 APRIL 1951

Chinese advance

Initial deployment

UN retreat

Re-formation

29th Brigade Main HQ

To Uijongbu

to 'button up tight' at night, and then in daylight to counter-attack strongly against any enemy who'd got through gaps in their line. Both the Fusiliers' and the Glosters' commanding officers urged Brodie to site the brigade more tightly, to deny penetration *between* battalions, and to deal with any outflanking movement by concentrated artillery fire, local counter-attacks and the brigade reserve. However, the brigade had no guns heavier than the 25-pounders and no means to call on heavier calibres from the neighbouring US division, and tighter siting would have meant bigger gaps between the brigade and the ROK and US divisions to left and right. Besides, Brodie, having commanded a brigade of Chindits, had lived with the idea of being encircled. It is just possible, therefore, that he saw no more reason to be dismayed at the prospect of Chinese penetration in hilly terrain than he had been at Japanese encirclement in the jungle.

The trouble was, among other things, that the corps line of defence didn't stand square to the Chinese axis of attack and route to Seoul. The line held in early April after 8th Army's counter-offensive, the 'Kansas Line', had been advanced some 10 miles in the centre in a further operation ('Dauntless') to form the 'Wyoming Line'. This created something of a salient, with its left on the confluence of the Hantan and the Imjin, the point where the Imjin turned from running north–south to meandering south-west. The 'hinge', as this bend in the line was called, meant that the brigade's right flank would be more than usually vulnerable. It is probably for this reason that Brodie sited the Belgians north of the confluence. They, in turn, would be out on a limb, but in a good position to delay any move round the right flank, and able to withdraw if necessary across the pontoon bridges constructed by the sapper squadron. In essence, they'd function as a strong standing patrol. Indeed, the Belgians' would prove the best-prepared position, dug and wired before they arrived by the Ulsters for just this purpose.

The underlying problem was that the brigade saw the Imjin as integral to the defence; yet the river itself was no obstacle, merely, in places, a slight hindrance. In defensive operations, however, rivers exert a strong pull. Brodie was relying on his two forward battalions to hold their ground, for the Belgians to disrupt a surprise flanking move, and for the Ulsters, with the Hussars, to act as a reserve from their 'anchor' positions in depth. But the Hussars' ability to move across country to support the Glosters was limited, not least because the rice paddy to the Glosters' rear, though not yet planted, was too soft going. With the brigade's focus being its right flank and Route 11, not least to safeguard the Americans' left, the Glosters were very much out on their own.

On the morning of the 22nd, the brigade – all of it – discovered just how wrong they'd been about what they were facing. For some weeks, the Chinese had been moving into position by night and by day hiding in caves and tunnels. Now, the recce patrols of the Glosters and the Fusiliers north of the river were astonished to see the enemy on the move in large numbers.

After their heavy losses on first crossing the Yalu, and again in Ridgway's counter-offensive, Mao and the PVA's commander, the 52-year-old Peng Dehuai, had concluded that only massive numerical superiority was likely to overcome the UNC's firepower and techno-logical superiority. By April, therefore, the PVA had been reinforced to some 1.3 million men, more than half of them in the fighting ech-elon of forty-two infantry divisions plus eight artillery and four anti-aircraft divisions, which gave them a three-to-one numerical advantage. Peng intended the spring offensive not just to take ground, but to threaten Seoul, drawing UN forces towards the capi-tal, which would then allow the PVA to encircle them and destroy them in detail. Critically, though, Mao believed that first annihilat-ing several UN divisions across the front would shatter 8th Army's morale and cohesion. As he put it, it was more effective to destroy one than defeat ten, a conventional war development perhaps of the old Chinese terror maxim: 'Kill one; frighten ten thousand.'

Consequently, the PVA's tactics would be first to fix the enemy and destroy him in place rather than to manoeuvre for advantage.* However, in failing to take advantage of their potential to infiltrate, this ironically would actually play to 8th Army's strength; and they, in turn, if they held their ground as Ridgway had told them, would be able to fix the Chinese rather than vice versa. Indeed, probably realizing this, some of Peng's subordinates argued that it would be better to draw 8th Army further north first and then encircle them. Peng, however, wasn't prepared to risk allowing UNC to gain the initiative.

Facing the 29th Brigade were the three divisions of the Chinese 63rd Army (more properly, army corps) – upwards of 50,000 men. These formed the left wing of the forty-year-old General Yang Dezhi's 19th Army Group, whose task was to destroy the UNC's I Corps and open the route to Seoul. When the first reports of enemy in strength reached Brodie, he ordered a 50 per cent stand-to-arms in the forward battalions, despite 8th Army's intelligence assessment that the Chinese main force was still 20 miles away, and that I Corps would face only probing attacks that night.

As darkness approached, indeed, the Belgians came under heavy attack, which thanks to the well-dug trenches and extensive wiring they were able to beat off. Then, towards midnight, the Chinese attacked in much greater strength, to the accompaniment of bugles and whistles. Again the Belgians managed to hold, with 45 Field Regiment firing both high explosive and illuminating rounds at a prodigious rate. Shortly after midnight, with cloud obscuring the moon, Brodie told

---

* Peng Dehuai's operational directive: 'First of all, we will mass our forces to wipe out the 6th Division of the Puppet [ROK] Army, the British 27th Brigade, the American 3rd Division, the Turkish Brigade, the British 29th Brigade and the 1st Division of the Puppet Army . . .': quoted in Farrar-Hockley, *Official History*.

the Ulsters to send a platoon in carriers to secure the pontoon cross-ings. The Chinese, though, had managed to slip round at the foot of the Belgians' hill and get there before them, inflicting heavy losses on the platoon, then pressing on to attack the Fusiliers' right rear ('Z') company. Further downstream, more Chinese troops managed to get across, and these attacked the Fusiliers' left forward ('X') company. Too far from the other companies for support, 'X' withdrew gradually closer into the centre of the battalion position, which in turn exposed the right forward ('Y') company. Pressure increased as the Chinese encircle-ment progressed, with each company having to fight by itself rather than in a concerted battalion action. Rather than being able to support 'Y' Company, for example, who were being attacked from the north-west, 'Z' Company was having to fight off separate attacks from the north. Slowly but surely, all but 'W' Company in the left rear, with a nearby battery of 45 Field Regiment, began to give ground. By dawn, the Fusiliers had been pushed off almost all the high ground, back towards Route 11.

Attempts by the Fusiliers to regain the ground that morning, with help from the 3rd (US) Division's reserve, failed. An attack by the 1st Battalion (US) 7th Infantry, however, helped extricate the Belgian battalion, who managed to withdraw to the west of the Ulsters' blocking position.

On the far left, the Glosters, further out on a limb than the Fusiliers, were fighting an even lonelier battle. Their commanding officer and adjutant were two men of extraordinary and complementary charac-ter: Lieutenant-Colonel James Power Carne and Captain Anthony Farrar-Hockley. Carne was forty-five, old for a commanding officer even in 1951, when the army hadn't yet settled back into its pre-war promotion routine. Pipe-smoking, taciturn to the point of apparent inarticulacy and utterly imperturbable, he'd commanded a battalion of the King's African Rifles in Burma. Farrar-Hockley, on the other hand, was as fiery as Carne was stolid. He'd enlisted under-age in the Glosters in the Second World War, been commissioned in the Parachute Regiment and won an MC at twenty. Pugnacious and uncompromising, he was the perfect adjutant for a man like Carne.

For the Glosters, the battle had begun well. The battalion was sited three companies forward (from left to right: A, D, B), each on its own hill, and one (C) in depth, with those elements of the support company not deployed with the rifle companies occupying a position close on their left (Hill 235), and battalion headquarters just to the rear of these two. Soon after dark the Glosters' standing patrol on the Imjin was able to throw back the first Chinese attempt to cross, alerting the companies in good time, and then to repel a further three attempts before running out of ammunition and having to withdraw. Soon afterwards, attacks began in earnest on A and D companies, and continued all night. Then B and C companies came under attack by Chinese troops who'd penetrated between D and B, or outflanked B to the east. By morning A and D companies had suffered severe casualties and were giving ground – critically at 'Castle Site', A's hill, which guarded the battalion's left flank. Farrar-Hockley, who'd gone forward to A Company soon after first light, gave a vivid account of the desperate business of trying to retake the hill, and of the conditions that characterized the fighting across the entire brigade front:

Phil [Lieutenant Philip Curtis, 1st Platoon commander] is called to the field telephone: Pat's [Major Pat Angier, 'A' Company commander] voice sounds in his ear. 'Phil, at the present rate of casualties we can't hold on unless we get the Castle Site back. Their machine-guns up there completely dominate your platoon and most of Terry's. We shall never stop their advance until we hold that ground again.' Phil looks over the edge of the trench at the Castle Site, two hundred yards away, as Pat continues talking, giving him the instructions for the counter attack. They talk for a minute or so; there is not much more to be said when an instruction is given to assault with a handful of tired men across open ground. Everyone knows it is vital: everyone knows it is appallingly dangerous. The only details to be fixed are the arrangements for supporting fire; and, though A Company's machine-gunners are dead, D Company [to their right] will support. Phil gathers his tiny assault party together. It is time; they rise from the ground and move forward to the barbed wire that once protected the rear of the forward platoon. Already two men are hit and Papworth, the Medical Corporal, is attending to them. They are through the wire safely – safely! – when the machine-gun in the bunker begins to fire. Phil is badly wounded: he drops to the ground. They drag him back through the wire somehow and seek what little cover there is as it creeps across their front. The machine-gun stops, content now it has driven them back – waiting for a better target when they move into the open again. 'It's all right, sir,' says someone to Phil. 'The Medical Corporal's been sent for. He'll be here any minute.' Phil raises himself from the ground, rests on a friendly shoulder, then climbs by a great effort on to one knee. 'We must take the Castle Site,' he says; and gets up to take it. The others beg him to wait until his wounds are tended. One man places a hand on his side. 'Just wait until Papworth has seen you, sir.'

But Phil has gone: gone to the wire, gone through the wire, gone towards the bunker. The others come out behind him, their eyes all on him. And suddenly it seems as if, for a few breathless moments, the whole of the remainder of that field of battle is still and silent, watching, amazed, the lone figure that runs so painfully forward to the bunker holding the approach to the Castle Site: one tiny figure, throwing grenades, firing a pistol, set to take Castle Hill. Perhaps he will make it – in spite of his wounds, in spite of the odds – perhaps this act of supreme gallantry may, by its sheer audacity, succeed. But the machine-gun in the bunker fires into him: he staggers, falls, and is dead instantly; the grenade he threw a second before his death explodes after it in the mouth of the bunker. The machine-gun does not fire on three of Phil's platoon who run forward to pick him up; it

302

does not fire again through the battle: it is destroyed; the muzzle blown away, the crew dead.*

Philip Curtis was twenty-four. He'd been seconded to the Glosters from the Duke of Cornwall's Light Infantry, and his action at Castle Site would be recognized by the award of the Victoria Cross. Years later, after his release from captivity, one of Curtis's men, Private Sam Mercer, who was badly wounded next day, recalled how the platoon put his body gently into a sleeping bag: 'We said a prayer and left him. There's never time in those circumstances to bury your dead. You can't.'

It wasn't going to be possible to retake the dominating ground. Major Angier spoke by radio to Colonel Carne. 'I'm afraid we've lost Castle Site. I want to know whether I am to stay here indefinitely or not. If I am to stay I must be reinforced as my numbers are getting very low.'

Carne told him in his quiet, measured way that the company must stay put.

Angier acknowledged, and then added: 'Don't worry about us. We'll be all right.' He was killed fifteen minutes later.

There was now only one officer alive and unwounded on A Company's position.

Fighting continued all day, until towards last light Carne, fearing they'd be overwhelmed in the dark, decided to pull back the forward companies to form a tighter defensive position on Hill 235. The remnants of A and D Companies did manage to withdraw, but B Company, on the right, couldn't disengage, fighting off seven separate attacks during the night. Daylight brought respite, and they were at last able to get back, but only seventeen of the company remained in action.

The deep Chinese penetration between them and the Fusiliers,

---

* From Jon E. Lewis, ed., *The Mammoth Book of Eye-Witness History* (New York, 1998), and in conversation with the author, 2005.

besides cutting off the Glosters, threatened the integrity of the brigade's defence. The 3rd Division's commander sent Brodie a task force – an infantry company and a troop of M-24 (Chafee) light tanks – from the Filipino 10th Battalion Combat Team to help restore the situation. Together with ten Centurions of the 8th Hussars they managed to make some progress, but 2 miles from the Glosters the lead M-24 was knocked out by Chinese fire, blocking the advance of the others. Restricted to a dirt road in a ravine, and against stronger resistance than expected, the task force was soon stymied. The official British history summarizes the rapid unravelling of the relief effort:

As no one else was helping, two of the Centurions squeezed past the other light tanks and, under their covering fire, the [crew of the disabled Chaffee] were able to join the main body. The 10 BCT's commanding officer [more correctly, detachment commander] proposed to Major [Henry] Huth [the British tank squadron commander] that his Centurions should assume the leading role, an offer wisely declined. The Centurions were too heavy and too wide for the track through the gorge, but even if, in this emergency, they attempted to move down it, the sides were so steep that they would be unable to apply fire effectively . . . At this point the relief operation on 24th April came effectively to an end.

The official US narrative of operations adds that 'the brigade commander considered it unwise to continue the effort to relieve the Gloucester Battalion and withdrew the relief force'.

Carne (and his adjutant) took the news philosophically. Receiving a radio message from brigade headquarters, he turned to Farrar-Hockley and said: 'You know that armour–infantry column that's coming to relieve us?'

'Yes, sir?'

'Well. It isn't coming.'

'Right, sir.'*

Throughout the 24th, the Glosters fought off wave after wave of Chinese infantry with the sole support of a single battery of 25-pounders, the only guns still in range, and a troop of heavy mortars.

Brodie had known full well since the morning of the 23rd that he – the whole division indeed – faced a full-blown offensive rather than just probing attacks, as did 8th Army's new commander, Lieutenant-General James van Fleet, who now ordered a limited withdrawal from the Wyoming Line to the Kansas Line, south of the Hantan river. It was even more important, therefore, that the 29th Brigade, at the very hinge of the two lines, held its ground, otherwise the left flank of the 3rd Division would have been entirely open.

The attacks continued on the brigade throughout the night of the 24th, and always to the unnerving shrill of bugles and fanatical screams. Farrar-Hockley, who as adjutant was the titular commander of the Corps of Drums, ordered the Glosters' drum-major (the drummers being also buglers) to answer each Chinese call with a defiant one of his own. And so everything from 'Cookhouse' to 'Officers Dress for Dinner' was sounded over the darkened hillsides. By morning, however, the game was up. At nine-thirty Carne received a message from the brigade commander saying the Glosters would soon lose their already limited artillery support as the remaining battery in range was having to pull back, and he would leave it to Carne's discretion whether – in truth, when – to withdraw.

Once an infantry battalion is without artillery support (or air, as here too) it can only fight the direct battle – in other words, what it

---

* From General Sir Anthony Farrar-Hockley, *The Edge of the Sword* (London, 1954), his account of the battle and his subsequent experience as a PoW (including his several escape attempts).

can see to its front. Even with its own mortars it can't much influence what the enemy is doing out of sight of its riflemen and machine-gunners. The enemy thus has freedom to manoeuvre and concentrate against the weakest point. And then, when small-arms ammunition, grenades and mortar bombs are finished, the bayonet buys only a few seconds more. The Glosters were down to three rounds a man, and the Bren guns to one and a half magazines (40–50 rounds). Carne, who'd now fired every round of his own pistol, ordered the companies to break out as best they could, and to go it alone.

But the Chinese were swarming so deep that evasion would prove all but impossible. Of the rifle companies, only the remnants of D – just forty men – made it. In all, that evening the Glosters would be able to muster just 150. Carne and Farrar-Hockley weren't among them. Both had been taken prisoner, and their experience of captivity would be almost as great an epic as the defence of, as it became known, 'Gloster Hill'.*

With continued Chinese pressure across the whole front, and multiple penetrations, early on the 25th the commander of I Corps ordered a general withdrawal to 'Line Delta', 10 miles south of the Imjin. The Belgians now took up blocking positions west and

---

* Although there was criticism after the battle that both Brodie and the divisional commander, Major-General Robert Soule, didn't do enough to relieve the Glosters, they'd tried initially, face to face, to make a plan for an all-arms force to break through, with infantry to secure the high ground, plus engineers and artillery, but the issue was one of time: such a force might get through – though in fact the Chinese were now to the rear of the Glosters in very large numbers – but not quickly enough. Hence the weak and restricted 10th BCT force and the Hussar squadron. The ROK's 1st Division, on the brigade's left, also sent a battalion-size force from the south-west to help, and they got to within 2 miles of the Glosters as well before being halted. Major-General Soule then ordered a much larger all-arms force, with air support, to be ready for a further effort at six-thirty the following morning (25th), but in the meantime the corps commander decided on a general withdrawal to Line Delta, and the attempt was therefore abandoned.

south-west of Brodie's main command post on Route II to cover the withdrawal of the rest of the brigade down the single road, with the Ulsters and Hussars (a fine Irish combination) as rearguard.

The withdrawal proved hazardous, to say the least, Chinese troops now holding the dominating ground almost the length of the line of retreat. Casualties mounted, including the Fusiliers' commanding officer, killed by mortar fire. Major Huth of the 8th Hussars summed up running the gauntlet of Route II succinctly: 'one long bloody ambush'. At one stage, with Chinese infantrymen crawling all over his Centurions trying to prise open the hatches, the tanks took to hosing each other down with their machine guns.

I Corps managed to rally in good order on Line Delta, however, where they held fast for twenty-four hours and then withdrew a further 15 miles to Line Golden, on which engineers had been working non-stop since the 23rd to dig a continuous line of strongpoints. But they withdrew in a series of well-coordinated bounds of 3–4 miles, with massive artillery and air strikes covering each move, then holding firm by night before beginning the next bound at first light.

By 30 April, I Corps was dug in firmly on Line Golden, and the Chinese offensive was petering out. The battle to save Seoul from occupation a third time – what Ridgway might have called a battle for honor – had been won.

POSTSCRIPT

In all, the 29th Brigade suffered 1,100 casualties in the battle of the Imjin River – including 140 killed, and 34 officers and 808 other ranks missing: a quarter of its fighting strength on the eve of battle. Of these, 620 were from the Glosters (of whom 522 were now prisoners of war, 180 of them wounded). Fifty-nine Glosters had been killed in action, and a further thirty-four would die in captivity. But the Chinese had bought their tactical victory dearly, for their casualties were estimated at some 10,000. As a result, the PVA's 63rd Army, which had begun the offensive with three divisions and 27,000 men, was pulled out of the front line.

The 29th Brigade's stand had enabled the 3rd Division to fall back to Line Delta without interference on their left flank (or, worse still, envelopment), in turn enabling I Corps to regroup and consolidate on Line Golden. Peng Dehuai's intention to surround and destroy I Corps had been frustrated, and Seoul never again fell. Imjin in one sense had been a tactical defeat – the brigade had had to abandon its ground – but in another it had been a success, a significant factor in the higher-level victory, the defeat of the Chinese spring campaign.

Through the rest of 1951 the fighting continued – a Chinese offensive in the east of the peninsula in May, a peninsula-wide counter-offensive by UNC in June and occasional Chinese return pushes, though never again south of Seoul and the Han river – with mounting PVA and KPA casualties, as well as civilian, and much of

308

the country both sides of the border laid waste. With the strategic bombing of North Korea and a tight naval blockade, a stalemate now developed. The failure of their spring offensive had demonstrated that the PVA and KPA simply didn't have the capacity to defeat the UN in battle.

Thoughts turned to a negotiated settlement, the Soviets telling Mao that they weren't prepared to escalate their support, and indicating to the UN that they were willing to seek resolution through arbitration. Negotiations began on 10 July, though Mao planned to go on fighting at the same time. When this proved too costly, however, he settled for an armistice of sorts along the 'contact line', just north of the 38th parallel. By the end of the year, talks got under way at Panmunjom, although guerrilla fighting continued in large parts of the south.

Those talks dragged on with little progress. In September 1952, fighting flared up again when the PVA launched an offensive in the east in an attempt to push back the UNC to the 38th parallel, though it met with little success. Nevertheless, with the change of US presidents in January 1953, Dwight D. Eisenhower succeeding Harry S Truman, the impetus for resolution increased, for Eisenhower wanted to focus on the Cold War in Europe. Stalin's death in March helped greatly: the politburo was determined to see an end to the war and told Mao that they'd withdraw all material support.

Yet Mao was still reluctant to give up, seeing Korea (as well as French Indo-China) as his opportunity to export the communist revolution. In May he launched one last offensive, which UNC brought to a halt after Chinese gains of a couple of dozen miles towards Seoul, and in late July the shooting war was more or less over, with peace negotiations beginning again, this time rather more in earnest.

And *there* and *then* – Panmunjon in the 'demilitarized zone' astride the 38th parallel, July 1953 – the Korean War (the Korean peninsula) has remained ever since, preserved in light-blue aspic. As the then UNC commander, van Fleet's successor General Maxwell Taylor, put it, the armistice was 'a suspension of hostilities – an interruption of the shooting'. Except that while today the South is a prosperous and sophisticated polity, the North remains an absolutist, repressive state, for the most part grindingly poor, and with an embryonic nuclear weapons capability. And US troops remain in the South – some 30,000 of them, with another 40,000 in reserve in Japan: a force equivalent in number to just about the entire strength of the British army.

Imjin was the British Army's bloodiest battle since the Second World War, its last major positional defensive battle (in brigade strength, against overwhelming numbers and over several days), and its last fighting withdrawal. The army's reputation at home and with allies had rarely stood higher. The Glosters were recognized by a United States Distinguished Unit (now Presidential) Citation:

> Without thought of defeat or surrender, this heroic force demonstrated superb battlefield courage and discipline. Every yard of ground they surrendered was covered with enemy dead until the last gallant soldier . . . was overpowered by the final surge of the enemy masses. The 1st Battalion, Gloucestershire Regiment and Troop C, 170th Independent Mortar Battery displayed such a gallantry, determination, and esprit de corps in accomplishing their mission under extremely difficult and hazardous conditions as to set them apart and above the other units participating in the same battle.

PART SIX

HELMAND

Operation Panther's Claw:
The Battle for the Population

19 JUNE–27 JULY 2009

Financially it is ruinous. Morally it is wicked. Militarily it is an open question, and politically it is a blunder.

Winston Churchill, on the Malakand campaign (1897)

Western societies have learned how to kill on an enormous scale, but they may still fight at a disadvantage against agrarian age armies who have not forgotten how to die and know well enough how to kill.

Professor Sir Michael Howard, 'How Much
Can Technology Change War?' (2004)

One of Britain's finest, most humane generals, James Wolfe, who died in the hour of his victory at the Battle of the Plains of Abraham, Quebec, in 1759 aged just thirty-two, said memorably and succinctly, 'War is an option of difficulties.' The war against the Taliban in

Afghanistan between 2001 and 2014, when the Americans, British and other contributing nations began withdrawing combat troops, leaving training and advisory teams to allow Afghan national forces to continue the fight, will undoubtedly prove to have been one of history's most problematic.* Just as Sword Beach is a textbook example of how the 'gearing' between the levels of warfare should work, so Afghanistan is a case study in how it should not. Panther's Claw, a lengthy operation by a brigade group whose insignia was a black panther (supposedly based on Bagheera from Kipling's *Jungle Book*), was front-page news in Britain for several weeks, not least because the casualties mounted by the day and the public had begun to doubt that the war was winnable. It was also evidently a battle that was in part shaped by political timidity and parsimony, and the prime minister accordingly began to feel the heat. But it was, too, the army's most intense and bloody fighting since the Falklands War of 1982. Why it took place and how it was conceived – what *shaped* it – is both a lesson in history and a study of professional soldiers dealt an option of difficulties.

---

* The Taliban are mainly but not exclusively Pashtun, Afghanistan's predominant tribe. The Pashtuns make up only 40 per cent of the population, however, and their tribal strength is largely in the south and west of the country

1

AN OPEN QUESTION

My dear boy, as long as you don't invade Afghanistan you'll be absolutely fine.

Harold Macmillan to Sir Alec Douglas-Home, October 1963.*

Every war is *sui generis*, 'of its own kind'; but equally, as William Faulkner wrote, 'The past is never dead. It's not even past.' And in Afghanistan, there's a lot of 'past'. Britain alone has fought four wars there: from 1839 to 1842, from 1878 to 1880, in 1919, and then the counter-insurgency campaign of 2002–14.

The first was pretty much a disaster. In 1826, after a decade of

---

* Harold Macmillan (69), prime minister of the United Kingdom, January 1957–October 1963, resigned the premiership due to illness, and arranged for Alec Douglas-Home (60), the Foreign Secretary, to succeed him without a formal ballot – a surprise choice to many, including Douglas-Home. Macmillan was known for his rather courtly, even arch, Edwardian manners, which were frequently a front; but also for his considerable classical education and historical sense.

civil war, Emir (originally simply 'commander') Dost Mohammad Barakzai – taking the title Dost Mohammad Khan – came to the throne, but soon found himself caught between Great Britain and Russia, both of whom were manoeuvring for influence in the turbulent kingdom on the frontier of their expanding empires. What exactly the purpose was of what became known as the 'Great Game' is really no clearer now than it was at the time. The term was first used by Rudyard Kipling in his novel *Kim* (1901) to describe the rivalry between the two. It captured the sense of sport which permeated Victorian society, fuelled by thrilling stories of clandestine exploits beyond the imperial Indian pale by officers and private adventurers alike, tales that frequently embellished (or even invented) accounts of Russian intrigues and the fickle loyalties of tribal chiefs.

The British, believing that Dost Mohammad was either hostile to them or unable to resist Russian pressure, were soon trying to intervene directly in Afghan affairs. First they negotiated, unsuccessfully, and then they invaded, intending to restore Dost Mohammad's predecessor to the throne. Facing widespread rebellion, in January 1842 they decided to quit Kabul. The retreat was very bloody indeed, on both sides, including the loss of 4,500 British and Indian troops and 12,000 camp followers. And although in the summer British troops reoccupied Kabul, the following year the new governor-general of India decided to evacuate entirely, and Dost Mohammad returned to the throne.

The 'Game' continued, but at lower intensity, until in 1878, with Russian influence growing, and with it the fear of the tsar's meddling in India itself, a second invasion was launched. This was carried out with considerably more efficiency than the first, and a settlement was quickly concluded in which the new emir agreed to conduct his foreign affairs, as the treaty put it, in accordance with the wishes and advice of the British government. The triumph was as short-lived as the earlier one, however. The following year the British envoy in

Kabul was murdered. Troops were once again dispatched, under General Frederick Roberts VC – later Field Marshal Lord Roberts of Kandahar – and after a short campaign occupied Kabul. A new emir was found, a new boundary line with British India drawn – accepted by Russia – and things settled down, more or less. Except that the boundary, the Durand Line, named after the secretary of the British Indian government, was a time-bomb. It cut through tribal areas and was never accepted by the Afghans as a whole. Twenty years later, Young Winston (Churchill) would earn his spurs in the province of Malakand on the North-West Frontier in a punitive confrontation astride the line, and though enjoying the thrill of being shot at without effect, was in no doubt about the expedition's iniquity.

Casualties in these later wars and expeditions weren't huge, but they nevertheless stung imperial pride, and cumulatively they could lead to weariness or excesses. The Afghans proved both recalcitrant neighbours in peace and elusive fighters in war – masters of ground, and expert shots gifted with seemingly preternatural long sight. A hundred years before the term was coined, Kipling wrote a poem about 'asymmetric warfare' that summed up the character of war in Afghanistan, the 'land of the Pashtuns'. With considerable prescience he called it 'Arithmetic on the Frontier' (1886):

> A great and glorious thing it is
> To learn, for seven years or so,
> The Lord knows what of that and this,
> Ere reckoned fit to face the foe—
> The flying bullet down the Pass,
> That whistles clear: 'All flesh is grass.'
>
> Three hundred pounds per annum spent
> On making brain and body meeter
> For all the murderous intent

Comprised in 'villanous saltpetre!'
And after – ask the Yusufzaies
What comes of all our 'ologies.

A scrimmage in a Border Station—
A canter down some dark defile—
Two thousand pounds of education
Drops to a ten-rupee jezail—
The Crammer's boast, the Squadron's pride,
Shot like a rabbit in a ride!

No proposition Euclid wrote,
No formulae the text-books know,
Will turn the bullet from your coat,
Or ward the tulwar's downward blow.
Strike hard who cares – shoot straight who can—
The odds are on the cheaper man.

One sword-knot stolen from the camp
Will pay for all the school expenses
Of any Kurrum Valley scamp
Who knows no word of moods and tenses,
But, being blessed with perfect sight,
Picks off our messmates left and right.

With home-bred hordes the hillsides teem,
The troop-ships bring us one by one,
At vast expense of time and steam,
To slay Afridis where they run.
The 'captives of our bow and spear'
Are cheap – alas! as we are dear.

And four years later, in 'The Courting of Dinah Shadd', Kipling has
Private Ortheris lamenting:

> I fired a shot at a Afghan,
> The beggar 'e fired again,
> An' I lay on my bed with a 'ole in my 'ed,
> An' missed the next campaign!

Afghan tribesmen certainly sharpened the British army's fighting skills. But the savagery of these wars became particularly marked. Kipling again:

> When you're wounded and left on Afghanistan's plains,
> And the women come out to cut up what remains,
> Jest roll to your rifle and blow out your brains
> An' go to your Gawd like a soldier.

When in 1914 Ottoman Turkey entered the war on the side of the Central Powers (Germany and Austria-Hungary), Constantinople did its best to incite *jihad* – that is, to make it a fight against the enemies of Islam, in particular with the British in India, on whose native army much of the empire now depended. Naturally, in Afghanistan there was widespread support for Turkey, but Habibullah Khan, emir since 1901, modernizing and pro-British, managed to maintain a policy of non-involvement which allowed Delhi to send a good many troops to the Middle East who would otherwise have been tied down on the North-West Frontier. However, Habibullah paid the price in 1919, assassinated by anti-British supporters of his son Amanullah Khan, who promptly seized the throne and declared total independence from Great Britain. This declaration launched the Third Anglo-Afghan War.

It was a short and relatively bloodless one – a series of skirmishes between an ineffective Afghan army and a British Indian army toughened by the First World War. But the RAF's bombing of several cities, including the emir's palace in Kabul, small-scale and primitive though it was compared with their efforts in the European war, introduced a new element of savagery.

In August a peace treaty was concluded recognizing the absolute independence of Afghanistan. Ominously, however, even before the ink was dry the Afghans concluded a treaty of friendship with the Bolshevik regime in Moscow, one of the first states to recognize the new Soviet government. From that, a 'special relationship' developed which ultimately helped no one. In 1973, the socialist prime minister Daoud Khan instigated a coup that overthrew the monarchy and made him president. Five years later the Communist People's Democratic Party of Afghanistan deposed him, but anticommunist Islamic guerrillas, commonly called *mujahideen* ('those who make jihad'), backed by the CIA, at once declared war on the Kabul government. Among these guerrillas was a Saudi Arabian, the seventeenth child (allegedly of more than fifty) of a billionaire construction magnate. His name was Osama bin Laden, and he was leader of the ultra-extremist Islamist network Al-Qaeda ('the base', or 'foundation'). In December the following year, 1979, the Soviet Union invaded Afghanistan in support of the communist government, prompting the CIA (and the Saudis, and the Pakistan Inter-Services Intelligence agency) to begin more active support of the *mujahideen*.

It was arguably the Soviet regime's worst misjudgement of the Cold War (which is saying something), a last roll of the 'Brezhnev Doctrine' of intervention to support a threatened communist government. It soon became the proverbial quagmire. The Soviet army suffered some 15,000 dead and countless wounded until in 1988 the United States, Pakistan, Afghanistan and Moscow signed an agreement by which Soviet troops would withdraw and Afghanistan would return to non-aligned status. That said, Mikhail Gorbachev, who'd become the Soviet leader in 1985 after Leonid Brezhnev and his two successors had died in office within three years of each other, continued giving financial support to Kabul until his successor, Boris Yeltsin, turned off the tap.

In 1992, in the wake of the collapse of the Soviet Union, various rebel Afghan groups, together with newly rebellious government troops, overthrew the communist President Najibullah. For a while it looked like another episode in 'the end of history',* with its supposition of a glide into universal liberal democracy. Western liberals took 'the end' to be a cue to rest on their arms reversed, while some conservatives – 'neo-conservatives' or 'neocons' – were eager to hasten the glide by military interventions. History, however, was not dead yet, especially in Afghanistan. The transitional government proclaimed an Islamic republic, but the *mujahideen* proved as fissiparous as Scots Presbyterians, and soon Kabul was a city under siege, while the countryside outside the capital slipped into chaos as the various factions warred among themselves and with what passed for government forces. The strongest faction proved to be the Taliban ('students'), a particularly puritanical Islamist group led by Mullah Mohammad Omar and supported by Pakistan. Augmented by volunteers from various foreign Islamist groups, by the middle of 1996 they'd seized control of most of the country and occupied Kabul. Just a small part of northern Afghanistan remained in the hands of a loose coalition of less militant *mujahideen*, known officially as the United Islamic Front for the Salvation of Afghanistan and unofficially as the

---

* *The End of History and the Last Man* (New York, 1992), by American political scientist Francis Fukuyama, argued that with the ascendancy of western liberal democracy attained by victory in the Cold War (1945–91), marked by the dissolution of the Soviet Union, humanity had reached 'not just . . . the passing of a particular period of post-war history, but the end-point of mankind's ideological evolution and the universalization of Western liberal democracy as the final form of human government'. The end-point was declared a little early.

Northern Alliance. Fighting continued for another five years of stalemate – until the world-changing events of 9/11.

The exact moments at which the two hijacked planes crashed into the Twin Towers on 11 September 2001 are now erased from mainstream media. Taste and decency demand it, and also reason: repetition risks dulling the senses. Yet although the choice of weapon and target far exceeded the evil of the Japanese surprise attack on Pearl Harbor (a day that in President Roosevelt's words would 'live in infamy'), the attacks on the World Trade Center and the Pentagon, and the heroically thwarted attack on the White House, shared with Pearl Harbor the shock of sudden vulnerability – and in consequence provoked the same seismic shift of US policy. Writing of the opening battle of the English Civil War, Edgehill, some 350 years earlier, Kipling had concluded that

> The first dry rattle of new-drawn steel
> Changes the world today!

Had he been alive on 9/11 he might have been moved to write something similar: that the blackened, twisted steel of the Twin Towers changed, if not the world, then America's view of it.*

Forty-eight hours after the attacks, a defiant President George W. Bush stood amid the rubble at 'Ground Zero' (significantly, the term used of the point of impact of a nuclear weapon), his hand on the shoulder of one of the New York firemen who'd borne the brunt of the heroic rescue effort, and spoke to the crowd through a microphone.

---

* Though this was not universally acknowledged at the time – a dangerous disconnect between British and American strategic thinking which at times continues still. In the immediate aftermath of 9/11 the author recalls listening in disbelief to a senior FCO official (later a key ambassador) disputing that anything fundamental had changed.

When a distant voice called out, 'George, we can't hear you!', Bush smiled and answered loudly: 'I can hear you! I can hear you, the rest of the world can hear you, and the people who knocked these buildings down will hear all of us soon!'

A week later, addressing Congress, Bush expanded on his extemporary remark:

Americans are asking, 'How will we fight and win this war?' We will direct every resource at our command – every means of diplomacy, every tool of intelligence, every instrument of law enforcement, every financial influence, and every necessary weapon of war – to the destruction and to the defeat of the global terror network. Now, this war will not be like the war against Iraq a decade ago, with a decisive liberation of territory and a swift conclusion. It will not look like the air war above Kosovo two years ago, where no ground troops were used and not a single American was lost in combat. Our response involves far more than instant retaliation and isolated strikes. Americans should not expect one battle, but a lengthy campaign unlike any other we have ever seen. It may include dramatic strikes visible on TV and covert operations secret even in success. We will starve terrorists of funding, turn them one against another, drive them from place to place until there is no refuge or no rest . . .

Sitting close by the president in Congress was Tony Blair, Britain's prime minister, who'd flown to Washington in a show of solidarity and to offer support (though critically he'd not taken with him the chief of the defence staff). Bush spoke of several countries that had shown their support, then added: 'America has no truer friend than Great Britain. Once again, we are joined together in a great cause. I'm so honored the British prime minister has crossed an ocean to show his unity with America. Thank you for coming, friend.'

Churchill, of course, had gone to Washington in the aftermath of

Pearl Harbor. Blair's ocean crossing would likewise define the British military response to 9/11, though he played his hand with less acumen than Churchill did in the Second World War. Unlike Churchill, Blair could never be criticized for taking a close interest in military detail.

Within a month of the attacks the United States had begun its counter-offensive, the 'War on Terror'. Afghanistan had been a haven and training ground for Al-Qaeda, which had carried out the 9/11 attacks as well as bombings and assassinations over the previous decade in East Africa, the Middle East and western Asia. The Taliban refused US demands to extradite Osama bin Laden, who'd again taken refuge in the country after his expulsion from Sudan in 1996. Bin Laden was the baby in the Taliban bathwater. Out, therefore, they'd both have to go.

At the instigation of the NATO Secretary General, the former British Labour defence minister Lord (George) Robertson, the US campaign to oust the Taliban (Operation Enduring Freedom) was endowed with additional legitimacy under Article 5 of the North Atlantic Charter,* and enjoyed widespread if not always vocal international support. (Bush had referred to the NATO resolution in his speech to Congress: 'Perhaps the NATO charter reflects best the attitude of the world: An attack on one is an attack on all. The civilized world is rallying to America's side.') The initial operation was a brilliantly conceived and well-executed application of high-tech intelligence, special forces (including British), air power (including RAF surveillance aircraft), and the armies of the various anti-Taliban warlords known as the Northern Alliance.

---

* This article states that 'an armed attack against one or more of [the allies] in Europe or North America shall be considered an attack against them all and . . . [each] will assist the Party or Parties so attacked by taking forthwith, individually and in concert with the other Parties, such action as it deems necessary, including the use of armed force, to restore and maintain the security of the North Atlantic area'.

By the middle of November 2001, Kabul was in the hands of the Americans and their allies, and by the end of December it looked as if all that was left was merely the mopping-up. Indeed, the historian and commentator Sir John Keegan, writing in the *Daily Telegraph*, compared the apparent victory with one of the great turning points in the military history of the British empire: 'The collapse of Taliban resistance in northern Afghanistan and the fall of Kabul may stand as one of the most remarkable reversals of military fortune since Kitchener's victory at Omdurman in the Sudan in 1898.'

But despite the ferocious battles in the mountains of south-east Afghanistan, in which lay the cave complex of Tora Bora to which many Taliban had bolted, the key Al-Qaeda leaders couldn't be found. Those Taliban who hadn't been killed in last stands at Tora Bora fled across the border into Pakistan.

US and British forces and their Afghan allies now began to con-solidate. A *loya jirga* (grand council) of tribal leaders and former exiles, in effect an interim Afghan government, was established in Kabul under the sophisticated tribal leader Hamid Karzai. At the same time, a NATO-led International Security Assistance Force (ISAF) was mandated by the UN Security Council to secure Kabul and the surrounding areas from comeback attacks by the Taliban, Al-Qaeda and factional warlords. Military attention also turned to civil projects to win over the hearts and minds of those Afghans fur-ther afield who were largely indifferent to who ruled in Kabul.

The Taliban hadn't given up, however, and both American and British troops were in action throughout 2002, although far enough from Kabul to reinforce the general impression that peace prevailed and that democratic and economic progress was being made. British efforts were in the main concentrated on 'provincial reconstruction', in which the army (with some 1,500 troops) was – in broad terms – meant to provide conditions of security within which the civilian agencies could operate. However, both London and Washington increasingly took their military eyes off the ball, while the civil agencies seemed unable or unwilling to play the game at all. The experienced British major-general in charge of the multinational ISAF, John McColl, was replaced by a newly promoted colonel to head the much-reduced British contingent.* The army was expecting to have to provide a division for the pending invasion of Iraq to oust Saddam Hussein (another campaign in the 'War on Terror'), and it still had a brigade's worth of troops on stabilization operations in Bosnia and Kosovo, as well as a battalion-sized presence in Sierra Leone. Troops were in short supply. In Afghanistan, the early symptoms of 'mission-accomplished' syndrome seemed to be in evidence.

It was a cruel illusion – for some, a *delusion*. President Karzai's new government began increasingly to struggle in its attempts to centralize authority against a surprisingly powerful Taliban counter-push – a full-blown insurgency indeed. And the military began increasingly to struggle in their attempts to get to grips with what Clausewitz said was the 'first, the supreme, the most far-reaching act of judgment that the statesman and commander have to make' – to work out what kind of war they were embarking on, 'neither mistaking it for, nor trying to turn it into, something that is alien to its nature'.

---

* So impressed with McColl was (by then) President Karzai – a republic having been established in 2004 after three years' transitional government – that he's reputed to have made enticing offers for him to pay back the Queen's shilling and take his instead. Blair later made McColl his special envoy to Afghanistan, and when Karzai turned down the former leader of the British Liberal Democrats, Paddy Ashdown, as the UN nominee for high representative in Kabul, the president asked instead for McColl (who was by then Deputy Supreme Allied [NATO] Commander Europe). Here were shades of the North–West Frontier and the 'Great Game'.

Left: The grand strategic level of war: President Franklin D. Roosevelt and British prime minister Winston Churchill meet off the coast of Newfoundland, August 1941 — four months before Pearl Harbor — to agree the political object of the war, in what would become known as the Atlantic Charter.

Right: The military strategic level: The British and US Combined Chiefs of Staff at the Casablanca Conference, January 1943. General George C. Marshall, US Army Chief of Staff and FDR's de facto principal strategic adviser, speaks across the table to General Sir Alan Brooke (in spectacles), CIGS and, as chairman of the British chiefs of staff committee, Churchill's principal strategic adviser.

Left: The military strategic level: Churchill and his chiefs of staff, and on his left Sir Archibald Wavell, C-in-C India, aboard the Queen Mary en route to Washington, May 1943.

Top: The operational (or campaign or theatre) level: The Supreme Allied Commander for Overlord, General Dwight Eisenhower, with (on his right) his deputy, Air Chief Marshal Tedder, and his single-service commanders: on his left, General Montgomery; on Tedder's right, Admiral Ramsay; on Montgomery's left, Air Chief Marshal Leigh-Mallory. On Leigh-Mallory's left is Eisenhower's chief of staff, (US) General Bedell Smith. On Ramsay's right is General Bradley, commander 1st (US) Army, who would command 12th (US) Army Group when Patton's 3rd Army landed in Normandy in July.

Inset: Lieutenant-General Frederick Morgan – 'architect of Overlord'.

Above: The tactical level: Major-General Rennie, 3rd Division, briefing staff before D-Day.

Left: The tactical level: Lieutenant-General Crocker, I (British) Corps, watching the fighting near Caen in July. The battle for Caen was Crocker's on D-Day, but it became Montgomery's when I Corps failed to take it.

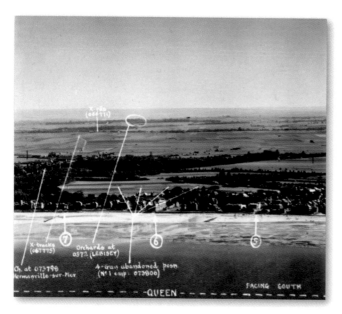

Left: 'No army in the history of war had such a wealth of intelligence on both the ground and the enemy, even if intelligence on the latter was ultimately incomplete.' Aerial photograph (by photo-reconnaissance Spitfire) of Queen Sector, Sword Beach.

Right: Commandos landing at H+30 on Sword Beach, which had been stormed at H-Hour by the 1st South Lancashires and 2nd East Yorkshires with the support of the semi-amphibious tanks of the 13th/18th Hussars. Some of 13/18H's incapacitated Shermans can be seen abandoned at the water's edge.

Left: Troops in the follow-up waves, possibly sappers, struggle ashore at Sword Beach. The congestion on the beaches was a major factor in the slow advance inland.

Left: House-to-house fighting towards Ouistreham. Note the lowered flotation screen on the 13/18H Sherman, and the propellers (hence 'DD' – duplex-drive).

Below: Troops of the 3rd Division, possibly 2nd Royal Ulster Rifles, pause in La Brèche d'Hermanville during the advance from Sword Beach.

Above: Infantry, probably of the 185th Brigade, move inland from Sword Beach. The bicycles were meant to speed the dash for Caen, but quickly proved an encumbrance as opposition stiffened.

Right: Only after much heavy bombing and costly outflanking operations were Caen and the dominating ground to the south-east taken towards the end of July.

Left: General Douglas MacArthur, C-in-C United Nations Command, with behind him the new commander of 8th Army, General Matthew Ridgway, who galvanized his shaken troops after the setbacks of December 1950.

Right: Chinese infantry, who dealt 8th Army a series of bitter blows in the winter of 1950–1.

Left: A Centurion tank of the 8th King's Royal Irish Hussars with men of the Gloucestershire Regiment ('Glosters') in March 1951 during the deceptively easy advance before the massive, surprise Chinese offensive at Imjin.

Left: The 29th Brigade's straight-line frontage was 9 miles, but because of the ground and the course of the Imjin River, in reality it was nearer 15 miles — far greater than a brigade would normally expect to hold.

Right: A 25-pounder howitzer of 45 Field Regiment Royal Artillery in action during the battle.

Left: 1st Ulster Rifles resting in their rearguard position towards the end of the battle.

Right: Roll-call of Gloster survivors — in all some 150 out of more than 800 — photographed possibly in Seoul towards the end of April.

HELMAND

Left: A convoy of Soviet armoured vehicles crossing a bridge at the Soviet–Afghan border, February 1989, during the withdrawal of the Red Army from Afghanistan.

Right: The London Conference, January 2006, jointly chaired by the British Prime Minister, Tony Blair, President Hamid Karzai of Afghanistan, and the United Nations Secretary-General, Kofi Annan.

Left: Key staff of the NATO Rapid Reaction Corps which led the International Security Assistance Force for nine months following the London Conference. Sir David Richards, ISAF's commander, is second from right; General Wardak, Afghan Defence Minister, far right. Painting by Brendan Kelly.

Right: Brigadier Tim Radford, whose reinforced 19th Light Brigade planned and executed Operation Panther's Claw in June–July 2009, at an Afghan shura (council) before the operation began. 'How do we know you'll stay?' was the question on the lips of every Afghan staking his future on the operation.

Right: The Chinook heavy-lift helicopter, key to the rapid deployment of troops (and casualty evacuation) during Panther's Claw, and for consolidation. There were not enough.

Left: A soldier of the Mercian Regiment fires a short-range 66mm HEAT (High Explosive Anti-Tank) rocket at an insurgent strongpoint near Babaji. 'Besides the constant IED threat, they would be opposed for most of the way by elusive fighters with, among other things, rocket-propelled grenades (RPGs), well able to destroy metal as well as flesh.'

Right: Light Dragoons, dismounted, covered by one of their Scimitar light tanks (strictly, CVR(T) — 'Combat Vehicle, Reconnaissance, Tracked') during the main phase of the operation.

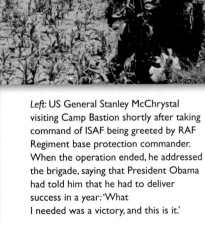

Left: US General Stanley McChrystal visiting Camp Bastion shortly after taking command of ISAF being greeted by RAF Regiment base protection commander. When the operation ended, he addressed the brigade, saying that President Obama had told him that he had to deliver success in a year: 'What I needed was a victory, and this is it.'

2

THE MOST FAR-REACHING
ACT OF JUDGEMENT

Macnaghten looked around him, and saw that 'everything was quiet from Dan to Beersheba'; and he rejoiced in the thought that he was about to quit Afghanistan for ever, and to carry with him no burden of anxiety and fear.

John Kaye, *History of the War in Afghanistan* (1857)

Operation Herrick, the codename by which Britain's military operations in Afghanistan were conducted from 2002, began inoffensively enough. At first its primary component was the 300 or so troops providing security in Kabul and helping to train the new Afghan National Army (ANA); but the following year the numbers more than doubled when several 'provincial reconstruction teams' (PRTs) and a rapid reaction force were established in north-western Afghanistan. Meanwhile, the number of troops based in Kabul was also rising – to 1,300 – and was augmented with an RAF detachment of six fighters at Kandahar airfield in support of the Americans.

Then, early in 2006, some 70 states and fifteen international organizations – not least NATO – took part in a conference in London chaired by British prime minister Tony Blair, President Karzai and UN Secretary General Kofi Annan to agree a concept of international cooperation. The conference concluded with the declaration that the participants,

Determined to strengthen their partnership to improve the lives of Afghan people, and to contribute to national, regional, and global peace and security;

Affirming their shared commitment to continue . . . to work toward a stable and prosperous Afghanistan, with good governance and human rights protection for all under the rule of law, and to maintain and strengthen that commitment over the term of this Compact and beyond;

Recognising the courage and determination of Afghans who, by defying violent extremism and hardship, have laid the foundations for a democratic, peaceful, pluralistic and prosperous state based on the principles of Islam;

Noting the full implementation of the Bonn Agreement [the initial series of agreements in December 2001 following the US invasion to re-create the State of Afghanistan] . . .;

Mindful that Afghanistan's transition to peace and stability is not yet assured, and that strong international engagement will continue to be required to address remaining challenges;

Resolved to overcome the legacy of conflict in Afghanistan by setting conditions for sustainable economic growth and development; strengthening state institutions and civil society; removing remaining terrorist threats; meeting the challenge of counter-narcotics; rebuilding capacity and infrastructure; reducing poverty; and meeting basic human needs;

Have agreed to this Afghanistan Compact.

As far as the various national military contingents in Afghanistan were concerned, however, the most significant specification – though its significance wasn't recognized and acted on initially with anything like the address that some expected – was that 'a professional and ethnically balanced Afghan National Army [ANA] with up to 70,000 soldiers is to be established and fully functional by 2010', while 'the police being formed is to provide reliable security in the country and at the borders'.

ISAF now moved up several gears to take over progressively more responsibility from the discrete but inevitably overlapping US Operation Enduring Freedom (the name extended beyond the initial intervention in 2001). It became a four-star command, and in May 2006 the multinational (NATO) HQ Allied Rapid Reaction Corps (ARRC) deployed from its base in Gloucestershire as the force headquarters for nine months, the first time a standing rather than an ad hoc headquarters would be in charge. In command was the British General Sir David Richards, with a mandate to align the campaign with the 'Afghanistan Compact', not least through his membership of the Afghan Presidential Advisory Group.*

---

* During the ARRC's nine-month stint, ISAF's area of operations doubled in size, encompassing the whole country, troop numbers growing from 9,500 to more than 35,000 as a result. Richards, a keen student of the British army's successful counter-insurgency campaign in Malaya (1948–60), put considerable effort into blending the different threads of the counter-Taliban campaign – political, military, security, humanitarian and developmental – at local, regional and national levels – and sometimes at international level, not least because with the expansion of ISAF's area of operations, for the first time there was a common border with Pakistan. It was not so

Meanwhile there was to be a major shift of emphasis for the British. Responsibility for the PRTs in the north-west was handed over to other national contingents to allow British troops to refocus on south Afghanistan. The defence secretary, John Reid, announced that Britain would send a PRT with several thousand extra troops to Helmand province for at least three years as part of the gradual expansion of ISAF's area of responsibility from Kabul to encompass the rest of the country. Reid planned an initial strength of 5,700 in all, stabilizing at about 4,500 for the rest of the deployment, on six-month rotation as before. Announcing the increase in parliament, he was at pains to explain that the 3,500 extra troops (a brigade's worth) were being deployed to help the reconstruction effort, but when visiting Afghanistan in April he added not unreasonably that

> Although our mission to Afghanistan is primarily reconstruction, it is a complex and dangerous mission because the terrorists will want to destroy the economy and the legitimate trade and the government that we are helping to build up. Of course, our mission is not counter-terrorism but one of the tasks that we may have to accomplish in order to achieve our strategic mission will be to defend our own troops and the people we are here to defend and to pre-empt, on occasion, terrorist attacks on us. If this didn't involve the necessity to use force we wouldn't send soldiers.

He distanced the operation from the US's Enduring Freedom, saying it was 'fundamentally different to that of the US forces elsewhere in Afghanistan . . . We are in the south to help and protect the Afghan people construct their own democracy.' But then, in a sort of

---

much like turning a supertanker as boarding a smaller one, setting a new course, then refitting and enlarging it while still at sea. But the nine months probably rescued ISAF from defeat, though victory still remains a long work in progress – to say the least.

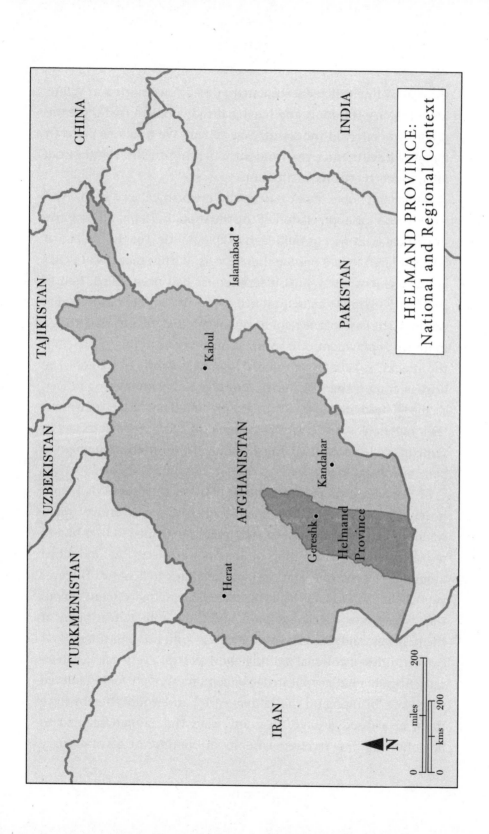

HELMAND PROVINCE:
National and Regional Context

throwaway line which encapsulated a decade's woolliness in White-hall's military thinking, and having already implied that there was no unity of effort in the country, he added: 'We would be perfectly happy to leave in three years and without firing one shot because our job is to protect the reconstruction.'

While such hopes of peace were wholly worthy, they'd soon reveal a dangerous misappreciation of the situation, in Helmand province in particular, as well as quite remarkable hubris. For the Taliban at once declared they'd oppose these efforts. Within months of Reid's announcement, forty British servicemen had been killed, half of them in Helmand in a single month, for 16 Air Assault Brigade, which was to be the basis of the reinforcement ('Herrick IV' – the fourth six-monthly deployment of troops), at once began trying to pre-empt the attacks, as Reid had intimated, as well as fighting them off. The brigade commander, Ed Butler, a former SAS commanding officer, seemed determined to take the fight to the Taliban rather than await their inevitable – as he saw it – counter-offensive, though in fact in terms of available 'bayonets' he'd not much more than an augmented parachute battalion.

In the late summer and autumn of 2006 there were daily and heavy firefights with the Taliban, and platoon-size (thirty men) standing patrols dotted about Helmand in defended houses had to resort increasingly to calling in fire from artillery, RAF and allied ground-attack aircraft, and the Apache attack helicopter. The ever younger Taliban fighters lacked tactical skill and marksmanship but they were almost suicidally brave, and there were a great many of them. It was, said the defenders, with the grim humour honed over two centuries of colonial fighting, 'Rorke's Drift every day'. Strategi-cally, Brigadier Butler appeared to be content, though, for he believed they were 'bringing on the Taliban early', and would thereby have them at a disadvantage. In many ways the Taliban seemed to be following the received wisdom of communist revolutionary warfare – although of course they were anything but communist: that the 'imperialist enemy' should be worn down by ambush and sabotage while the revolutionary forces built up enough conventional strength to take on and defeat them in open battle. It had been notably successful in Mao's campaign against the nationalist forces in China, and in Ho Chi Minh's in French Indo-China. If the Taliban were trying to follow this blueprint, however, they were dangerously accelerating the process in hurling their fighters against a preponderance of conventional firepower. Butler claimed tactical success, but it would be short-lived. Besides, while huge amounts of ordnance killed Taliban in large numbers, the 'collateral damage' – in terms of civilian casualties – was also heavy. This served as a recruiting serjeant for the Taliban, and what little progress there was in reconstruction and nation-building – the whole object of the process, according to Reid's announcement – was soon either put on hold or even reversed.

There were criticisms of the way Brigadier Butler spread his forces in 'penny packets' around Helmand, but he himself appeared to feel that in the absence of strategic clarity he'd been given no choice. In his post-operational report he wrote of 'the lack of early, formal political direction and a strictly enforced manning cap [upper limit of troop numbers], established upon apparently best case rather than most likely or worst case planning assumptions and taking little account of the enemy vote'. He also complained that there'd been delays in getting the right equipment and in the right numbers, the Ministry of Defence (MoD) and Treasury being unwilling to commit funds to urgent operational (equipment) requirements prior to any formal political announcements. But he put his finger on the real essence of the problem when he spoke of 'unrealistic time-scales that foresaw no offensive operations'. He might well have cited Clausewitz's first rule – 'to enter the field with an army as strong as possible' – and he might well have added ruefully, just as Clausewitz had, that 'This [dictum] sounds very like a common place, but still is really not so.'

Plus ça change . . .

Butler resigned his commission eighteen months after returning from Afghanistan, as did the commanding officer of the Parachute battalion, who'd also been dismayed at the inadequate treatment of his wounded soldiers on evacuation to Britain. However, the army's leadership hadn't entirely endorsed Butler's appreciation, or his tactics, and resignations often follow from disappointment in future promotion prospects.

The preoccupation of British troops in Helmand that first summer had been 'kinetic' – fighting the Taliban. To a large extent this was inevitable. Until the Afghans were themselves able to provide security for the people of Helmand, the British (and their allied contingents) would have to do so. A forward presence was therefore necessary. However, the Taliban opposed that presence as an 'article of faith', as well as seeing the province as a key test of their ability to take and hold territory from NATO-led Afghan national security forces (ANSF: the ANA and police); and so the fighting would grow in intensity to the detriment of training the ANA. Indeed, the more the Taliban could distract ISAF, the longer it would take to make the ANA capable of taking responsibility for security.

In the later nineteenth century British army officers began developing subtle skills in 'humint' – intelligence gathered direct from human sources via interpersonal contact, as opposed to that gained by indirect, technical means – mastering tribal languages and acquiring considerable cultural understanding. Especially so in India, sometimes on secondment to the Indian Political Service as district administrators or as advisers to the princely states independent of the British Raj. And of course as players in the 'Great Game'. Understanding and respecting local ways – speaking the language, literally and metaphorically – became a point of pride, the politically nuanced officer thereby able to punch above his weight in dealing with feudal rulers, while confident of the real weight that backed him. The concept entered the collective mind of the army. On withdrawal from empire, however, it largely left that mind, except in special forces.

Thus the British army had embarked on a mission of subtlety in Helmand, but initially without the tools for the job or an agreed understanding of what those tools were, even of what the job was. That autumn, 2006, they started to reach 'cessation of hostilities' agreements with local Taliban forces around the district centres that they'd held in the summer. Under the terms of the agreements, both sides were meant to withdraw from the conflict zone. It was a tacit acceptance that troop numbers were just too low to hold the key bases in Helmand that President Karzai had requested. It was also a setback for the Taliban, though, who'd been desperate to consolidate their gains but had been losing men in disturbing numbers. They would have to play a longer game – and they believed they could, that time was on their side. And they composed a taunting mantra exalting the war's asymmetry: 'You have the watches, but we have the time.'

Although it wasn't strictly true – with time, the ANSF would be getting better – it was clever, because it played on what the Taliban knew would be the weakness of the international community: strategic impatience. The United States was still haunted by the long war in Vietnam and severely pressed by the insurgency in Iraq following the 2003 invasion, a theatre which the British were eager to quit.* So the Taliban began to adapt their tactics. Instead of hurling

---

* British troops in quasi-divisional strength had assisted the US in the invasion of Iraq in 2003, which Washington viewed as part of its 'War on Terror' – as well as 'unfinished business' from the First Gulf War (1991) – and found themselves seriously on the back foot in Basra when they underestimated the scale and nature of the post-invasion insurgency.

themselves at strongly defended positions, they considered the 'arithmetic on the frontier'. The term 'asymmetric warfare' describes conflict between conventionally equipped, 'high-tech' regulars and an enemy who takes them on, deliberately or through lack of choice, at a lower level of military technology. The boy David's sling against the chink in the giant Goliath's armour isn't a bad comparison. The low-tech force relies on patience and pinprick attacks, often the improvised explosive device (IED) – which in the terrain of Helmand could be huge – to exhaust the opponent's political will to continue the fight in the face of steady, if comparatively quite small, losses. The conventional force must either bring the low-tech force to battle 'in the open' (the low-tech force believing themselves ready for the 'one big push' to finish the job), or else adapt the enemy's own tactics to fight at the low-tech level even better than he does. The latter especially requires a great deal of humint, as the enemy's methods of communicating and operating probably won't be as amenable to non-human penetration.* Humint was at a premium as far as ISAF and the ANSF were concerned. One officer, writing of this more asymmetrical phase, gave the Taliban handsome praise:

The average Taliban fighter is sly, fearless and a master of camouflage and concealment. He is not stupid and understands our rules of engagement as well as we do. Unless he will lose face or ground that he wishes to retain, he will simply blend into the local population and observe you. If he spots a perceived weakness, however, he will react. The trick then is to convince him that you are weak enough for him to take you

---

* That said, a low-tech enemy does rely for its electronic communications on commercial systems, with limited encryption – and insurgents in Iraq after the 2003 invasion paid a high price in consequence; but there again, a patient, low-tech insurgency will be less reliant on electronic communications than conventional forces.

on; not that easy to do as nobody wants to initiate a well-prepared ambush on ground of the enemy's choosing, and if you suspect that he is there, the natural reaction is to look for him in strength. Contacts were most frequently therefore initiated at extremely close range and in extremely close country.*

And movement was thereby made constantly tense by the IED threat.

Fighting continued throughout the winter of 2006–7, British and allied troops – including special forces – increasingly proactive. By this time 16 Air Assault Brigade had been replaced by the 3rd [Royal Marines] Commando Brigade, as eager to get to grips with the enemy as their great rivals the Parachute Regiment had been. They in turn were replaced in April 2007 by the 12th Mechanized Brigade, and although the expected spring offensive by the Taliban didn't materialize, almost certainly owing to the large number of casualties their 'foot soldiers' had taken in their frontal assaults the previous summer, the tour was just as 'kinetic'. By 2008, indeed, the rotational and by now hugely augmented British brigades for Helmand – referred to as Task Force Helmand (TFH) – were training primarily with the expectation of intense combat in up to brigade strength, rather than of work under the original Reid vision that 'our mission is not counter-terrorism' but one of 'reconstruction'. The TFH certainly continued to take casualties, if nothing like the numbers the Taliban had taken in 2006, and these were beginning to tell with public opinion and therefore political confidence at home. By 2009 the number killed in action in Afghanistan since 2001 was approaching 200. In cold statistical terms this was hardly alarming; during the three decades and more of Operation Banner (Northern Ireland, 1969–2007), some 1,400 servicemen had died, over half of them in IRA attacks

---

* Author's archive.

(most of the rest in operational and training accidents), and the Falklands War of 1982 killed 250 in just over six weeks. Yet proportional to the numbers deployed, the figures were troubling, not least because serious (life-changing) casualties were also increasing alarmingly, as was their public profile. These casualties, usually involving amputations, sometimes of more than one limb, were almost always the result of IEDs, and ten years earlier would likely as not have resulted in death. The increased survival rate was testimony to the remarkable first-aid expertise of the troops on the ground, which had undergone a revolution in the previous decade, as well as to the RAF's skilful and fearless helicopter casualty evacuation ('casevac'), the trauma surgery and nursing at the main base of British forces in Helmand – Camp Bastion – and subsequently the RAF's medical flights to England, with casualties often in an induced coma.

In the public mind, these grave injuries came on top of the nearly 200 deaths in Iraq, a campaign that had gone badly wrong.* And without doubt the sometimes brave but faltering British performance in that insurgency had stung the army's leadership into wanting out as fast as possible in order to restore self-confidence and reputation in what appeared to be a more straightforward if bloody tactical challenge in Afghanistan. Commanders on the ground in Helmand were in no mood to give any impression of unwillingness to get to grips with the enemy, as had sometimes appeared evident in Iraq. And because there was no permanent two-star (division equivalent) headquarters to give consistency and continuity to the campaign,

---

* Also called the Second Gulf War (2003–11), the conflict consisted of two phases. The first was a brief, conventionally fought campaign (March–April 2003), in which a combined US–British force (with token contingents from several other countries) invaded and rapidly defeated Iraqi military and paramilitary forces. The second phase, the US-led occupation, faced an unexpected (or unexpectedly large) insurgency, which was not quelled until 2007, after which the US and Britain gradually reduced their military presence.

with complete brigades rotating every six months rather than the headquarters staying put while the constituent units came and went in rotation – a departure from all previous counter-insurgency practice* – TFH commanders themselves were naturally focused on shorter-term offensive operations at brigade level. This was the time of the making of names – 'seeking the bubble reputation in the cannon's mouth'. And why not? For reputation – individual, regimental, army and national – was an implicit, and sometimes explicit, part of the mission. Unfortunately, it didn't conduce to coherence and consistency in the campaign.

That said, there was no want of thoughtfulness at the head of TFH. Indeed, the commander of Herrick VI during the fighting summer of 2007, Brigadier (later Lieutenant-General Sir) John Lorimer, had read Arabic and Islamic Studies at Cambridge, and in 2018 would become defence senior adviser for the Middle East, an appointment which, if closer to home than Afghanistan, acknowledged at least a marked degree of cultural awareness. But the situation at the beginning of each six-month tour was as he and others found it, and for the most part they could only make the best of a bad job.

By the middle of 2008, with the situation not improving, the commander of Herrick IX, Brigadier Gordon Messenger, whose Royal

---

* The reason given by the then CGS, Sir Richard Dannatt, was that because brigades had to mount brigade-size operations, they had to train as brigades prior to deployment, thus making it unfeasible for their individual units to 'trickle' rotate. The reason why command was not vested in a fully functioning permanent two-star headquarters is still a mystery. The key decision-makers in the process weren't army and could see no need for it; and the political imperative of limited liability trumped what was perceived as army 'gold-plating'. The numbers had become the strategy. The result was a brigade headquarters of over 200 strong – a divisional headquarters in all but name – facing a command challenge that was too great. Without a headquarters above them looking upwards and outwards, brigade commanders were too often distracted from the tactical-level fight on which they should have been focusing. As a result, TFH too often lacked focus and agility at the tactical level.

Marines were expending a good deal of ammunition in many a fire-fight, evidently considered it was time for a rethink. Although the original plan in the spring of 2006, developed by ISAF headquarters and encouraged by the Afghan government (notably President Karzai), had been to focus on the population centres, British forces had got drawn into the 'platoon house [Rorke's Drift] strategy', and General Richards in Kabul had only with some difficulty been able to pull them out of it. But Richards had left Kabul in February 2007, and the US General Dan McNeill had taken his place. His approach was decidedly more aggressive, and McNeill's own successor in June 2008, General David McKiernan, also American, was no less inclined to the mailed fist.

Perhaps, being a Royal Marine, Messenger was able to take a step back from what might have been perceived as 'army' strategy and think afresh.* In any event, he concluded that the strategy was flawed, and persuaded both London and the NATO chain of command in Afghanistan to return to the original (Richards) concept of focusing on the centres of population rather than the peripheries – in the case of Helmand, the so-called Afghan Development Zone, the triangle formed by the provincial capital Lashkar Gah, Gereshk (the economic hub of Helmand) and Camp Bastion, 20 miles north-west of Lashkar Gah. This, however, needed more troops than he actually had, and he was only able to put a battle group (an all-arms force based on a battalion) into Nad-e Ali on the other side of the Helmand river west of Lashkar Gah by asset-stripping elsewhere. He was also keen to make their presence less kinetic. 'Our reaction to being fired

---

* Messenger hadn't been intended for the job, but was hastily transferred from the operations directorate of the MoD when the brigade commander was almost killed in an accident during pre-deployment leave. He'd also been involved in the initial planning for Helmand while serving in the Permanent Joint HQ at Northwood, just outside London.

on is still to react in kind, sometimes disproportionately, alienating sections of the population as a consequence,' he said – the very thing that British commanders had been critical of the Americans doing, here in Afghanistan as well as earlier in Iraq.

Messenger's intentions would be endorsed by his successor in the summer of 2009, Brigadier Tim Radford, commanding the 19th Light Brigade. Radford, described by one not uncritical defence correspondent as 'soft-spoken and cerebral',* brought to the campaign a politics degree as well as a special forces background and the accumulated experience of the Northern Ireland 'Troubles', Iraq, and a spell as assistant director of counter-terrorism in the MoD.† The rotation to Herrick X also coincided with a change of command in ISAF: in June, President Obama, frustrated by the lack of progress and encouraged by his Defense Secretary, Robert Gates – who, unusually, had continued in post from the previous administration of President George W. Bush – removed McKiernan and appointed instead a special forces officer, General Stanley McChrystal.

Steeped in counter-insurgency theory and practice, McChrystal quickly reset the thinking: 'We are fighting for the population and that involves protecting them both from the enemy and from unintended consequences of our operation.' He coined the term 'courageous restraint' to characterize the approach he wanted.

London too knew that things weren't working. TFH wasn't just a brigade but a civil–military mission coordinating the UK's so-called 'comprehensive approach'. The civil side operated under the lead of the Foreign and Commonwealth Office (FCO), with the Department for International Development (DfID) and its PRTs trying desperately

---

* Toby Harnden, *Dead Men Risen* (London, 2011).

† As a four-star general, Radford would in 2020 become Deputy Supreme [NATO] Allied Commander Europe (DSACEUR), and Messenger Vice-Chief of the Defence Staff in 2016. Helmand was a proving ground for a generation of senior officers.

to work 'normally' and with minimal military profile. Indeed, DfID personnel had frequently been reluctant to engage with the counter-insurgency side of the comprehensive approach. By early 2009, senior British officers were increasingly voicing concern that the FCO and DfID 'didn't quite have the equation right', that better security was needed to protect the Afghans' reconstruction and governance; and for that, more troops were needed. Parliament voiced concern, too, but with a slightly different emphasis, concerned that there was 'too much kinetic activity going on . . . they needed to see the evidence of reconstruction and development . . . that is what the government has presented to the British people'.* In April, a report entitled *UK Policy in Afghanistan and Pakistan: A Way Forward* confirmed London's commitment to the counter-insurgency strategy, focusing on Lashkar Gah and other population centres in Helmand, including Gereshk; but the comprehensive, civil–military effort just wasn't getting results. Indeed, in July the House of Commons Foreign Affairs Committee concluded that 'the security situation [in Helmand] is preventing any strengthening of governance and Afghan capacity' and that the 'security situation makes it extremely difficult for civilians to move around the province, and as a result civilian projects suffer'. In other words, to stabilize Helmand and improve security, British forces needed to go all out on combating the insurgency.

Winning the population ought to have been like pushing at an open door, for by and large the Taliban were hated. That much had always been understood; but the door was easily jammed. Indeed, at worst it could actually swing back and close for good if tactical methods continued to kill large numbers of ordinary Afghans, however inadvertently. In other words, reliance on heavy ordnance, particularly aerial bombing, no matter how precision-guided, wasn't

---

* See Jeffrey Dressler, *Afghanistan Report 2* (Washington DC, 2009).

an option – not of first resort, certainly. Troops on the ground would have to close with the enemy and be tactically discerning.

In this fight for the population, and for the whole nation-building project, 2009 would therefore be a – perhaps *the* – defining year. The elections for both the presidency and the national and provincial councils taking place in August were fundamental to the project. If these were to have any chance of success, in Helmand in particular, it wouldn't be enough simply to guard the polling stations; the Taliban would have to be ejected from the province so that Afghans – an estimated 80,000 in TFH's area of operations – would be able to move freely to and from them. Thus an ambitious operation would be launched in the two months prior to polling, both to clear out the Taliban and to allow the ANSF to occupy and hold the ground, thus linking the provincial capital with the economic capital, which had hitherto been 'bandit country'. It would take the codename Panther's Claw – in Pashtun, *Panchai Palang* – and would be carried out by Radford's brigade, due to arrive in theatre in May.

As planning began at the 19th Brigade's headquarters in Northern Ireland, long before deployment, there were indications of another Taliban offensive against Lashkar Gah. Intelligence reported that Mullah Omar intended making Helmand the focus of his main effort, and that several hundreds of Taliban fighters would assault the provincial capital from the north-west and from Marjah across the Bolan desert to the south-west, and mount rocket attacks against the brigade base. Radford's staff therefore began planning to clear the area of Babaji and the so-called Chah-e Anjir Triangle ('CAT') – roughly equilateral, 5 miles a side – to strengthen the security of the provincial capital. Any threat to Lashkar Gah had to be taken seriously, for obvious political as well as military reasons. Besides, Helmand's governor, Gulab Mangal, had for months been pressing Kabul for additional ANA troops. Any provincial governor's position at this time was precarious, to say the least, and while it was inconceivable that the Taliban could actually capture the town, let alone hold it, any disruption to daily life might make Mangal look weak. (His own compound would be within range of Taliban rockets fired from the Bolan bridge across the Helmand river.) President Karzai eventually sent two more *kandaks* (battalions: approximately 600 men each) to the province.

If Mangal felt there was 'strategic' pressure on his position as governor, British officers – from commanders in Afghanistan to the most senior in Whitehall – most certainly felt the pressure. Iraq had not been the army's finest hour. Subtle and effective in the initial capture of Basra in the south, the divisional-size force had rapidly got out of its depth in the subsequent Shia insurgency. It wasn't so much the fault of the troops on the ground – although the lack of operational 'grip' was at times very marked, with the many acts of heroism (including one meriting the award of a VC) marred by acts of thuggery – as the effects of confusion in the interconnecting corridors of political and military power in London. In particular, the withdrawal from the city of Basra itself to the security of the airport, though well conducted tactically, was little short of a strategic disaster in terms of British relations with US commanders. However much it was presented as 'tough love', forcing the Iraqi security forces to take responsibility for the city, it was impossible to counter the impression – the accusations – that the army had pulled out because they weren't prepared to fight, to shed blood, and then had to be bailed out by Americans coming down from Baghdad. Or, as one senior American special forces officer put it, 'The British wrote cheques they couldn't cash.'

The fact was that those at the top in London – particularly in the MoD – had decided that Iraq was 'unwinnable'. They'd not expected to face an insurgency, troop morale was now suffering, and external support was disappearing. But cutting and running from Iraq couldn't be an option unless there was something else to focus on, in a sense to redeem the army's reputation as being competent and willing to fight – in other words, its reputation in the eyes of the public, the Treasury, the world; and in particular the Americans, the military partnership with whom was at the heart of security policy. Afghanistan in 2006 had seemed to offer just that opportunity – a smaller-scale affair well suited to recent British experience of 'operations other than war', notwithstanding the bloody noses in Basra. The last thing Radford needed now, three years later, as he planned for Herrick X, was the threat of McKiernan, who was then still in post, sending US troops in large numbers into Helmand to 'kick ass', giving the impression that the Brits couldn't cope – the impression of another Basra.

Herrick X also coincided with something of a sea-change in the approach to the campaign in London. Frustrated with Whitehall's – not least the MoD's – view that Afghanistan was just one of a number of continuing commitments (one that just happened to be uniquely bloody), an 'operation' rather than a war, General David Richards, by then the army's commander-in-chief, and later to become Chief of the General Staff and then Chief of the Defence Staff, persuaded the MoD that the army needed to be put on an 'operational footing', focusing almost entirely on counter-insurgency, to get fully to grips with the campaign. At first he'd wanted to call it a 'war footing', but that was judged a foot too far. But with 'Operation Entirety', as it was called, Richards gave notice that the army had to move into a much higher gear.

This, too, would have its effect in shaping Panther's Claw – the sense of at last having some proper 'top cover' at home (although, as it would prove, still not enough). As would the belated realization by the prime minister, Gordon Brown, that under-resourcing the campaign from the outset was now having awkward political consequences.

To begin with, the 19th Light Brigade's order of battle would be larger than hitherto, consisting of a tracked armoured reconnaissance regiment (the Light Dragoons) and five infantry battalions – 1st

Welsh Guards, 3rd Royal Regiment of Scotland (Black Watch), 2nd Royal Regiment of Fusiliers and 2nd and 4th Rifles, with in addition elements of 2nd Battalion Mercian Regiment and 2nd Battalion Royal Gurkha Rifles as mentoring teams with the ANA and police, an armoured infantry company of the 2nd Royal Welsh, and strong artillery and engineer support. Also, directly supporting the brigade, as they had its predecessors, would be the Army Air Corps' Apache helicopter-gunships and an RAF squadron of Chinook heavy-lift helicopters, with the joint Harrier force at Kandahar airfield on call.

The area of operations – the battlefield – was compact enough: an area about the same size as the Isle of Wight, but complex, a wedge-shaped plain some 24 miles long from Lashkar Gar in the south to Gereshk to the north-east. Bounded by the Nahr-e Bughra canal on the north side and the Helmand river on the south, it was some 14 miles wide at its south-western end (its southern border formed more or less by the Shamalan canal north-west of Babaji – although the CAT is immediately to the west of the canal), tapering to just a couple of miles at its north-eastern tip. It was an ancient, agrarian, exceptionally fertile district, a place of open fields and irrigation channels, 'the green zone', with those who farmed the land and tended their animals living in traditional, square-built *qal 'ah*s ('fortresses'). It was certainly not an empty space, and it had been under Taliban control for years, their corridor for operations along the Helmand river. However, the Taliban didn't wear uniforms, and they'd advanced from their earlier strategy of suicidal frontal assaults. The Afghan was famed for his long-range sniping; now he'd also become adept at the indirect method, the threat underfoot – mines, some retrieved from the Soviet era, some home-made, the IEDs. The effect of these wasn't just physical but psychological. Troops in Helmand in particular had become very IED-conscious, both on foot and in wheeled armoured personnel carriers (APCs). The IED threat wasn't new, as those who'd served in the border areas of Northern Ireland during the

'Troubles' – and there were still a few – could testify. But in South Armagh the IEDs had been 'command detonated': an IRA man at the end of a long length of buried cable, or with an electronic device, initiating the explosion. On the whole the IRA were keen to minimize casualties among a civilian population who in those parts were largely sympathetic; but also, they didn't want to waste their resources. Booby traps were rare, therefore. In Helmand the Taliban used command detonation, but also – like the Viet Cong in Vietnam – pressure-plates and tilt-switches, having warned the local population to keep clear.

In the two months preceding 19th Light Brigade's arrival in theatre, the 3rd Commando Brigade (on their second tour within eighteen months) carried out a number of preliminary operations to take and hold ground to give Radford's troops a better chance of success. Notable was a four-day action to establish a checkpoint on a key route into Lashkar Gah which would then be manned by Afghan forces 'mentored' by the British to prevent infiltration and to disrupt any spoiling attack the Taliban might make once Panther's Claw was under way – representing an unusual degree of cooperation, overlap and continuity between brigades.

Radford's brigade began arriving in early April, and at once started the delicate job of taking over the ANSF mentoring responsibilities. They had two months in which to refine the plans made at home, to gather more intelligence and adjust to changing circumstances, and to accustom the troops of the brigade to Helmand. Their final exercise on Salisbury Plain had been as realistic as ground and climate allowed – the 'green zone' would have fitted comfortably into the dimensions of the training area, though the plain in winter snow wasn't the green zone in summer – and reading the actual ground and its people takes time. Radford also had to be sure of his allies. Not only did he have to get the measure of the ANA and police commanders, he would also have Danish and Estonian troops under command – a Danish battle group, with a troop of German-made Leopard II tanks and an integrated Estonian recce platoon. At the same time, Radford's commanding officers had to turn the concept of operations they'd understood before deployment into concrete plans once they'd accustomed themselves to the ground and the threat.

Some were distinctly troubled by what they saw – especially the mismatch between demands for helicopters and their availability. There was unlikely to be more than a battalion's-worth of lift at any one time, and although the operation would be sequenced ('phased'), with the helicopters switched between the battle groups, the logistic needs remained. Resupply would therefore have to be by road, which was both dangerous and slow. Helicopters had indeed become a political issue at home, with mounting accusations that the Treasury had cut procurement funding.* There was also a complete lack of surveillance equipment covering the approaches to the compounds serving as the brigade's forward operating bases, which meant the Taliban had an easier job planting IEDs under cover of darkness. Nevertheless, the operation would have to begin in June to have any chance of clearing out the Taliban and then consolidating the gains before the August elections. Like those planning for D-Day who knew they didn't have all the landing craft they'd like, Radford and his staff had to make a plan for Panther's Claw with the resources they were given.

Several more months of intelligence-gathering, not only by special forces but from Afghans displaced by the Taliban (and fear of the fight to come) from the green zone and now in refugee camps, proved even more valuable than expected. In many respects local knowledge was still poor, however, for despite being in the province since 2006, TFH

---

* The Treasury had effectively cut the defence budget in 2003/4, and the (joint) chiefs of staff chose to cut much of the funding for the future helicopter programme.

hadn't been able to immerse itself deeply in the classic counter-insurgency way. One unexpected bonus, however, was the cooperation of a US marines task force, some 4,000 strong, which McKiernan had ordered south before his sudden departure. Originally intent on an aggressive operation of their own, they were persuaded by Radford to deploy instead west of the Helmand river to cover Lashkar Gar from diversionary Taliban attacks.

In essence, Panther's Claw was a 'cordon and search' operation, a type the British army knew well from many a campaign, but on a new scale and against unprecedented odds, particularly the IEDs. And against an enemy who was expecting it, and was more determined to resist than escape. 'Hammer and anvil' comes to mind.

The first phase of the operation, to get the cordon in place, began in the early hours of 19 June, with special forces inserted by helicopter to eliminate known Taliban commanders. Soon afterwards, four companies of the 3rd Scots, some 350 men, flew from Camp Bastion in ten US and RAF Chinooks to secure key crossing points of the Nahr-e Bughra canal prior to a direct assault on a Taliban-controlled drugs bazaar – one of their logistics and financing centres – at Babaji in the Luy Manda wadi just to the west of the Helmand.

They met with some resistance as they landed, but managed to consolidate while the remainder of the battle group in armoured vehicles, and ANSF, linked up with them for the push on Babaji. Despite the continual Taliban attacks, by 23 June the Scots had gained their objectives, though not without casualties. There were, however, far fewer casualties among civilians than there might have been, since most had quit the area in the days and weeks before – indeed, in sudden numbers on the eve of the Scots' fly-in, as drone surveillance had reported. The implication was that they were forewarned of the assault: in other words, there'd been a breach of security, always a factor in operations with local forces, and corrosive of trust.

Two days later, on 25 June, the Welsh Guards began advancing up

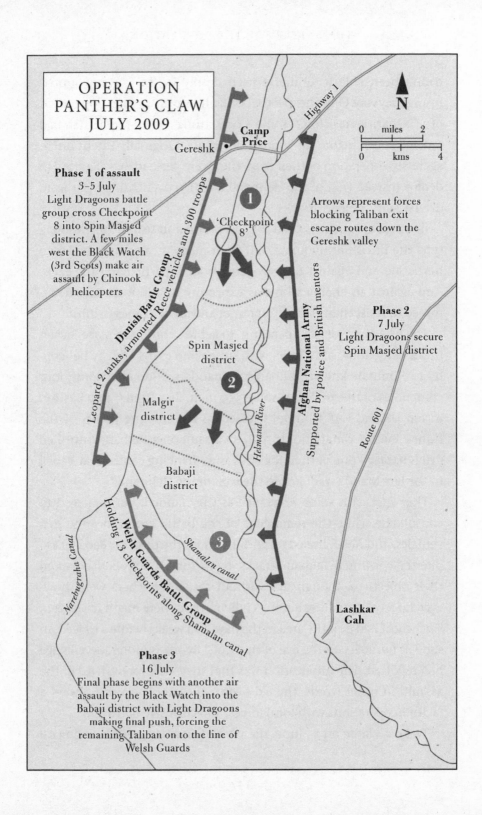

OPERATION PANTHER'S CLAW JULY 2009

Phase 1 of assault
3–5 July
Light Dragoons battle group cross Checkpoint 8 into Spin Masjed district. A few miles west the Black Watch (3rd Scots) make air assault by Chinook helicopters

Camp Price

Gereshk •

Highway 1

0   miles   2

0   kms   4

N

'Checkpoint 8'

Arrows represent forces blocking Taliban exit escape routes down the Gereshk valley

Danish Battle Group
Leopard 2 tanks, armoured Recce vehicles and 300 troops

Afghan National Army
Supported by police and British mentors

Phase 2
7 July
Light Dragoons secure Spin Masjed district

Spin Masjed district

Helmand River

Malgir district

②

Babaji district

Route 601

③

Shamalan canal

Welsh Guards Battle Group
Holding 13 checkpoints along Shamalan canal

Narehagraha Canal

Lashkar Gah

Phase 3
16 July
Final phase begins with another air assault by the Black Watch into the Babaji district with Light Dragoons making final push, forcing the remaining Taliban on to the line of Welsh Guards

the Shamalan canal, securing more crossing points to cut off Taliban lines of supply and thus prevent more fighters coming into the Babaji area. The Welsh had taken casualties to IEDs even before their push began – on the first day of the operation, indeed – including a company commander killed. Then on 1 July the commanding officer himself, Lieutenant-Colonel Rupert Thorneloe, was killed accompanying a resupply column. News of these high-profile losses frayed yet more nerves in Westminster.

Next day, the helicopter carrying the brigade commander ran into heavy fire and came close to being shot down. As expected, the Taliban were resisting hard. Mullah Omar had staked his and their reputation on dominance in Helmand that summer.

Meanwhile the Danish battle group (with its troop of tanks) left Camp Price outside Gereshk, heading south to clear Spin Masjed district, midway between Gereshk and Lashkar Gah, and to secure two further crossing points on the Nahr-e Bughra canal. The tanks were proof against the largest IEDs or mines – the most they could lose probably was a track – and their main armament, at 120 mm, could demolish a strongpoint at 2,000 metres. Indeed, their heavy machine guns too could bring down walls, but it was their menacing 'overwatch'– their observation and threat of fire while themselves invulnerable – that was their first strength. They'd no need of concealment – the Taliban had no weapon to deal with them – so could site themselves in a dominating position, traversing the turret as if minutely scanning the ground, which indeed they could with their advanced optics, and at night, reassuring the ground troops to their front and intimidating any would-be snipers. And in the event of IEDs and casualties, they could sprint to the scene with immunity and provide physical protection, something an Apache gunship, which could also menace, wasn't able to do. It remains another mystery why the Danes, who hadn't been at war since 1864, recognized the value of well-armed, well-armoured fighting vehicles – tanks – in Afghanistan, while the British, who'd only had one year (1968) in more than a century when they'd not lost a man in action, didn't.

While the boundaries of the battlefield were being secured, on 2 July the US marines, now with the same strategic intention as Panther's Claw, launched Operation Khanjar ('Sword Strike') in the Helmand valley south of Lashkar Gah. In the absence of any real command from the two-star headquarters in Kandahar, it was an impressive piece of Anglo-American coordination by the respective brigade commanders and staff. The task force from the 2nd Marine Expeditionary Brigade and an ANA *kandak* swooped into the area by helicopter and armoured vehicles, the biggest offensive airlift by the marines since the Vietnam War. Besides clearing the way for the August elections, Khanjar would put paid to any large-scale Taliban counter-attack on the 19th Brigade.

The Panther's Claw battlefield had now been shaped. Or rather, the waterways that gave the green zone its shape were now secured (the Helmand river itself by ANSF and their British mentors), forming a massive cordon. Now the main phase could begin: a push by the Light Dragoons battle group from north-east to south-west between the Nahr-e Bughra canal and the Helmand to clear the entire area up to the Shamalan canal – in other words, to kill or capture the Taliban fighters, or to drive them on to the troops at the cordon – a drive of almost 10 miles.

It would prove tough going. The Light Dragoons were equipped with up-armoured Scimitar 'light tanks' (10 tons apiece, with 30 mm cannon and coaxial machine gun), an assortment of lightly armoured wheeled vehicles and a dismounted demi-company, and were reinforced by engineers and two companies of the Mercian Regiment with their ANA mentorees. Besides the constant IED threat, they would be opposed for most of the way by elusive fighters with, among other things, rocket-propelled grenades (RPGs), well able to destroy metal as well as flesh. The brigade post-operation report conceded that, contrary to the planning intelligence assessments, '[there] were a large number of INS [insurgents] determined and motivated to resist friendly forces advance. They had not buckled under the advance of two battle-groups, were not deterred by the presence of armour, AH [attack helicopters] and aviation, and continued to fight despite heavy losses.'

Indeed, said Radford later, 'The Light Dragoons were engaged in an extremely hard fight for five days . . . an incredibly hard fight.'

The direct fight was one thing, but the indirect fight proved the more inhibiting. On the second day, a Scimitar was destroyed by a huge IED; fortunately the crew, almost miraculously (for the Scimitar, even up-armoured for Afghanistan, was still a light vehicle), survived with relatively minor injuries. The Danish armoured repair and recovery vehicle, a variant of the Leopard tank, that came to recover it was disabled later that day by another IED.

During those five days the battle group would come across sixty-nine IEDs, a good many of which detonated before they were found. The effect of an IED on an already methodical operation is almost always to slow it down further, even if the IED has first been detected. If it hasn't been detected, it can bring the operation to a halt. Irrespective of the explosion's physical damage, there is first the threat of a follow-up IED, or a small-arms attack, to deal with. Next are the casualties to treat and evacuate, and the consequences of the casualties to manage – the moral effect on the survivors, the loss of numbers and perhaps key capabilities, especially if the casualties include the tactical commander. In a conventional attack – those, for example, on D-Day and in Korea – there is a naturally strong forward momentum, and casualties do not always slow the advance; but in a methodical operation such as Panther's Claw, dealing with ambush and casualties can *become* the operation. On 4 July, in a well-sited ambush consisting of about twenty Taliban, an RPG hit one of the Dragoons' Spartan APCs, the troop-carrying variant of the Scimitar.

It detonated a box of grenades inside, killing Private Robert Laws of the Mercians, aged eighteen, and wounding four others. The Spartan's commander, Lieutenant Guy Disney, though badly wounded, managed to extricate it from the ambush and report the contact by radio, adding: 'I need a heli. I think I've lost my leg' (which he had, the lower part). Others rushed to them over a bridge across an irrigation ditch, including the Dragoons' commanding officer, Lieutenant-Colonel Angus Fair. A casevac Chinook arrived quickly and the wounded were got away. A few minutes later, as one of Fair's signallers, Lance-Corporal David Dennis, crossed the bridge, an IED exploded beneath. He died during the second casevac flight, which also took out others caught in the blast, including the Mercians' company commander and serjeant-major. Fair ordered the company to withdraw 200 metres to a farm compound where they could reorganize and recover. Of the 2 kilometres that he'd planned to clear that day, they'd managed only one.

The advance continued next morning, although there was no let-up in the Taliban fight-back, or the problem of IEDs. At the far end of the battlefield an explosion killed Lance-Corporal Dane Elson of the Welsh Guards and wounded several others. As news of the casualties reached London, anxiety began to mount in Downing Street. On 13 July, Brown rang Radford to ask if he had enough helicopters. Radford replied that he'd made his plans with what he'd got, and that although it was enough he could do with more helicopters and also more manpower to build on the results of the operation.* This

---

* In parliament on 15 July, with casualties now a daily concern of the national media, the leader of the opposition, David Cameron, pressed the prime minister on the issue: 'Is not the basic problem this: the number of helicopters in Afghanistan is simply insufficient? Will the Prime Minister confirm that the American marines, who have approximately the same number of troops as us in Helmand, are supported by some 100 helicopters, whereas our troops are supported by fewer than 30?' To which the PM replied that he'd spoken to Radford, who'd said '[he] has sufficient to get on with the

was the first major offensive operation in the history of the British army in which heliborne forces played a sustained and integrated part. Without helicopters it would have taken an entirely different shape and course – if indeed it had been carried out at all.*

On 10 July a strong company-group of the 3rd Scots was lifted by Chinook forward of the Light Dragoons to confuse the Taliban; and Radford told the battle group to 'pause' in Malgir area to recuperate and resupply, and to allow the Mercians and their ANA contingent to secure checkpoints and compounds in the cleared zone. The IEDs had taken their toll on momentum as well as flesh. It was the old story: 'Objectives that were meant to have been overwhelmed in an hour took more than a day to seize,' as the MoD's Media Ops (London) blog reported. 'We were essentially manoeuvring in a giant minefield,' added one of the Light Dragoons. And in temperatures of almost 40 degrees.

By 14 July the Dragoons had reached their objective, a line from the Nahr-e Bughra canal south and east to the Helmand river, just before the river turns further south and the green zone widens. From here, other elements of the brigade would take on the final push

---

task . . . he's been given'. This, of course, omitted the material point, that more helicopters were needed to do the job properly. Radford had also told the PM that he needed 'more and better ANSF in order to lead to transition and more helicopters which would greatly enhance our tactical effectiveness' (Radford's diary). In choosing to represent the conversation with Radford in this way, ignoring its import, the PM laid himself open to accusations of disingenuousness, which persist. While tactical operations aren't a 'no-go area' for policy, the manner of contact needs special care, not least to avoid misunderstanding by a policy-maker not familiar with tactical matters. The question ought to have been asked of the Chief of the Defence Staff, who would then have been obliged to answer fully, and held to account by parliament. And the CDS ought to have insisted on it.

* The army and Royal Marines had, of course, had a good deal of experience in helicopter operations – in Malaya, Suez, Borneo, Northern Ireland and the Falklands – but Panther's Claw was a considerable gear change.

towards the Shamalan canal. A week later, the brigade had cleared a further hundred compounds and the remaining 7 miles of the green zone, but at continuing and increasingly high-profile cost. On 18 July, 26-year-old Captain Harry Parker of the Rifles was severely wounded, losing both legs. His father was Lieutenant-General Sir Nick Parker, the army's deputy C-in-C, who was about to take over as McChrystal's second-in-command in Kabul. When the news was broken to him, he said it made him even more determined that they did the job properly.

The final phase to take key ground surrounding Babaji could now be launched: heliborne assaults by the 3rd Scots behind the Taliban to pin them in place, while the company-group from the 2nd Royal Welsh in sixty armoured vehicles, including the well-protected Warrior tracked armoured infantry fighting vehicle, pushed into the area from the south-east. By 27 July Babaji itself was secured. Intelligence estimated that in all some 200–300 Taliban had been killed, out of perhaps some 500 active in the green zone (the actual body count was low, with the Taliban always trying to recover their dead), and resistance was clearly crumbling. Radford called a halt. It was time for consolidation.

POSTSCRIPT

Arguments continue as to just how successful Panther's Claw was. When the operation ended, McChrystal came down from Kabul and addressed the brigade. He said President Obama had told him that he had to deliver success in a year: 'What I needed was a victory, and this is it.'

It was certainly a tactical success in driving out the Taliban, holding out hope that Lashkar Gah and Gereshk could be joined up, and making for continuity with the brigade that would replace the 19th in November. But voter turnout on 20 August proved low, probably because of a remaining Taliban presence sufficient to intimidate and coerce the local population. After all, the operation had been expected and its strategic purpose well understood, and besides resisting the brigade's attempt to clear the area, the Taliban must have calculated on enough of them being able to lie low or re-infiltrate once the operation was ended. Radford had always understood this: 'How do we know you'll stay?' had been the question on the lips of every Afghan staking his future on the operation. One of his answers had been what he called 'hot stabilization', the immediate follow-up by the PRTs to begin the development projects that the Taliban's presence had prevented. It was on a par with 'courageous restraint'. But holding cleared territory was meant to be the responsibility of the ANSF, with British support and mentors, and they proved not yet up to the task in number, commitment or reliability. Indeed, their heart, and that of the

Afghan civil authorities, wasn't yet in it. Nor, evidently, had been that of the commander of ISAF Regional Command (South), a Dutch major-general, who might have allocated more resources to the operation, including helicopters and explosive ordnance disposal, if he'd judged it represented his command's main effort.

British officials, military and civilian (FCO, which of course had the notional lead), had stressed that Panther's Claw and continuing operations in the summer and autumn months would be crucial, not just in taking decisive military action against the Taliban, but also to convince public opinion in Britain that the ANSF would be increasingly responsible for their country's security. The task for British and other alliance troops would then be to train these forces and develop a proper civil infrastructure. Panther's Claw showed, however, that there needed to be another reset – or at least considerable retuning – of the campaign.

It also showed that the British army was indeed prepared to shed blood. But the casualties had been more than expected – back in Britain, that is. They were high-profile and particularly harrowing, with reports of multiple amputees, and they continued after the operation was declared at an end. In fact, the casualties during Panther's Claw weren't significantly greater than during the brigade's six-month tour as a whole (seventy-six killed and 340 notifiable casualties, of which thirty were amputees). But they caused great political difficulties for the prime minister, Gordon Brown, for now the unpopularity of the Iraq War, which was seen as 'Blair's war', its opprobrium accordingly attaching not to him but to his predecessor, had attached itself to the Afghan War. And the same unforced errors of the Iraq War, notably the slow fielding of adequately protected vehicles and second-rate care and support for wounded troops on return, and their families, were remorselessly censured by the media and opposition parties. Helicopters were the totemic issue. By now it was clear to all but the purblind that there weren't enough, and never had been enough, and the government's attempts to persuade people otherwise made matters even worse, for there was now to all intents and purposes a breakdown in civilian–military trust. And Gordon Brown could expect no quarter, for as chancellor of the exchequer during the first ten years of Labour government from 1997 he'd insisted on defence cuts that had led to those very reductions in capability; although, that said, a lack of interservice spending coherence and botched procurement certainly hadn't helped.

British military policy in Afghanistan – or, perhaps better, the focus of the campaign's strategy – now changed very decidedly. The emphasis switched almost exclusively to training the ANSF and getting them to take the lead, with October 2014 set as the date for withdrawal of all combat forces – 'tough love'. Thereafter, just a few hundred trainers and advisers would remain, the minimum to honour the continuity promised to the Afghans. (Sceptics – cynics perhaps – had argued for some time that the 'exit strategy' for Afghanistan should be to declare victory then quit.*) In November 2009, the British Major-General Nick Carter took over Regional Command (South). This was a significant move. Carter's operational experience was huge, and he was both willing and able to take command of what in effect was a division, rather than leaving matters for subordinate commanders to arrange among themselves.

McChrystal gave him command of Operation Moshtarak, to be launched in February to clear the Taliban from Marjah district, a

---

* In November 2020, despite the wishes of the joint chiefs, President Trump announced further cuts to troop numbers (to a maximum of 2,500 in January 2021), with an aspiration for total withdrawal by 1 May 2021. In April 2021, President Biden announced that there would be total withdrawal by the highly symbolic date of 11 September – '9/11'. As it would be nigh impossible to maintain the mission in the absence of the United States, all the other NATO nations announced the departure of their own troops too – a further 7,000. The UK's political and military leaders strongly opposed the US withdrawal. General Richards declared it 'a sorry moment for Western grand strategy'.

major stronghold. Moshtarak – 'Together', significantly, in Dari, Afghanistan's lingua franca – involved two simultaneous offensives, one by a US marines task force in Marjah south of Nad-e Ali, and one by TFH in the north of Nad-e Ali. Both McChrystal and Carter were determined that Moshtarak would be a politically led effort in full partnership with ANSF – hence the name. Crucially, and in contrast with Panther's Claw, the Afghan government pledged to hold any territory seized during the assault with Afghan forces, which meant both raising more of them and diverting existing forces to Helmand from elsewhere, notably Kabul and the east. In turn, even greater emphasis on 'courageous restraint' would enhance legitimacy. It was no coincidence that on Moshtarak the use of high-explosive artillery shells went down by more than 60 per cent, while the use of smoke shells to mask movement went up by nearly 70 per cent. Critically, though, Carter, who nine years later would become Chief of the Defence Staff, also took great pains to secure, as it were, his home flank – UK public opinion. He wanted Moshtarak to end when it had achieved its strategic object, rather than when nerves frayed in Whitehall. In that respect, too, Panther's Claw had shaped Moshtarak, both directly in terms of tactical lessons learned, and indirectly by its impact at home.

Battles always have strategic consequences, because strategy is the employment of the battle as the means of attaining the object in war – the object being the first element of policy. And policy, while not precisely the same as politics, is ultimately political. Policy shapes battles by design. Battles shape politics by chance.

CONCLUSION

People . . . give us our edge.

Defence in a
Competitive Age (2021)

'The narratives speak for themselves,' I wrote in the preface; and I trust they do. I said that I didn't intend to compare and contrast, or to draw over-arching conclusions that are in any way prescriptive; and I'm not going to. Nevertheless, I think a few concluding thoughts are in order.

I didn't choose the battles to make a particular point. They're battles that have long interested me – Helmand, the most recent, because my own (descendent) regiment, the Light Dragoons, was so closely involved, and I wrote about it at the time for the *Daily Telegraph*; Hastings, the earliest, because it's the first battle in England that we really know anything much about, and because the events of 1066 were so dramatic and Anglo-Saxon military organization was so impressive. Towton was the battlefield nearest my boyhood home, and I walked it many a time 'under instruction'. The field of Waterloo, likewise, I've trodden length and breadth – and indeed ridden, which offers a different perspective, literally and figuratively. No soldier could find Waterloo anything but absorbing. As for Sword Beach, the first regiment to land – the 13th/18th Hussars in their DD Shermans – was that which I had the privilege to command forty-five years later. There were many veterans to talk to. And Imjin River was of great professional interest to so many of us in the British Army of the Rhine during the Cold War. Besides, Anthony Farrar-Hockley's *The Edge of the Sword* (1954) had gripped me as a subaltern. Each is, of course, a battle of its time and place; but each also offers both echoes and auguries.

The first thing that strikes me, not surprisingly, is just how true Michael Howard's words are: that only by understanding the combatants' cultures can one come to understand what it was that they fought about and why they fought in the way they did.* I made the point generally in the preface, but also specifically in connection with Towton, whose blood-letting would otherwise pass all understanding. But it's equally if not perhaps so obviously the case with the battles that follow. For example, Britain in the Napoleonic Wars had come to see itself as a nation very much apart from its continental allies – Shakespeare's 'fortress built by Nature for herself / Against infection and the hand of war . . . set in the silver sea' – in which commerce and the liberty of the individual made for a sort of semi-detached way of war: the Royal Navy the prime strategic instrument, the army in effect its auxiliary, and war made indirectly, thriftily, *cautiously*. Not for nothing was Wellington called 'the Fabian general'. Yet when battle on the grand scale came at last, at Waterloo, the solid corps of the duke's professionals knew how to stand their ground against human waves the like of which they'd never previously seen. Nature's fortress had raised a defiant breed (characterized, later, with the adjective 'bulldog'). In *The Battle* (2006), the Italian Professor Alessandro Barbero wrote:

---

* The Chairman of the US Joint Chiefs of Staff, General Mark Milley, made the same point in a different way in his remarks on the 'Five Myths of War': 'Armies don't fight wars [nor navies and air forces]. Nations fight wars.' See *Proceedings of the RUSI Land Warfare Conference* (London, 27 June 2017).

However proletarian and semiliterate he may have been, the English [*sic*] soldier, well nourished with meat and beer, stimulated with gin, and *convinced of his own racial superiority to the foreign rabble he had to face* [emphasis added], was a magnificent combatant, as anyone who has ever seen hooligans in action at a soccer match can readily imagine.*

I wouldn't dispute that there was a racial element, except that with Welsh, Scots and Irish in the mix it was rather more complicated, but it seems to me that the British soldier at Waterloo was more convinced of his *national* and his *military* superiority. It was one of the reasons that Wellington was confident he could give battle as he did that day. Rough men, 'the scum of the earth',† he called them, led by 'gentlemen's sons', for the most part younger sons of the gentry who knew their duty – first and foremost, to be brave.

The parallels with Imjin River nearly 150 years later are really quite striking, though I don't suggest the troops there were stimulated by anything stronger than tea, pride and desperation. And indeed, it's not difficult to see some of the same in Helmand – a war fought by men apart from society, and whom society would rather forget, and sometimes has forgotten, unless to sentimentalize them. Which is why Sword Beach stands out as so interesting an exception, fought at a time – only the second time, indeed – when Britain was a nation in

---

* Chroniclers of Hastings said much the same of Harold's line on Battle Hill. Without discipline, however, his warriors likely threw away their advantage in a precipitous charge downhill.

† Wellington was a realist, but he wasn't without humanity, and he knew his Bible. The words are his – though used by many before him, including John Wesley – but the sense is that in St Paul's First Letter to the Corinthians (4: 13): 'Being defamed, we intreat: we are made as the filth of the world, and are the offscouring of all things unto this day. I write not these things to shame you, but as my beloved sons I warn you.' In other words, see what can be done with unpromising material when held to account (in the soldier's case by military discipline and good leadership).

arms. The sense of shared effort is palpable. The planning and execution, too, reflected the considerable intellectual talent that the army had acquired – and a particular cast of intellectual talent: liberal, independent-minded, humane. Oxford, Cambridge and the rest of academe had emptied their lecture halls, and their graduates too had put on uniform. This time, though, they'd not been thrown willy-nilly into the great threshing machine, as in Kitchener's New Armies of the First World War. The RAF was especially clever in harnessing technical intellectual expertise, but the army too was quick to promote and appoint men of marked intellect. The most celebrated case is probably that of Enoch Powell, who in just under five years rose from second lieutenant to brigadier, in military intelligence. And later, of course, in the early 1960s, he became a government minister. There were many others, such as Captain Edward Burn, aged twenty-one, who'd read Classical Mods in one year at Oxford before enlisting and who was plucked from a battalion of the Oxford and Buckinghamshire Light Infantry in the run-up to D-Day to be the intelligence and operations officer of the 3rd Division's logistics brigade at Sword Beach. In due course he became an influential law don at Oxford, where he was noted for being an almost infallible proof-reader of legal texts. Such qualities on the staff of Montgomery's divisions saved lives before the battle even began.

But such qualities also served the apparently less cerebral business of the bullet and the bayonet. The distribution of grey matter (and sensitivity) among the PBI – the 'Poor Bloody Infantry' – saved lives *during* battle. Few will know, for example, that the Cambridge music scholar Sir David Willcocks, famous for the Christmas Eve broadcasts 'Carols from Kings', won the Military Cross not long after D-Day with the Duke of Cornwall's Light Infantry. Or that Edwin ('Dwin') Bramall was bound for Oxford with a scholarship to read history but instead landed on Sword Beach on D+1, aged just twenty and in command of a platoon of the King's Royal Rifle Corps. After the war he decided not to return to Oxford but to make the army his career, something he'd never previously contemplated; and in 1982 he became Chief of the Defence Staff. When the Chairman of the US Joint Chiefs of Staff, Ivy League graduate General Mark Milley, stresses the need for 'mass', as he frequently does – 'numbers matter, because people count' – I don't imagine he means human waves like the PVA at Imjin or the Taliban's 'Rorke's Drifts' in Helmand. And when Montgomery said that 'battles are won primarily in the hearts of men', we can be sure that if he hadn't been striving for brevity he'd have said 'hearts *and minds*' – good minds.

The precise nature of that grey matter isn't of course a straightforward business. Enoch Powell's type of classical brilliance (professor of Greek in his twenties) doesn't unfailingly translate into practical soldiering. William Neville, Lord Fauconberg, had no great formal schooling; he'd spent his life in the profession of arms. Yet at Towton his *coup d'œil* changed the shape of the battle – as it did, indeed, at Ferrybridge and Dinting Dale too – and yet others no less experienced than he failed in their reading of the battle that day, as have others ever since. It is one of the fascinations of the subject.

The *coup d'œil* is a tactical gift, whether acquired or bestowed (and I think it's largely the latter, though a gift that improves with cherishing). What, then, is the equivalent at the campaign level and above, where the seeds of battle are sown? What is it that gives a general the art of strategy, which, in Churchill's words, consists in foreseeing the outlines of the future and being prepared to deal with it? Not the least element of this is the ability to recognize how to exploit success in battle; how, as it were, to fit success into the overall concept of the campaign. If we seek another French ocular expression, perhaps *la longue vue* would be apt. It would certainly fit with Wellington's experience. And although at such a distance in time it can only be very conjectural, *la longue vue* was what in the end Harold Godwineson fatally lacked. Dwin Bramall was very clear about the role that history has in this: 'You can't form a rounded view of current and future strategy without it.'*

But just as it's not possible fully to understand the battle without understanding the war (and the societies engaged in that war) and the campaign within which it was fought, so success at any one level doesn't guarantee ultimate success in the absence of understanding what exactly is going on at the other levels. By his own reckoning, Ridgway in Korea took about a fortnight to comprehend fully how and why the gearing between strategy and tactics – the campaign – wasn't working, and then to get it going properly. Without strategy, tactics fumble blindly, bloodily and with no assurance of success; and the same can be said for the proposition reversed – strategy without tactics. Afghanistan is recent witness to both. If Sun Tzu, the sixth-century BC Chinese author of what's rendered in English as *The Art of War* (*Bing-fa*) really did exist – and there's a doubt, in which case there's a genius to fame and fortune unknown – then his picturesque encapsulation of the relationship between strategy and tactics really can't be bettered: 'Strategy without tactics is the slowest route to victory. Tactics without strategy is the noise before defeat.'

But what of the future? I said in the preface that this book is my study of why some battles were fought as they were, and as battles to one degree or another will always be fought. Is this latter – 'will always be fought' – tenable, though, in any meaningful sense? Following the so-called Integrated Review by the National Security Council,† the Ministry of Defence published its blueprint for what might be the most profound shift in British military policy since the formation of NATO, possibly even since before the First World War:

---

* See the final interview before his death (with the author): 'Wise Old War Horse', *The Spectator*, 16 Dec. 2017.

† Cabinet Office, *Global Britain in a Competitive Age: The Integrated Review of Security, Defence, Development and Foreign Policy* (London, 2021).

Defence in a Competitive Age. The section on 'The Future Battlefield' begins boldly with the statement: 'The future operating environment will not be limited by lines on maps or by geography.' What follows is persuasive, not least because of 'the newer domains of cyberspace and space' and the likelihood of being 'confronted by complex and integrated challenges below, and potentially above, the threshold of armed conflict'. The battlefield in the old sense, a place where opposing forces do battle, seeking to destroy or neutralize one another by fire, manoeuvre or both, is clearly going to be an increasing competition between concealment and detection; and one in which the overhead threat is as great as or greater than the threat to front or flank. There again, the Lancastrian line learned the lesson of the overhead threat at Towton; and yet the longbow disappeared from the battlefield the following century.

I'm not suggesting that the character of war, as opposed to its nature, won't change as much as is being predicted. There *are* people who know what the next battlefield will be like; but those having to make plans now don't know who they are, any more than *they* do themselves. Clausewitz wrote that war 'is a mix of instinct, art and reason', the so-called Clausewitzian trinity. War in his view is first an affair of 'primordial violence, hatred and enmity . . . a blind, natural force'; its art is in the 'play of chance and probability, within which the creative spirit is free to roam'; and it is only as an instrument of policy that, theoretically, war is 'subject to pure reason'. The struggle in the future, as in some degree in the past, will be between the 'blind, natural force' and the control that the militaries try to exert over it in the 'newer domains' and with the already 'complex and integrated' weapons systems (not least artificial intelligence and autonomous weapons – 'killer robots' as comic-book copy has it) that technology is developing at accelerating speed.

And yet . . .

In 1944, just before D-Day, the essayist A. P. Herbert wrote an encouragement to the 'PBI' as they prepared to breach the Atlantic ('West') Wall:

> Hail, soldier, huddled in the rain,
> Hail, soldier, squelching through the mud,
> Hail, soldier, sick of dirt and pain,
> The sight of death, the smell of blood.
> New men, new weapons, bear the brunt;
> New slogans gild the ancient game:
> The infantry are still in front,
> And mud and dust are much the same.
> Hail, humble footman, poised to fly
> Across the West, or any, Wall!
> Proud, plodding, peerless PBI –
> The foulest, finest job of all.

Herbert had been an infantryman in the First World War. He didn't imagine that things had changed much in their essentials since then, only that a few lessons had been learned to spare the PBI the worst. In Helmand, the infantry – or perhaps more accurately the 'boots on the ground' – weren't facing such a formidable wall, but mud and dust were much the same, as were flesh and blood. Some of the troops had micro-drones that could be launched from the hand to peer into compounds, sending real-time images back to view on a screen in the same hand. The Duke of Wellington would have approved: 'The whole art of war,' he said, 'consists of guessing at what is on the other side of the hill.' But not having to guess doesn't then eliminate the need for action. The man will undoubtedly remain the first weapon of war, and the prime shaper of the battle.

And, as *Defence in a Competitive Age* confidently asserts, 'People . . . give us our edge.'

ACKNOWLEDGEMENTS

The publishing of a book is not unlike the practice of war. There are broadly the same levels – the Strategic, the Operational, and the Tactical.

At the strategic level I must thank Peter Straus, my agent at Rogers, Coleridge and White, who (to paraphrase Churchill) foresaw the outlines of the book's future and was prepared to deal with it. Likewise, the strategic advice of my editor at Penguin Random House (Transworld division), Simon Taylor, was decisive: 'An object may be very desirable strategically; but that which is strategically desirable must be tactically possible with the forces and means available' (Montgomery).

At the operational level, where strategy is 'geared' into tactics (and sometimes, vice versa), as ever I'm obliged to the managing editor at Transworld, Katrina Whone.

At the tactical level, my copy editor, Gillian Somerscales, has once again worked tirelessly to prepare the words for battle. No parade could be inspected with a more critical eye than hers. Phil Lord, design manager, has smartly regimented the internal layout of the book, commissioned the maps and marshalled the plate sections. Phil Evans, senior production controller, has regulated the movement of words into line through typesetting and printing. Auriol Griffith-Jones has yet again mapped the campaign with a fine index. Richard Shailer has camouflaged the whole with a masterly cover, and Sally Wray, my publicist, has worked heroically in communications for Publication Day.

It would be a very long list indeed if I attempted to pay tribute to the many people who have helped me, directly and indirectly, actually to write this book, some on terms of confidentiality. I have therefore decided to trust to their understanding and not name names. I am nevertheless hugely grateful.

PICTURE ACKNOWLEDGEMENTS

Any illustrations not specifically credited below are in the public domain or the copyright holder is unknown. Every effort has been made to trace copyright holders; any who have been overlooked are invited to get in touch with the publishers.

Section 1

Page 1, top—Death of Edward the Confessor, detail from Bayeux Tapestry: funkyfood London/Paul Williams/Alamy Stock Photo.

Page 1, middle—Harold Godwineson is crowned the day of Edward's funeral, engraving: May Evans Picture Library.

Page 1, bottom left—Harald Hardrada defeats the northern earls at Gate Fulford, detail from Matthew Paris's *Chronica Majora*: © Cambridge University Library.

Page 2, top—William of Normandy's knights attack King Harold's shield wall at Hastings, detail from Bayeux Tapestry: World History Archive/Alamy Stock Photo.

Page 2, bottom—The last stand of King Harold, as imagined by Richard Caton Woodville: Hulton Archive/Stringer/Getty Images.

Page 3, top—At the butts: archery practice, Luttrell Psalter detail: © British Library Board. All Rights Reserved/Bridgeman Images.

Page 3, middle—Death of Edmund of Rutland, 19th-century engraving: Nastasic/Getty Images.

Page 3, bottom left—Edward, Earl of March (Edward IV): Hulton Archive/Stringer/Getty Images.

Page 4, top—The old bridge at Ferrybridge: © British Library Board. All Rights Reserved/Bridgeman Images.

Page 4, bottom—*The Earl of Warwick's Vow Previous to The Battle of Towton* by Henry Tresham: © Manchester Art Gallery/Bridgeman Images.

Page 5, top—Lord Fauconberg at the Battle of Towton, illustration by James William Edmund Doyle: Heritage Image Partnership Ltd/Alamy Stock Photo.

Page 5, middle—Henry VI, painting: © Guildhall Art Gallery/Bridgeman Images.

Page 5, bottom—The slaughter in the Cock Beck as imagined by Caton Woodville: The Print Collector/Alamy Stock Photo.

Page 6, middle—The Earl of Uxbridge, 1st Marquess of Anglesey, by Henry Edridge: © National Portrait Gallery, London.

Page 6, bottom—Battle of Talavera, 28 July 1809, pen and wash by E. Walker: © National Army Museum/Bridgeman Images.

Page 7, top—*Summoned to Waterloo, Brussels*, chromolithograph after Robert Hillingford: Historic Collection/Alamy Stock Photo.

Page 7, middle—*Wellington and Blücher meeting before the Battle of Waterloo* by Robert Hillingford: incamerastock/Alamy Stock Photo.

Page 7, bottom—*Ligny* by Ernest Crofts (windmill on the heights of Naveau): The Picture Art Collection/Alamy Stock Photo.

Page 8, top inset—Duke of Wellington: GL Archive/Alamy Stock Photo.

Page 8, main image—Battle of Waterloo: Hulton Fine Art Collection/Getty Images.

Section 2

Page 9, top—President Franklin D. Roosevelt and Prime Minister Winston Churchill meet off the coast of Newfoundland, August 1941: Freemantle/Alamy Stock Photo.

Page 9, middle—Casablanca Conference, January 1943: Courtesy of the Library of Congress.

Page 9, bottom—Churchill and his chiefs of staff aboard the *Queen Mary* en route to Washington, May 1943: © Imperial War Museum A 16709.

Page 10, top (main image)—The Supreme Allied Commander for Operation Overlord with his senior officers: Popperfoto via Getty Images.

Page 10, top (inset)—Lieutenant-General Frederick Morgan – 'architect of Overlord': © Imperial War Museum EA 33078.

Page 10, middle—Major-General Rennie briefing divisional staff before D-Day: © Imperial War Museum H 38094.

Page 10, bottom—Lieutenant-General Crocker, I (British) Corps watching the fighting near Caen: © Imperial War Museum B 7753.

Page 11, top—Aerial photograph (by photo-reconnaissance Spitfire) of Queen Sector, Sword Beach: © Imperial War Museum MH 1997.

Page 11, middle—Commandos landing at H+30 on Sword Beach: © Imperial War Museum B 5103.

Page 11, bottom—Troops, possibly sappers, struggle ashore at Sword Beach: Pictorial Press Ltd/Alamy Stock Photo.

Page 12, top—House-to-house fighting towards Ouistreham: © Imperial War Museum MH 2012.
Page 12, middle left—Infantry, probably of the 185th Brigade, move inland from Sword Beach: © Imperial War Museum B 5078.

Page 12, middle right—Troops of the 3rd Division, possibly 2nd Royal Ulster Rifles, pause in La Brèche d'Hermanville during the advance from Sword Beach: © Imperial War Museum B 5039.

Page 12, bottom—Heavy bombing in Caen: © Imperial War Museum B 6727.

Page 13, top—General Douglas MacArthur, C-in-C United Nations Command, with behind him the new commander of 8th Army, General Matthew Ridgeway: Everett Collection Inc/Alamy Stock Photo.

Page 13, middle—Chinese infantry, Korea, February 1951: Courtesy of the Australian War Memorial.

Page 13, bottom—A Centurion tank of the 8th King's Royal Irish Hussars with men of the Gloucestershire Regiment ('Glosters') in March 1951 at Imjin: © Imperial War Museum KOR 649.

Page 14, top—View of the Imjin River: © National Army Museum/Bridgeman Images.

Page 14, 1st middle—A 25-pounder howitzer of 45 Field Regiment Royal Artillery: © National Army Museum/Bridgeman Images.

Page 14, 2nd middle—1st Ulster Rifles resting: Courtesy of the Royal Irish Regiments Archive.

Page 14, bottom—Roll-call of Gloster survivors: © Associated Press.

Page 15, top—A convoy of Soviet armoured vehicles crossing a bridge at the Soviet–Afghan border, February 1989, during the withdrawal of the Red Army from Afghanistan: AFP/Stringer/Getty Images.

Page 15, 1st middle—The London Conference, January 2006: Reuters/Alamy Stock Photo.

Page 15, 2nd middle—Key staff of the NATO Rapid Reaction Corps, painting by Brendan Kelly: © Brendan Kelly.

Page 15, bottom—Tim Radford at an Afghan shura (council) consulation: PA Images/Alamy Stock Photo.

Page 16, top—The Chinook heavy-lift helicopter during a resupply to ground forces during Operation Panther's Claw: Crown Copyright 2009, http://www.nationalarchives.gov.uk/doc/open-government-licence/version/3/.

Page 16, 1st middle—A soldier of the Mercian Regiment fires a short-range 66mm HEAT rocket at an insurgent strongpoint near Babaji: Crown Copyright 2009, http://www.nationalarchives.gov.uk/docopen-government-licence/version/3/.

Page 16, 2nd middle—Light Dragoons, dismounted, covered by one of their Scimitar light tanks during the main phase of Operation Panther's Claw: Crown Copyright 2009, http://www.nationalarchives.gov.uk/doc/open-government-licenceversion/3/.

Endpapers—The slaughter in the Cock Beck as imagined by Caton Woodville: The Print Collector/Alamy Stock Photo.

INDEX

ABOUT THE AUTHOR

A professional soldier for thirty-five years, Allan Mallinson began writing while still serving. His first book was a history of four regiments of British light dragoons, one of which he commanded. His debut novel was the bestselling *A Close Run Thing*, the first in an acclaimed series chronicling the life of a fictitious cavalry officer before and after Waterloo.

His *The Making of the British Army* was shortlisted for a number of prizes, while *1914: Fight the Good Fight* won the British Army's 'Book of the Year' Award. Its sequel, *Too Important for the Generals*, is a provocative look at leadership during the Great War, while *Fight to the Finish* is a comprehensive history of the First World War, month by month.

Allan Mallinson reviews for the *Spectator* and the *TLS* and also writes for *The Times*. He lives on Salisbury Plain.